The Story of Man

By the same author

Charles Darwin

A Book of Scientific Curiosities

THE
STORY
of
MAN

CYRIL AYDON

CARROLL & GRAF PUBLISHERS
NEW YORK

For Reg Gwilliam and Tamara Moon

Carroll & Graf Publishers
387 Park Avenue South, 12th Floor
New York, NY 10016
www.perseusbooks.com

First published in the UK by Constable,
an imprint of Constable & Robinson Ltd 2007

First Carroll & Graf edition 2007

ISBN-13: 978-0-78672-085-9
ISBN-10: 0-7867-2085-9

Printed and bound in the EU

Contents

Maps and Diagrams

Maps

Diagrams

TABLES AND CONVERSION TABLE

TABLES

CONVERSION TABLE

Imperial	Metric
1 inch	2.54 centimetres
1 foot	0.3048 metres
1 yard	0.9144 metres
1 mile	1.609 kilometres
1 acre	0.405 hectares
1 sq. mile	2.59 sq. kilometres
1 cubic inch	16.38 cubic centimetres
1 pound	0.454 kilogrammes
1 ton	1.016 tonnes

A C K N O W L E D G E M E N T S

A book like this, written by someone who is not a professional historian, inevitably draws heavily on the work of those who are. It is, therefore, a pleasure to acknowledge the debt I owe to the people whose books are listed in the Further Reading section. I have also been helped by my reading of many other excellent texts, including: *Maps of Time*, by David Christian; *The Fontana Economic History of Europe*, edited by Carlo Cipolla; *Rising Sun and Russian Bear*, by Richard Connaughton; *The Chinese Experience*, by Raymond Dawson; *The First Industrial Revolution*, by Phyllis Deane; *A Short History of Technology*, by T.K. Derry and T.I. Williams; *The Crusades*, by Geoffrey Hindley; *Forces of Change*, by Henry Hobhouse; *The Language of the Genes*, by Steve Jones; *The Ancient American Civilisations*, by Friedrich Katz; *Ship*, by Brian Lavery; *The Great Wall*, by Julia Lovell; *The Human Web*, by J.R and W.H. McNeill; *A World History*, by W.H. McNeill; *The Shaping of America*, by D.W. Meinig; *After the Ice*, by Steven Mithen; *Eternal Egypt*, by Pierre Montet; *The Discovery of India*, by Jawaharlal Nehru; *Empires of the Word*, by Nicholas Ostler; *A History of Russia*, by Nicolas Riasanovsky; *The Holocene*, by Neil Roberts; *Identity and Violence*, by Amartya Sen; *Marx*, by Peter Singer; *Conquests and Cultures*, by Thomas Sowell; *Early India*, by Romila Thapar; *An Unfinished History of the World*, by Hugh Thomas; *Neanderthals, Bandits and Farmers*, by Colin Tudge; and *Europe and the People Without History*, by Eric Wolf.

Among the friends who have helped to make this a better book than it would otherwise have been, I am indebted to two in particular. Reg Gwilliam has added to more than half a lifetime of favours the service of reading every word of the draft manuscript, and gently pointing out a number of solecisms it contained. Jim Honeybone has done the same, making this the third book of mine that has been shaped by his critical intelligence. It must not be thought that either of them agree with all of the opinions expressed within these pages. Peter Thoday and Martha Nochimson have read, and made helpful comments on, some of the text, but they are entitled to the additional disclaimer that there are substantial sections that they have not seen. Others whose comments have helped in the shaping of the book include Deborah and Sue Aydon, Mike Fenner, Alec Muir, Patrick Neale and Tom Troy.

Jan Chamier and her team at Constable & Robinson have never faltered in their support for the project, and have demonstrated a degree of skill and care that one might have thought was no longer possible in today's fiercely demanding marketplace. My editors, Becky Hardie and Hannah Boursnell, have deployed an exemplary combination of helpful suggestion, unfailing courtesy and firm control. Christopher Feeney's long experience of history publishing has enabled him to contribute far more to the finished book than a copy-editor could reasonably be expected to offer. Chris Summerville not only drew the maps, but improved the quality of the information contained in them. And my desk-editor, Claudia Dyer, has overseen the production process with calm efficiency. The final element in the team effort that this book represents has been contributed by Joyce Aydon, whose moral support and IT skills have lightened the task of actually writing it.

INTRODUCTION

This is the story of how human beings spread around the world from their original home in Africa, and of the adventures and misadventures that the human race has experienced since then. It is also the story of some of the ideas that have governed people's lives, especially ideas about religion, about politics and about the workings of the natural world.

Strictly speaking, this is *a* story, not *the* story, since every story-teller sees things differently. A really objective history of the human race would be the most boring thing imaginable: a list of names, places and dates. It would also be wellnigh useless. The only kind of history that is of any use is the kind that tries to explain, not only *what* happened, but *how* things happened and *why* things happened in the way they did. But every such explanation is inevitably coloured by the background, and prejudices, of the person doing the explaining – and this book is no exception.

It is my belief that the history of humanity has been shaped by two enormous changes. The first was the emergence of settled agriculture in several different parts of the world in the period we know as the neolithic. The second was the Industrial Revolution that occurred in Europe in, and around, the eighteenth century. These two developments are the hinges on which my story turns. It is in the hope that I may be able to help readers to a better understanding of these two landmarks in human history that I have chosen to write the story of man in this particular way.

While giving precedence to these two transformations of the material basis of human existence, I have been able to find room for a host of other fascinating stories. Some, such as the history of the Black Death or the repeopling of the Americas, will be familiar to many readers, though perhaps not in such great detail. Others, such as the Industrial Revolution in first-century China or the origin of the modern Olympic Games, will, I feel sure, come as a revelation to most.

It is possible that we are close to another great transformation of human fortunes. The runaway growth of human population and industrialization during the last half century, with its implications for climate change and environmental pollution, raises the spectre of a possible collapse of civilization before some parts of the world have even begun to feel its benefits. Strictly speaking, this is the subject matter of futurology, not history. But it would be an incomplete account of the human journey that ignored such implications, and I have tried to do justice to this hugely important and very contentious topic in the final chapter.

Whatever readers may feel about the way I have chosen to tell it, I feel sure that they will agree with me that it is one hell of a story.

1

African Origins

Wherever we may live in the world, we are all Africans. Africa is the home of our closest relatives, the chimpanzees and the gorillas, who are in turn more closely related to us than they are to orang-utans or any other apes. And it was in Africa, some 6 million years ago, that the split occurred between the line that led to chimpanzees and the line that led to modern humans. Since then, many humanoid (human-like) species have evolved, lasted for a while, then died out. Which of them were our direct ancestors, and which just cousins, is still uncertain. But what is certain is that around 150,000 years ago, on the wide grassy plains of East Africa called the savannah, there were human beings who looked very much like us.

Proof that Africa is the original home of the human race is provided by genetic analysis. There is a greater genetic variety among the inhabitants of Africa than elsewhere in the world. This is exactly what one would expect if human beings had originated there, and lived there for a long time, before they lived anywhere else. If one ignores first- and second-generation immigrants, the difference between the genetic makeup of the inhabitants of some African villages 20 miles apart is greater than that between some European nations.

During the nineteenth and early twentieth centuries, when biologists and historians tended to be well-off westerners, confident in the superiority of their own tribes, there was a widespread belief in the separate origin of so-called 'white', 'black' and 'yellow' races of mankind. We now know much more about genetics, and about human origins, and all talk of such 'races' can be dismissed as the product of ignorance or delusion.

We are still a long way from being able to construct a family tree showing the line of descent of human beings since that branching-off 6 million years ago. We know from human remains that sometimes during the past three or four million years there have been several species of sort-of-humans in existence simultaneously. But these remains – partial skulls and incomplete skeletons – are not numerous, and we will need far more examples before we can begin to claim that we have established humanity's ancestral line. Bearing in mind that only a tiny proportion of the human beings alive as recently as 100,000 years ago can have any living descendants, the chances that any fossil creatures yet found were literally direct ancestors of ours are vanishingly small. It may be that some represent species that collectively were ancestral to our own, but confirmation of that must lie a long way in the future.

Remains of early pre-human species have been found in various parts of East and South-east Africa. These extinct species have been given Latin names in accordance with the system devised by the eighteenth-century Swedish naturalist, Carl von Linné, who is generally known by his Latin name, Linnaeus. In the Linnaean system every plant and animal carries a two-part description. The first part indicates the genus, or kind, and the second the species, or precise biological character. Dingoes, greyhounds and St Bernards are all in the genus *Canis,* meaning dog. But dingoes are classified as a separate species – *Canis dingo* – whereas greyhounds and St Bernards are both classified as *Canis familiaris* ('domestic dog') – two varieties of the same species.

When Linnaeus came to classify the primates (lemurs, monkeys, humans, etc.), he placed human beings in the genus *Homo* (which means 'human'), and gorillas and chimpanzees in the genus *Gorilla* and *Pan* respectively. But he placed gorillas, chimpanzees and humans in the same sub-order, *Anthropoidae* (Latin for 'human-like'). In doing so, he went against the religious teachings of his time, which held that human beings were unique among the animal creation. According to the Christian faith, as derived from the Bible, humans had been created 'in the image of God', 'to have dominion over all the beasts of the earth'. In Linnaeus's view, humans were not sufficiently different from the great apes to justify any greater separation in their biological description.

Had the science of genetics existed in Linnaeus's day, he would not even have separated gorillas, apes and humans this far. Common chimps and pigmy chimps (bonobos) share 99.3 per cent of their genes. Both kinds of chimp share 98.4 per cent of their genes with humans. This 1.6 per cent difference between chimps and humans is only about half the difference between chimps and humans on the one hand and gorillas on the other. There can be little doubt that, if Linnaeus had been classifying the primates in the 1990s, rather than in the 1750s, common chimps, bonobos and humans would now all be included in the genus *Homo*.

Biologists still reserve the description *Homo* for modern humans and their nearest extinct relatives. Some more ancient species are placed in the genus *Australopithecus* ('southern ape'). These Australopithecines had brains only a little larger than those of chimpanzees. They had long arms, which presumably meant that they could still easily move about in trees, and, as with most apes, the males were much bigger than the females.

But they did share some characteristics with the later *Homo* group, including an upright gait and smaller front teeth. These species somehow developed the habit of walking upright and the changes in body shape that went with it. One theory has it that, as climate changed and forest gave way to tall grass, apes with a tendency to walk upright could see further. The resulting ability to avoid predators would have increased their chances of survival, and their chances of passing on this tendency as an inherited characteristic. But it is also true that walking upright consumes only about half the energy of four-limbed movement. It may be that this energy-efficiency was a powerful driver of the trend to upright walking.

Around 4 million years ago, there was an upright-walking, ape-like species of this kind living in East Africa, known as *Australopithecus Afarensis*, 'southern ape from Afar' (a district in Ethiopia). This is the species to which 'Lucy', the most famous of all fossil hominids, belongs. Lucy was discovered at Hadar in Ethiopia in 1974, by a joint American/French team led by Donald Johanson and Maurice Taieb. (Donaldson was listening to the Beatles song 'Lucy in the Sky with Diamonds' at the time.) We don't know for sure that Lucy *was* female. The skeleton is incomplete and the assumption was made on the basis of her diminutive stature – about $3^{1}/_{2}$ feet tall. This species, on average about 4 feet tall, or a species like it, has left us an evocative proof of its upright walking habit. Near the Olduvai Gorge in Tanzania, in 1976, the anthropologist Mary Leakey discovered three sets of footprints, 3.7 million years old, that appeared to be those of two adults and a child. They extended for 164 feet (54 yards) across a patch of volcanic ash that a shower of rain had turned into quick-drying cement.

Two and a half million years ago, a rather more

human-looking creature – *Homo habilis* ('handy human') – lived in Kenya and Tanzania. The number of fossil remains classified as belonging to this species is small, and some palaeontologists question whether they represent a single, identifiable species. On the assumption that they do, they suggest an average brain size of around 40 cubic inches, about 40 per cent larger than a chimpanzee's, but less than half the brain capacity of a modern human. These creatures probably possessed the beginnings of speech. All primates have the gift of language, but the limited range of sounds and signs available to chimpanzees and gorillas does not constitute speech. The development of speech had to wait upon two evolutionary steps: complicated changes in the structure of the jaw and the larynx, and changes in the structure and organization of the brain. Just when these occurred, how they interacted and what drove them is still obscure. From the evidence, it is possible that people identified as *Homo habilis* had crossed the boundary that separates animal communication from human speech.

Homo habilis was also a tool-maker. Chimpanzees use sticks and stones *as* tools, but this species fashioned stones *into* tools. Though very simple in form, these tools represented an advance on the practice of previous tool-using species. The material from which they were made was chosen with great care, and their shape, though simple, was crafted with precision.

Homo habilis was a long-lasting species, surviving for something like a million years, and confined to Africa, as were all human-like creatures before 1.5 million years ago. The first such species to venture out of Africa seems to have been *Homo erectus* ('upright human'). The oldest remains of this species, dating from around 1.6 million years ago, are found in Africa. It later spread very widely, and has been discovered right across

Europe and Asia. As well as being widespread, *Homo erectus* was another long-lasting species. Fossils dating from as recently as 200,000 years ago have been found in China, Java and the Caucasus, which implies that there were people of this kind living somewhere in the world for around 1.5 million years.

Two of the most famous humanoid fossils, 'Java Man' and 'Peking Man', belong to this species. The remains of Java Man were discovered in a cave in 1891 by a young Dutch doctor and keen palaeontologist named Eugène Dubois. Other specimens since found on the island indicate that the species lived there from about 1 million to about 500,000 years ago. Peking Man was first identified as a new human fossil from a single tooth found in a cave at Chou-k'ou-tien, near Beijing, in 1927 by the Canadian Davidson Black, also a doctor. The identification was subsequently confirmed by a number of finds at the same site. These remains have been variously dated from about 900,000 to about 130,000 years ago. One of the most amazing discoveries in the cave was a 20 feet thick layer of ash, which not only showed that the cave had been occupied continuously over a long period of time, but that these early humans were already confident users of fire.

As well as being a fire-user, *Homo erectus* was a moderately sophisticated tool-maker, making hand-axes and a variety of roughly shaped tools from flint, chert and quartzite. In both height and brain size *Homo erectus* came about half-way between *Homo habilis* and modern humans, and the species quite possibly had a fairly well-developed power of speech, albeit much more primitive than ours.

The subject of brain size brings us to another hugely significant change that occurred somewhere along the evolutionary path from our ape-like ancestors. Big brains call for big heads. But big heads cause difficulties, as any new mother can verify. In a bipedal ape, there is a limit to the size of head that the pelvic girdle can deliver. But a big brain gave its possessor such an enormous advantage in the survival stakes that there must have been strong evolutionary pressure for brains to grow as large as practicably possible. The outcome of this two-way contest between the advantages of a big brain for the child and the advantages of a small infant head for the mother was in a real sense a premature birth. The nine-month term was followed by the delivery of an offspring whose brain has to complete its development over a period of many months, during which the child is totally dependent on its mother, or mother substitute. No other mammal is born at such a premature stage. If human babies were born at the same stage of brain development as other mammals, they would grow in the womb for at least eighteen months. The fact that they don't is the result of a trade-off between the vulnerability of prolonged dependency and the advantages of a highly developed brain.

It is not known whether *Homo erectus* was a direct ancestor of modern humans, or whether the *sapiens* line and the *erectus* descended separately from a common ancestor species (*Homo habilis*, or a near relative) somewhere between one and two million years ago. But whatever the actual line of descent, the succession did not occur in all the parts of the world where remains of *Homo erectus* have been discovered. New species do not develop in parallel in different locations. Speciation – the development of a new species from an established one – is a unique event that occurs in one location only. Only after a new species has evolved in a particular location does it spread to occupy other territories. If the line to our own species does descend from *Homo erectus*, it can only have originated in one place, and that place has to be somewhere in Africa. In terms of timing, the transition from *Homo erectus* to *Homo sapiens*, if that is what happened, probably occurred more than 500,000 years ago. Fossil remains of that age discovered in Africa display a mixture of *erectus* and *sapiens* characteristics.

It is not until around 150,000 to 120,000 years ago that we find, in Africa, the remains of creatures whose bodily structure is so like ours that biologists feel justified in placing them in the species *Homo sapiens* ('wise human'), and in giving them the label 'modern humans'. When they wish to be very precise in their classifications, biologists call these modern humans *Homo sapiens sapiens*, to distinguish them from the earlier versions of *Homo sapiens* that were around three or four hundred thousand years ago. Greater precision than this cannot be expected. Even if we had a lot more specimens than the handful we possess at present, we would still be confronted with the problem of defining just what constitutes a modern human. The range suggested here – 150,000 to 120,000 years ago – is as precise a date for the appearance of anatomically modern humans as the present fragmentary evidence justifies.

It is important to understand what is meant when one calls this group of people who lived in Africa 150,000 or so years ago 'modern humans'. Human evolution did not stop 150,000 years ago. Our species has undoubtedly changed since then, and not just in obvious superficial ways such as the development of differing skin colours and hair textures. There may also have been significant changes in intellectual and verbal abilities. What we can say for sure is that well before 100,000 years ago our ancestors had achieved a physical form very like our own.

When we move away from the question of physical characteristics, the degree of confidence with which we can characterize these early modern humans is much reduced. We can only guess at the extent of their language skills, their view of themselves, their religious beliefs and practices, their social arrangements, their artistic abilities and the part that music and dance played in their lives. But we can say with confidence that they did have what we would recognize as language, self-consciousness, religious beliefs and practices, social arrangements and music and dance. Why? Because humans throughout history, including the native peoples of Australia and isolated tribes everywhere, have had these things, so they must have been part of the lives of our ancestors well before that party of them left Africa 60,000 years or more ago.

Two opposing contemporary schools of thought compete to interpret the very limited evidence we have. One theory is encapsulated in the phrase 'the great leap forward', coined in the 1990s by the American physiologist and writer on evolutionary biology Jared Diamond in his book *The Rise and Fall of the Third Chimpanzee*. It is a theory that has received powerful endorsement from the eminent American philosopher of language Noam Chomsky. Supporters of this theory believe that somewhere around 50,000 years ago there was a step-change in human evolution, sparked by genetic changes that caused a 'rewiring' of the human brain. The evidence to support this view is rather thin, as is the evidence to refute it. People who see things this way attach great importance to the much greater variety of stone and bone tools employed from around 50,000 BC and the technical skill involved in their manufacture. They also point to what appears to be a sudden flowering of artistic talent, especially as displayed in the magnificent cave paintings in places like Altamira in Spain and Lascaux in France, made by the peoples of the European culture known as the Cro-Magnon from around 30,000 BC. Chomsky, in particular, has forcefully argued that the kind of language ability possessed by present-day humans could not be the product of a gradual evolution over scores of thousands of years, but must have been the outcome of changes in the structuring of the human brain attributable to specific mutations in the human genome.

This interpretation of the very limited evidence leads some to accept the description of our ancestors of 150,000 or so years ago as 'modern humans'. But they qualify the description by making it 'anatomically modern humans', and insist on a different term – 'behaviourally modern humans' – to describe the human beings who have lived since around 60,000 years ago.

The opposite school of thought is represented by people like Robin Dunbar, Professor of Evolutionary Psychology at the University of Liverpool, who argues in his book *The Human Story* that the evidence will equally well support the view that the development of language, of self-consciousness and of intellectual capacity took place gradually over a much longer period. Viewed in this way, there is no case for invoking a 'great leap forward' and no need for a category labelled 'behaviourally modern humans'. The difference between our ancestors of 100,000 to 150,000 years ago and us becomes one of degree rather than one of kind.

Both genetics and neuroscience are still young sciences, and these matters will probably be much better understood in forthcoming generations. It is reasonable to expect that we will by then have assembled a much more informative collection of fossil evidence. In the meantime, we are all at liberty to listen to the arguments, and either keep an open mind or take up a position on one side or the other, without allowing ourselves to be too much intimidated by the eminence of the contesting parties. For this writer, the theory of a great leap forward around 50,000 BC seems for the moment to rest upon too flimsy a body of evidence to be really convincing.

2

THE PEOPLING OF THE EARTH

Those modern humans who lived in East Africa 100,000 years ago, suitably dressed, and well-groomed, could have stood at a supermarket checkout without giving rise to much concern. But though they would not have frightened peak-hour shoppers, shopping would have frightened them. Crowds were something they had no experience of. In the whole of East Africa 100,000 years ago, there were probably no more than 10,000 people – the population of a small town – spread over an area twice the size of France. And scattered among that 10,000 was a handful of people who were the direct ancestors of everyone alive today.

Like chimpanzees, these ancestors of ours lived a wandering life, in family groups of twenty or thirty. Like chimpanzees, they lived off the land, on a largely vegetarian diet. This was supplemented by meat from small animals they caught or scavenged from the remains of larger prey left by carnivores such as lions and leopards. But compared with their primate cousins, they had much more control over their environment, and over their way of life. They had brains as big as ours, and it seems reasonable to assume that they could communicate in a pretty sophisticated way. As a result, they could co-operate, and share information, far more effectively than creatures with small brains and no language. It was large brains and language that enabled them to seek out, and share information about, edible

2.1 The Peopling of the Earth

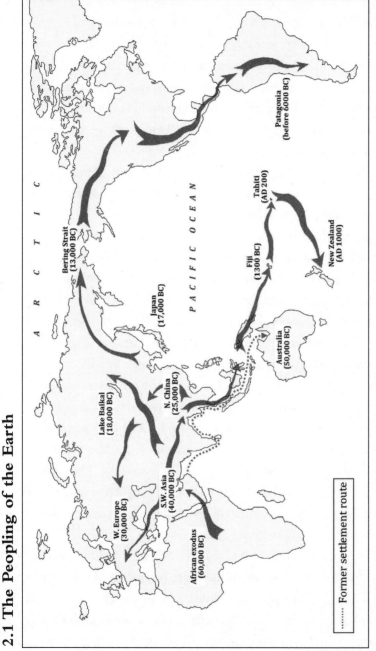

This map shows the likely pattern of spread of modern humans after leaving their original African homeland. All dates shown are subject to possible major revision, as evidence accumulates from future genetic studies and fossil discoveries. The dotted line shows the now submerged route by which Australia was probably first settled. Sources: pattern – S. Oppenheimer, *Out of Eden* (Robinson, 2003); dates – various.

plants. It was large brains and language that enabled them to kill animals as big as, or even bigger than, themselves: by digging pits for them to fall into; by driving them over cliffs; or by cornering them and throwing stones from a safe distance. And in a hot climate, humans have an advantage over other large mammals: they sweat profusely, and lose heat quickly, so that sometimes all they had to do was patiently pursue their prey until it collapsed from exhaustion.

Language skills and a large brain did not just mean efficient gathering and hunting. They made possible two other things – having ideas and sharing ideas – that would henceforth distinguish human beings from the rest of the animal kingdom, and set the human race on the roller-coaster of change we are still riding today. Big brains could think up ideas, not just about things that existed, but about things that might be invented. And language made it possible to pass ideas on to later generations.

It was not just in comparison with chimpanzees that these early humans were better equipped to succeed in whatever surroundings they found themselves in: they were better equipped than most humans are today. They had a rich culture that included a wide range of tools and skills. And they had a large stock of accumulated knowledge, much of it – like the use of fire – inherited from their pre-human ancestors. They knew the location, and the edibility, of hundreds of different kinds of plants, giving them a mastery over their environment that a modern city-dweller might envy.

It is tempting to think that the life of these forebears of ours must have been one of hardship, but in many ways it was anything but. The land they lived in was one of warmth and comparative plenty. Fruit and edible plants were there for the picking; small animals for the catching; and clothes were unnecessary. Their diet was varied, to an extent unimaginable by the farmers who came later. Their teeth were sounder, and their health was better. The necessities of life could be secured by a few hours' work a day, leaving ample leisure for talking, dancing, love-making, story-telling and playing with children: all the things that 'civilized' people have difficulty finding time for. Admittedly, there were lions and leopards, but if one knew how to keep out of their way, life on the savannah 100,000 years ago had much to recommend it.

Africa is almost completely surrounded by ocean, so most creatures that were born there stayed put. But there is one spot where a wandering animal is not brought up short by an expanse of ocean: the corner where Africa meets Asia, on the shores of the Red Sea. From time to time, small groups of creatures – including humans – have found themselves in that corner, and have been led by their curiosity into other continents, where their descendants are still to be found.

The ease with which people could move out of Africa has varied over time. For reasons connected with changes in the shape of the earth's orbit, and the tilt of its axis, the amount of heat received from the sun in the more northerly and southerly regions varies over long periods of time. Particularly important is the amount of heat received by the land masses adjacent to the North Pole. If there is a reduction in the amount of summer melting, ice sheets will spread and more sunlight will be reflected back into space, further intensifying the cooling effect over the whole earth. As a result of such influences, the northerly and southerly regions experience periodic, but not regular Ice Ages, which are interrupted by short, warmer periods known as interglacials when the effects are operating in reverse.

Since human beings evolved, there have been a number of Ice Ages, and we have the good fortune at present to be living in an interglacial that began around 11,000 BC. The amount of water locked up in the form of ice has varied with these fluctuations in the climate. When the ice sheets were at their greatest extent, sea-levels were much lower, and large areas of the earth's surface that are now submerged were dry land. Japan was joined to the Asian mainland; Australia and New Guinea were one continent; North America and East Asia formed a continuous land mass; and the Red Sea was dry, creating a highway from Africa into Asia.

From time to time, during the million or so years before modern humans evolved, early hominids had wandered across this land-bridge. Most of them belonged to the species identified as *Homo erectus*, and between Ice Ages some of these found their way into distant corners of Europe and Asia, where their descendants lived, and where their remains are occasionally unearthed. *Homo erectus*, and all the other species that found their way out of Africa – apart from our own species – eventually succumbed to later Ice Ages. One such group was made up of the ancestors of the people known as Neanderthals (from the Neander Tal, a valley in Western Germany, where their remains were first found in 1856). The Neanderthals constitute a separate species, *Homo neanderthalensis*. They had strongly built bodies and even bigger brains than ours. They were descended from a line that separated from our own in Africa about half a million years ago. They evolved *outside* Africa 250,000 years ago, just before the time that modern humans evolved *within* Africa.

There are remains that suggest that a few modern humans may have found their way out of Africa into the Levant (the area at the eastern end of the Mediterranean) 100,000 years ago. If they did, there is no trace of them in the genes of people alive today. It was not until about 60–70,000 years ago – at least 50,000 years after our species first evolved – that a small number (perhaps a few hundred) made the journey out of Africa that enabled human beings to colonize the rest of the world. Some of their descendants appear to have made their way along the coast of South and South-east Asia. (Sea-levels were lower than they are today, and much of what was dry land is now ocean bed, so we have no evidence of their journey.) In an amazing feat of exploration, some appear to have made it all the way to Australia (over many generations, of course), where their remains have been discovered in deposits 50,000 years old. Despite lower sea-levels, this journey would still have involved crossing more than 30 miles of open sea, beyond which the only indication of land was presumably the smoke from natural bush fires.

There is evidence that a second wave of settlement may have occurred in around 40,000 BC, but apart from that, we can say that the native peoples of Australia are the inheritors of a culture that developed more or less undisturbed for almost 50,000 years. By the time later parties of humans reached South-east Asia, the melting of the ice sheets had drowned many of the land-bridges. This turned the crossing to Australia into a severe challenge that only much later developments in boat building and seamanship would overcome.

The settlement of the rest of the world was a long-drawn-out affair. It was not until around 40,000 years ago that modern humans began to make their way into Europe and South-west Asia. They reached western Europe just around the time, about 30,000 years ago, when the last of the Neanderthals disappeared from the scene. From what we can deduce from their remains, the Neanderthals displayed many of the characteristics that we would regard as being peculiarly human. They were skilled tool-makers, even though their tools were less refined than those developed by modern humans. They seem to have cared for their disabled elders, and they buried their dead with grave goods. Given that their ancestral line diverged from our own only half a million years ago, they presumably had a capacity for speech. But how closely their language skills – and for that matter, their brain power – matched our own, is something we can never know. Whether our own ancestors played any part in their demise is also unknown.

Some people have expressed puzzlement that the Neanderthals became extinct, while our own species, *Homo sapiens*, which was around at the same time, managed to survive. No dramatic explanation is called for. Most species that ever existed are now extinct, and this is true of every hominid species apart from our own. Neanderthals had originated in more northerly regions, where they were vulnerable to a deteriorating climate, and their disappearance coincided with the most severe stage of the last Ice Age. Modern humans tended to live in warmer regions, where life was easier, and their numbers would have been correspondingly greater. The question is not why Neanderthals became extinct, but why our own species survived. And the answer is that it was probably down to luck, as much as to any natural advantage. Those scattered bands of Neanderthals, tough and intelligent though they undoubtedly were, may, like many species before and since, have simply been in the wrong place at the wrong time.

As a result of recent discoveries, we now know that the Neanderthals were not the only other human species around at the time when our own ancestors were beginning their exploration of the world. In 2004, an Australian team discovered the remains of pigmy humans in a cave on the island of Flores, in Indonesia. This species, which they named *Homo floresiensis*, and nicknamed 'the Hobbit', appears to have occupied the cave from some 70,000 until about 12,000 years ago. The only sensible conclusion from this amazing find is that there must have been other human species still around at this time, whose remains have yet to be located.

As modern humans spread around the globe, and generation succeeded generation in widely differing environments, differences in physical appearance became more pronounced. The inhabitants of Africa were already well on the way to the variety they display today: brown alongside black skin; short squat bodies as well as tall rangy ones; and so on. Outside Africa, further variations arose, including new skin colours, face shapes and body builds. Like the varieties of flowers, these bred true, and, over time, the total number of such true-breeding varieties multiplied. The most striking differences – outside Africa – were those that characterized the inhabitants of the Australian land mass, as one might have expected, given the small size of that continent's population, and the long time that they had been cut off from other African emigrants.

All of these differences arose in small isolated populations. Some were undoubtedly the consequence of the process that Charles Darwin called natural selection: the gradual spread of genetic differences that give some creatures an advantage in the survival stakes. Many were probably the result of Darwin's other, lesser-known theory, sexual selection. But it is safe to say that a lot of them arose by pure chance, in the process known as genetic drift: a random trend in the genetic make-up of small groups that owes nothing to selective pressures of any kind.

Isolation in small groups did not just speed up the rate of physical evolution; it also quickened the pace of language change. All languages change over time. But when populations are separated by physical obstacles such as rivers and mountain ranges, they develop in different directions, forming dialects, and eventually, mutually unintelligible tongues. Thus it was that a shared language divided into dialects that became the parent forms of the great language groups we know today: Indo-European, Sino-Tibetan, and so on. These split in turn, so that, for example, Indo-European gave rise to Latin – the source of both French and Spanish – and to Sanskrit – the source of Hindi and Bengali.

As human beings became more widespread, they also became more numerous. Thirty thousand years ago, the population of the world was probably around half a million. With so few remains, we have only a sketchy idea of their way of life. Some settled near water and lived on fish. But most were foragers: people who moved camp every few weeks, as they exhausted the food resources around them. And for most of them, gathering, rather than hunting, was their major source of sustenance. The phrase 'man the hunter' that is sometimes applied to these early ancestors of ours has only two things wrong with it: the word 'man' and the word 'hunter'. It overstates the contribution of men to the feeding of their families, and it exaggerates the importance of hunting in the lives of most foraging communities.

Some were already making pots and weaving baskets. They wore beads and bracelets, and made ivory carvings. In ice-bound regions such as south Australia and present-day

Russia, they had no fruit, but had ample supplies of meat, and wore tailored clothes of fur. But no matter what their way of life, our forebears of 30,000 years ago had one thing in common: they still lived in small family groups, or 'bands', as their ancestors had done for thousands of years before them.

These bands were not completely isolated. There is evidence, in the tools and other objects they left behind, that they were in contact with others, in trading networks that extended over considerable distances. These contacts were of great importance in the accumulation of knowledge and the maturing of what we would call a shared culture. A striking example is provided by the small statuettes known as 'Venus figurines', found across Europe, from the Pyrenees to the northern shores of the Black Sea.

Like twentieth-century gatherer-hunters, these bands presumably got together from time to time in social gatherings of a few hundred, for celebrations in which song, dance and story-telling featured strongly. In regions with seasonal rains, groups of this size would sometimes have lived around a water-hole for weeks at a time.

Although these wider networks of trade and socializing were important in the diffusion of culture, the business of everyday life was still carried on in small groups. Settlements, in so far as they existed, were very small. And vast areas of the world had yet to feel the imprint of a human foot. South and South-east Asia were home to scattered human populations as early as 40,000 years ago, and there is evidence that their descendants had reached the area of modern Beijing by around 25,000 years ago. But most of Central Asia, and all of North and South America, were still 'undiscovered'.

The spread of human beings into these other parts of the world took another 15,000 years. These 15,000 years included the period from 25,000 to 18,000 years ago, when the last Ice Age was at its most severe, and when the challenge for much of humanity was to survive in existing territories, rather than explore new ones. But these people were made of stern stuff. By 18,000 BC, at the latest, some of them had penetrated Central Asia as far as Lake Baikal, in present-day Siberia.

The question of when human beings first reached the Americas is still hotly debated. If one goes by the archaeological evidence, it would seem that it was not until around 13,000 BC that people reached the eastern extremity of Siberia and made the crossing of the then existing land-bridge into North America. But the genetic evidence, particularly from South America, suggests that the Americas may have had more than one founding population, and that at least one of these may have made the crossing as early as 20,000 BC. Whichever theory should ultimately turn out to be correct, we can say with confidence that long before 6000 BC, human beings had made it all the way to the furthest extremity of South America.

Africa's colonization of the world was now almost complete. Only the islands of the Pacific and the lands around the Poles still awaited their first human visitors. By 6000 BC, a chain of settlements stretched from Cape Horn to Hudson Bay, and from Newfoundland right across North America, Asia and Europe as far as the West of Ireland. By this time, the world's population was around 10 million.

The way of life of most of this 10 million still conformed to the gatherer-hunter model that describes the life of early humans 100,000 years before, although the details of their lives varied greatly. In East Africa, food gathering – the collection of

fruit and edible plants – still played the major role, and cloth-
ing was a minor concern. In Siberia and the Canadian Arctic,
life revolved around hunting and fishing. There, the ability to
skin large animals, and turn those skins into coats and trousers,
was a matter of life and death. The mammoth-hunters of
southern Russia passed the winter in tents made of skins, with
mammoth bones for pegs and poles, eating meat from the
freezer (storage pits in the permafrost) which they thawed out
over the fire. In Australia, the descendants of that 'first fleet' of
50,000 years before dined off wild duck, which they hunted
with boomerangs. Their contemporaries in the American
Midwest hunted bison with spears.

But whatever the food, and whatever the implements and
weapons used, over most of the earth, human life was still the
life of the small band, consisting of no more than twenty or
thirty adults and a few children. Permanent settlement was the
exception, not the rule. And children were few, because having many children would have been a liability. These bands
needed to travel light. In a world full of predators, a woman
with a child at her breast and a toddler to watch over was a
luxury a wandering band could ill afford. The baby that arrived
too soon after an older sibling carried its own death warrant.

In spite of these difficulties, world population continued to
grow, from an estimated 500,000 in 30,000 BC to 10 million in
6000 BC. Such a rate of growth may appear unexceptional by
the standards of the last few hundred years, but compared with
what had gone before, these were dramatic figures. Something,
clearly, was working in humanity's favour. That something was
the most important revolution in human history.

3

PUTTING DOWN ROOTS

Most of the increase in human population between 30,000 BC and 6000 BC occurred towards the end of that period. Before 11,000 BC, ice sheets covered the whole of northern Europe (including most of Britain), Central Asia and northern North America, and this limited the amount of land suitable for human existence. Cave-dwelling bands, who clothed themselves with animal skins and knew how to use fire, were able to survive in the ice-covered regions, but their numbers were small. As time went by, improvements in hunting technology – the invention of the bow and arrow, the spear-thrower and the harpoon – enabled more people to live off a given area of land. But for hunting and gathering to support a substantial increase in population, the amount of land available had to increase. From around 11,000 BC, as the ice retreated, new feeding grounds opened up to the animals that were the hunters' prey, and their numbers increased. As the hunters followed them, their numbers increased, too. As frozen rivers thawed out, fishing grounds became more widespread, and fish – and fishermen – became more abundant. For those who were not merely hunters but gatherers as well, there was a double benefit: as the grasses spread into new areas, so did the fruit trees and the wild cereals.

The benefits of climate change were widespread. A side-effect of the icy conditions in regions near the Poles had been reduced rainfall in lands nearer the equator. This had limited the range of many plants, and the animals that fed on them. But as the climate warmed, many places enjoyed increased rainfall, with a consequent increase in the richness of plant and animal life.

Suddenly, there was more of everything. Clever people continued to invent tools and weapons, enabling more mouths to be fed. But this did not amount to a new way of life; they were simply improvements to ways of life that had persisted for thousands of years. No matter how efficient gatherers and hunters became at their traditional pursuits, they were never going to become property agents or software engineers. For this, something fundamental had to change.

Suppose a band of hunter-gatherers find themselves on the banks of a lake teeming with fish, where reeds flourish and animals come to drink. Their reaction will be to linger. What is the point of running miles after food, when the food insists on coming to you? After a while, other people arrive; but food is plentiful, and so is space, so there is no need to fight over either. Old habits die hard, and, at first, individual family groups keep their distance. After a few years, thatched dwellings line the lakeside, and the smell of grilled fish and steak and the laughter of playing children fill the air. Soon, the children of neighbouring families are playing together; and the more gregarious parents are inviting the parents of their children's friends to fish suppers.

But doorstep delivery of meat and fish is only one of the delights of this new location. Like all communities, this one contains people who like cooking, and others who have a special feeling for plants. Between them, they discover that the countryside around them is full of wild cereals that are good to eat, especially if cooked. Soon, they are making porridge. The plant-lovers – who are about to become gardeners – naturally select the cereals with the biggest ears, containing the plumpest seeds. Sometimes, when they come back from a harvesting trip, they spill some of the grain on the ground, which is rich with nutrients brought down by the river that feeds the lake and spread by its floods. Some of this grain, already carefully selected, takes root. Soon the area around the settlement is home to an interesting crop of grass, with more than usually big ears, containing noticeably plump grain. One day, a particularly bright gardener-in-the-making hits upon the idea of selecting the very best ears from this already choice collection not for eating, but for planting. The next year, someone suggests that the best grain from that crop should be set aside, and used as seed for the following year.

It is obvious where this is leading. Locate the lake shore in Palestine – or make it a river valley in central China – and we have a speeded-up version of the Agricultural (or Neolithic) Revolution: the fundamental change in living habits that made our modern world possible.

While the term 'Agricultural Revolution' is used by historians and archaeologists, it doesn't signify the overnight initiation of a new process. The term 'proto-farming' is used by some writers to describe the long transitional period during which gatherers must have experimented with relocating and irrigating wild plants, before they settled down to practise farming as a permanent way of life. The process was a series of steps, adapting to changing circumstances over an extended period.

One of the reasons why people tend to over-dramatize the emergence of settled agriculture is that they start from a misinterpretation of the term 'hunter-gatherer'. The Agricultural Revolution was not a sudden switch from a lifestyle in which *men* chased antelopes, to one in which *men* got their kicks from growing bigger vegetables than their next door neighbours. In most hunter-gatherer societies, food gathering is as important as hunting, and in many, it is overwhelmingly more important. Cultures such as the Inuit of North America, in which meat accounts for most of the food intake, are not typical: they were forced upon people by a harsh environment. In the softer climates where settled agriculture first arose, there must have been a long learning period during which women *and* men acquired a profound understanding of wild food plants and the ways of gentler animals. When they found themselves in places where the idea of settlement seemed attractive, they were already in possession of most of the knowledge they needed to embark upon an agricultural way of life.

Although our thought experiment shows *how* the change to a farming culture could have happened, it does not explain *why*. *Why* questions are usually about motivation: 'Why did you do that?' or 'Why did the chicken cross the road?'. We can't ask that kind of question about the Agricultural Revolution, because it wasn't the result of deliberate intention. Nobody said, 'I'm fed up with hunting and gathering – let's invent urban civilization.' No one *chose* this new way of life. Changes over long periods of time are the result of thousands of individual choices about desired outcomes next week, or next year. Such changes occur gradually, without anyone willing them, and usually without anyone realizing that they *are* occurring.

The question we now need to ask is 'Where, and when and in what kinds of environment, did the changes take place that led to the replacement of hunter-gathering by agricultural civilizations?' Thanks to the discoveries made by archaeologists during the past hundred years, this is a question we are well on our way to answering.

There was not one Agricultural Revolution, but several, in various parts of the world. Each took place in a different way, and involved different crops and methods of cultivation. Table 3.1 contains a list of six regions where we know that independent revolutions of this kind occurred, though there were undoubtedly others. Of these six, the one that has been most intensively researched occurred in the 'Fertile Crescent' – the stretch of country extending from southern Palestine, through Syria, southern Turkey and northern Iraq, into western Iran. The others occurred in the Yellow River Valley, in north China; in the valley of the River Yangtze, in central China; in central Mexico; on the Andean Plateau, from Colombia, through Peru, to northern Chile; and in Africa south of the Sahara.

The dates shown in the table are approximately when the populations of the various regions made the change from a wandering lifestyle to a settled system of agriculture. These dates are provisional. The starting date in each case could well be pushed further back, as a result of future discoveries. This applies particularly to north and central China, which have not been subjected to as much archaeological exploration as the Fertile Crescent.

How did the change take place? The geography and climate of each region were different, as were the plants and animals available to the settlers, but one factor was common in all of them: the process of domestication, the incorporation of plants and animals into a partnership with human beings. It was

3.1 The Emergence of Agriculture

Region	Period of Emergence	Key Domesticates	
		Plants	**Animals**
1 The Fertile Crescent (Palestine to Iran)	*c.* 8000 BC	Wheat Barley	Goats Sheep Cows Pigs
2 Central China (Yangtze)	*c.* 6500 BC	Rice	Pigs Water-buffaloes
3 North China (Yellow River)	*c.* 6500 BC	Millet	Chickens Pigs
4 Central America (Mexico)	*c.* 3000 BC	Maize Squash Beans	
5 South America (Peru/Chile)	*c.* 2500 BC	Potatoes Quinua	Llamas Alpacas Guinea-pigs
6 Sub-Saharan Africa	*c.* 2000 BC	Sorghum Millet	Cows

Source: B. D. Smith, *The Emergence of Agriculture* (Scientific American Library, 1995)

only when men and women (with the help of their children) domesticated wild species that farming truly began.

Domestication has two elements: *manipulation* and the *creation of dependence*. Manipulation means the careful selection of the most desirable specimens from successive generations of plants and animals so as to breed more useful varieties. In the case of wheat, wild species were grown in carefully prepared

soils, and the seed for subsequent crops was selected for qualities of size, hardiness and high yield. By continued repetition
of this process, new varieties were created that yielded more,
and better, flour, and – most importantly – could be relied
upon to breed true to type. In the case of sheep, new varieties
gave bigger joints and juicier meat. Later on, they were bred
to have thick woolly coats, in place of the mostly hairy skins
of their wild ancestors. In western Asia, they were even bred
to give copious supplies of milk, which the peoples of the
region were able to digest (something many adults elsewhere
in the world have never been able to do). The most striking
example of human manipulation of a wild species – the wolf –
was also one of the earliest. This was another creature with an
instinct to follow a leader. Cubs from a pack caught hanging
around a camp could be taught to follow a human leader
instead. In this case, breeding experiments over many generations resulted in a totally new species – the dog – that could be
relied upon not to eat the sheep, and also to prevent wolves
from eating them.

Important as manipulation was, its contribution to the
making of the Agricultural Revolution should not be exaggerated. Much of the selection that led to the evolution of new
varieties of animals and plants must have been unintentional.
Every time a herdsman killed a big, bad-tempered bull, or an
unusually menacing ram, he was automatically reducing the
incidence of genes for large size and aggression in the population at large. (Early domesticated varieties were invariably
smaller than their wild forebears.) Every time a woman collected wild wheat and kept some of the seed for planting, she
was automatically selecting for genes that caused the grain to
remain firmly in the ears until it was harvested.

The other defining feature of domestication is the creation of dependence. As selective breeding continues down the generations, animals and plants become more dependent upon human beings. Dogs might still be able to manage in the wild individually, if they had to, but they would rather not. And if they did have to, they might not survive for long as a separate species. In the case of sheep, a stage is soon reached at which the new variety is unable to survive without human protection. The same can equally be true of a crop like maize, where the tight heads of domesticated varieties are unable to release their seed without human help. This is what distinguishes the cultivation of wild plants, and the management of wild herds, from true domestication. Domesticated varieties are human creations, and most of them would quickly cease to exist without human intervention.

But for domestication to be possible, there had to be settlement. Because towns and cities could not have come into existence without an agricultural base, it is often assumed that agriculture must have come first, and that settlement must have followed. But that was true only of large settlements. Until human beings settled in specific places and created villages, agriculture could not exist at all, so in a very real sense the village is the source of civilization.

The earliest agricultural village so far discovered is in the West Bank area of Palestine, 15 miles north of Jericho. There, on the site of the ancient city of the same name, beneath more than twenty layers of later settlements, lie the remains of a village that, around 8000 BC, was home to at least 300 people. They lived in mud-brick houses, on the edge of a spring-fed lake. They grew figs, two kinds of wheat and two kinds of barley, which they harvested with wooden-handled flint sickles.

3.1 Early Agriculture in South-west Asia, 8000BC – 6000BC

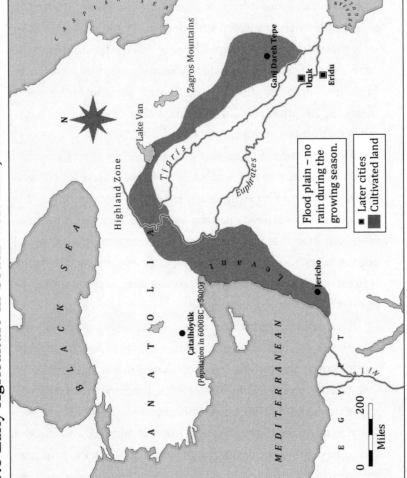

One of several regions of the world in which agriculture arose independently. The shaded area – 'The Fertile Crescent' – was almost certainly the earliest such region. Source: B. Smith, *The Emergence of Agriculture* (Scientific American Library, 1995).

CASPIAN SEA

BLACK SEA

Highland Zone

Lake Van

Zagros Mountains

ANATOLIA

Tigris

Euphrates

Ganj Dareh Tepe

Uruk

Eridu

PERSIAN GULF

Çatalhöyük
(Population in 6000BC = 5000)

LEVANT

Jericho

MEDITERRANEAN

EGYPT

SIN

Flood plain – no rain during the growing season.

■ Later cities
■ Cultivated land

N

0   200
Miles

They introduced excitement into their lives, and variety into their diet, by hunting the wild sheep and gazelle that lived nearby.

Although Jericho is the oldest farming village so far discovered, other settlements have been dated around that time in the western portion of the Fertile Crescent, which archaeologists call the Levantine Corridor. That this region, so bare and arid today, should have been the birthplace of the world's first agricultural villages might seem strange. But 'Fertile Crescent' is an apt description of the area from Palestine to western Iran as it was then: a green, wooded country, filled with game.

Despite its name, the region did not have a particularly fertile soil. The plains to the south, fed by the flooding of great rivers, were potentially much richer, but they received little rain, so were irrelevant in an age without artificial irrigation. The foothills around the Fertile Crescent, on the other hand, enjoyed reliable year-round rainfall, and had a soil in which wild forms of wheat and barley were perfectly at home.

Scientists who have considered the history of manipulation of wild species believe that 300 years is all that would have been needed to develop domestic strains from the wild varieties that existed in the surrounding countryside. It is a conclusion that would not surprise a modern plant breeder. It also makes sense. It is difficult to imagine a Stone Age farmer having the patience to persevere in breeding generations of cereals that displayed little improvement in the course of an entire working life.

Just as the development of arable farming depended upon locally available wild cereals, so the development of livestock farming depended upon a supply of animals suitable for domestication. In this respect, too, the countries of the Fertile Crescent were a farmer's dream. The ideal candidate for domestication is a docile, slow-moving animal that is easy to catch, tolerant of confinement and breeds happily in captivity. It helps if it is not too fussy about what it eats, and if its instinct is to follow a leader. That such a creature should exist in the wild sounds too good to be true; but the settlers in the Fertile Crescent found themselves in the company of not one, but three: the sheep, the goat and the cow. With such a store of live meat, and such a variety of wild grains, the area was like an outdoor supermarket. It is no wonder that the human beings who discovered it decided to park on its doorstep, and concentrate on improving the stock.

Although the earliest agricultural settlements are found at the western end of the Fertile Crescent, and although it was there that cereals were first domesticated, it was at the eastern end that a system of mixed farming, combining field crops and livestock, first appeared. Excavations at Ganj Dareh Tepe, a site in west-central Iran, dating to around 7000 BC, have yielded evidence of domestication of both goats and barley. This was a region with a long history of the herding of wild goats, and from here the practice of keeping goats later spread to the Levant.

The last of the three animals to be domesticated was the cow. This was a daring venture, and an impressive achievement. The wild ancestor of the cow was the aurochs, a massive creature standing 6 feet high at the shoulder, with long, curved, forward-pointing horns. It survived in the wild until the seventeenth century, a formidable beast whose domestication is a tribute to the spirit and determination of those early farmers who fenced it in, and bred from it the smaller, more docile creature we know today.

A different kind of agriculture arose in the valley of the River Yangtze, in central China. There abundant rain created a region of wetlands and inter-connecting lakes unique outside

3.2 Early Agriculture in China, 6500BC – 5500BC

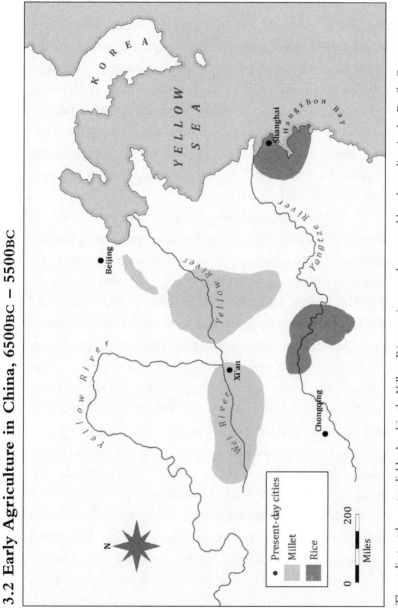

The earliest settlements reliably dated in the Yellow River region are almost as old as the earliest in the Fertile Crescent.
Source: B. Smith, *The Emergence of Agriculture* (Scientific American Library, 1995).

the tropics. The naturally occurring cereal was rice, and there is evidence of the harvesting of wild rice as early as 12,000 BC. Rice likes to have wet feet during the growing season. Water was something the Yangtze Valley had in abundance, so the settlers there set about providing their improved rice strains with the environment they appreciated, building retaining walls on the valley slopes to create flooded fields while the rice was growing. Then they breached the walls, releasing the water and enabling the rice to dry out. This was the origin of the paddy-field system of rice cultivation, which is such a feature of the Chinese landscape today.

The oldest farming villages so far uncovered in the Yangtze Valley date back to around 6500 BC. This is a thousand years later than the earliest excavated in the Levant, but it is possible that future excavations will cause this date to be pushed back. Like the Fertile Crescent, the Yangtze region had wild animals that tasted good and were amenable to domestication. The heaven-sent species in this case were the wild pig, with its ability to transform all kinds of refuse into delicious meat, and the water buffalo, a creature that seemed purpose-made for day-long toil in the fields, with shoulder blades that made perfect spades for working them.

Four hundred miles to the north, in the valley of the Yellow River, nature had set out another tempting stall. This was an area of sparse rainfall and cold winters – no place for rice. However, it contained several species of wild millet – a plant that thrives in dry conditions. For the people who settled there, millet provided a useful addition to a diet already rich in fish, venison and assorted wild plants. In the intervals between fish suppers and venison roasts, they passed the time with experiments designed to improve the yields of the wild millets, and in cross-breeding them to produce new varieties. These experiments yielded two varieties – broomhorn and foxtail – that would later assume an importance in the economies of East and South-east Asia second only to rice. Both are valuable food sources in their own right and can also be fed to pigs and chickens. Pigs and chickens ran wild in the Yellow River Valley and it did not take a genius to make the connection between them and domesticated millet. By 5000 BC, the chickens and the pigs were in pens, and chicken drumsticks and spare ribs had become a staple of the local diet. The discarded bones are a familiar sight on archaeological digs today.

4

THE WORLD IN 4000 BC

By 4000 BC, settled agriculture was an established way of life throughout the entire length of the Fertile Crescent, in the Nile Valley, and across wide areas of central and northern China. The most significant consequence of this was a speeding-up of the rate of cultural change. To understand why this occurred, we need to think in terms of networks. 'Networking' sounds like a modern invention, but it is older than the first human settlements. Networking is what hunter-gatherers did 20,000 years ago, when they traded tools and information with people they met on their travels. But the number of such transactions increased when people began to live in villages only a few miles apart. When bright people could discuss ideas daily, the rate of innovation increased. When travellers met up two or three times a month, rather than two or three times a year, the rate of spread of new techniques rocketed. Whereas the way of life of scattered food gatherers might remain essentially unaltered for hundreds, or even thousands of years, these farming communities were caught up in a process of continual change. It must have been somewhere about this time that old people could first be overheard saying, 'I remember when none of this was fields.'

Just as it had taken only a few hundred years to domesticate the plants and animals that became the basis of this new way of life, so it took only a few hundred more for the new cultures to spread across whole regions. And they did so against a background of climate change that was continually opening up new areas for settlement. In the older centres of population, it was not only the number and density of villages that increased; so did their average size. As they grew, the character of the largest of them altered. They became small towns: centres of trade, gossip and amusement, housing the world's first market traders and door-to-door salesmen.

As villages grew into towns, the lives of their inhabitants changed. The informality of village life could no longer cope effectively with all that needed to be done. Organization became essential. Markets worked better if they were held at regular, advertised intervals. Projects like the building of town walls called for planning and leadership. Tasks such as tool making, fishing and cereal growing could be performed much more effectively if they were left to specialists working full-time at one trade. Once the population of settlements was measured in thousands rather than hundreds, all these things became possible. It was with the development of the first towns that three notable features of our modern world – bureaucracy, occupational specialization and a boss class – appeared.

The benefits of agriculture were obvious. The lands where it was adopted were able to support a much larger population. Depending on the environment, a hunting and gathering band of two dozen people needed a territory of anything up to 30 square miles to ensure a reliable supply of food; a farming family of the same size could get by on 50 acres. Their food supply was also more secure. Crops could be stored in granaries and meat could be stored on the hoof. And in a settled environment, babies that arrived in quick succession were no longer a liability; they were useful bird scarers and animal minders.

In the short term, it must have seemed all gain. But these benefits had a fearsome downside, one that would not be revealed until the process had gone too far to be reversed. Close proximity to animals meant close acquaintance with their parasites, and the diseases those parasites carried. Some of these diseases were transferable to humans. So long as people lived in scattered villages, the danger was slight. Any outbreak of disease was likely to peter out, from lack of new people to infect, before it could do much damage. But when people, and their beasts, began to live in towns, and towns began to multiply, conditions were created in which diseases could spread quickly, creating havoc in populations that had not yet acquired immunity.

The densest concentration of villages and towns in 4000 BC was in the Fertile Crescent. It had been the scene of the first agricultural settlements, and its people were now pioneers in urban living. From southern Palestine, through Anatolia, to the Persian Gulf, hundreds of large villages and small towns dotted the landscape. At least one of them – Eridu, on the banks of the Euphrates, in what is now southern Iraq – boasted 5000 inhabitants. Among the crops the people of this region had added to their creature comforts were domesticated varieties of two plants that grew wild there: the vine and the date palm. Some of their improved vines supplied table grapes; one – *Vitis vinifera*, the wine grape – offered even greater delights. The date palm was a cornucopia of useful products, including fresh and dried fruit, timber for making furniture and leaves for basket making.

As well as helping them to furnish their homes, the date palm also provided the material for making rafts. These river-valley people were unacquainted with the horse, and we have no evidence that they possessed carts. The earliest image of a wheel so far found dates from around 3500 BC. In 4000 BC, loads too heavy to carry were moved on hand-drawn sledges. In the absence of wheeled vehicles, and the roads that went with them, rafts were an essential form of transport for both people and materials. This dependence on water transport was a key factor governing the location of many of the first towns.

In terms of technology, this was an age of stone. The tool-boxes of the craftsmen of Eridu, and the tool sheds of their farming neighbours, contained a wide range of implements, but those that were not made of wood were fashioned from stony materials such as flint, granite and obsidian. Obsidian, a black volcanic glass that could be worked to produce a fiercely sharp edge, was particularly prized, and it was traded over hundreds of miles from its source on the shores of Lake Van, on the borders of present-day Turkey and Iran.

Metallurgy and metalworking were as yet undeveloped. In some parts of the world, such as West Africa and northern Iran, where copper occurred in its natural form, it had been in use for at least 2000 years for ornamental purposes. But it was too soft to be able to compete with stone as a general-purpose material for tools, and the happy discovery of techniques for strengthening it by combining it with other metals lay far ahead.

Living as we do in a world dependent upon metals, it is easy to slip into the habit of thinking that a 'Stone Age' culture must be a primitive one. For some people, the term 'mud brick' carries similar connotations. Such thinking does less than justice to the lives of these town dwellers of 6000 years ago. Their lives were lightened by music, song and dance, as ours are. They had paintings and wood-carvings, textiles woven on the loom, jewellery and elegant hand-thrown pots. They constructed their houses and their public buildings out of mud bricks, not because they couldn't think of any other way to do it, but because sun-dried bricks were cheap and easy to make, and the land they lived in was not blessed with accessible sources of stone.

These people of the Fertile Crescent had without doubt the most sophisticated culture of their day, but a plainer version of their way of life was followed right across Europe, from Spain to the Ukraine. To work their fields, these European farmers had a recently invented tool: the plough. With a wooden frame, no wheels, no mouldboard and a deer antler for a share, it was not strong enough to turn the soil and bury weeds. But it was a much more effective way of preparing a seed bed than the digging stick used by their ancestors, and the productivity that resulted greatly increased the number of mouths that a given area of land could feed. They had no towns to match those in the Fertile Crescent, but their villages, located in forest clearings, were numbered in thousands.

In 4000 BC, the culture of farming established on the European mainland had not yet found its way to the continent's offshore islands. Britain and Ireland had been cut off from the mainland by rising sea-levels since around 8000 BC. Both were clothed in dense woodland, patrolled by bears and wolves. These woods were no place for humans; but on the open moors above them, a few thousand people maintained the hunting and gathering lifestyle their ancestors had brought with them before the seas had risen.

The farming practices of the Fertile Crescent had spread, not just north and west, but south and east as well. Prior to 5000 BC, the region that is now the Sahara had been a country of open savannah, interspersed with great lakes and teeming with wildlife, where a farming people cultivated cereals and herded wild cattle. The Nile Valley, by contrast, had been a forested swamp. But rising temperatures, combined with reduced rainfall, had started a process of drying out. As the first patches of desert appeared, and the river valley became drier, the farmers and their families decamped. As they cleared the forests, they discovered that they had moved to a land whose rich soil was annually refreshed by the river floods. Inspired by the example of their neighbours in Palestine, they had planted peas and beans, as well as wheat and barley. They had domesticated sheep, pigs, goats and cattle, and had become skilled at catching fish. In this rich new environment, their numbers had exploded, and in their riverside villages and small towns they were now laying the foundations of a brilliant civilization.

In East Asia, the farming culture that had arisen along the Yellow River had spread to much of northern China. Further south, the rice-and-pork lifestyle of the Yangtze had diffused over a wide area, but rice still formed only a modest portion of the food intake of the people there. Rice is a hugely productive grain, with a far greater yield than other cereals, but it requires a massive investment of labour to create the conditions in which it gives of its best. It would take many centuries for it to become a staple of the Chinese diet and to support a nation of city-dwellers. China in 4000 BC was, like Europe, still a land of villages rather than towns.

Across the sea in Japan, life revolved around fishing and hunting. The rise in sea-levels at the end of the Ice Age had isolated the country, and its inhabitants had developed an indigenous culture based on coastal life in small villages. The seas that had cut them off from foreign ideas had in turn deprived their neighbours of awareness of their lifestyle, which included a culture of pottery-making far in advance of anything in mainland Asia.

In the countries to the south of China, the dominant culture remained that of the hunter-gatherer. The barriers to the movement of people and ideas were formidable, and it would be another thousand years before wet rice farming would find its way into South-east Asia.

Across most of South Asia, too, food gathering was still the predominant way of life. But in the north-west corner of the Indian subcontinent there was an established culture of settled agriculture. Our knowledge of the early history of this part of the world is fragmentary, and much of the evidence has been swept away by the floods that have periodically devastated the region. But recent excavations in Balochistan, in north-west Pakistan, make it clear that there is a story to be told of ancient domestication of animals and plants. Whether it will turn out to be yet another example of the independent development of agriculture, or whether, as seems more likely, it will prove to have been an extension of developments in the Fertile Crescent, we cannot at present say.

One continent – Australia – was never to have an Agricultural Revolution. The rise in sea-levels had completely isolated it, and it would be thousands of years before the agricultural way of life would touch its inhabitants. The fact that they did not develop a farming culture of their own is no reflection on their energy or intelligence. Farming has emerged independently only half a dozen times in the history of the world, and it has done so only in fertile regions where there were animals and plants that lent themselves to domestication. And even then, it required a 'critical mass' of settlements of an appreciable size for the process of agricultural innovation to develop real momentum. On a score of one to ten for the factors required for an Agricultural Revolution, the environment of most native Australians was close to one. Given the hand that nature had dealt them, it is no surprise that the Australians of 4000 BC were still gatherers and hunters, as the first Australians had been 50,000 years before.

Australian agriculture at this time was an example of the system known as 'slash and burn', an unfortunate term to apply to what is in fact a deliberate system of environmental management. What sounds as if it was a wanton, destructive assault on the environment was a calculated process, based on centuries of accumulated experience, in which areas of forest were cleared by a mixture of tree felling and fire, to create an open landscape, fertilized by ash, where new growth of a desired kind could establish itself. In Australia, as in many other regions of the world, it was the work of people who knew what they were doing, and it represented a domestication of the landscape as profound as the domestication of animals and plants performed by settled peoples.

On the other side of the Pacific, the vast continent of the Americas was home to many different cultures. Most were characterized by an itinerant life style, based on their relationship with the large mammals with which they shared their homelands: the caribou in the North, the bison in the Midwest and the guanaco and the vicuna on the Andean Plateau. (The llama – the product of a cross between the guanaco and the vicuna – had not yet been invented.) The people of the Americas were all either hunters or hunter-gatherers. Historically speaking, they were also newcomers, and it would be hundreds of years before their descendants would embark upon the experiments that would take them into their own Agricultural Revolutions.

This whistle-stop tour has focused on two sharply

4.1 The Development of Human Cultures

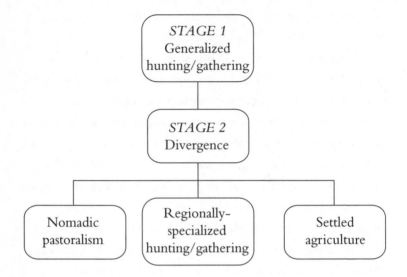

4.2 The Transition to Settled Agriculture

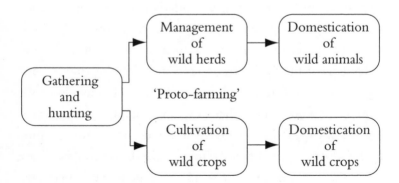

The transition from gathering and hunting to full-time farming was a gradual one, via a long period of part-time 'proto-farming'.

contrasting kinds of existence: farming, and hunting, or hunting and gathering. But it would be a misleading history that concerned itself solely with these two. A third way of life has been followed by millions of people in the past, and is still widely practised today. It is called nomadic pastoralism, and its practitioners have contributed to some of the most dramatic events in human history.

Pastoralists are livestock farmers who travel with their beasts. Whereas other farmers keep their herds and their flocks in the same locality from one year's end to the next, nomads move theirs from place to place, to take advantage of seasonal grazing. Their homes are portable, and their characteristic dwelling is a tent made of skins. They don't all live in small bands. Their flocks and herds can be huge, and their own numbers can be correspondingly large.

The historical relationship between pastoralism and other cultures is illustrated in Diagram 4.1. Both pastoralism and farming grew out of hunting and gathering, and both were based on careful science. Both were concerned with the quality of their stock, and were equally knowledgeable in matters of breeding. Wealth could be accumulated in either activity. The owner of a flock of fine sheep had no reason to feel disadvantaged alongside the owner of a large farm; for a poor peasant farmer, he might feel nothing but pity.

In Africa, and in the lands bordering the Fertile Crescent, as well as across much of Central Asia, pastoralism would later become the established way of life of many different peoples, but their story belongs in a subsequent chapter. In 4000 BC, the people whose descendants would go on to adopt pastoralism were still basically food gatherers. Only in one part of the world, southern Russia, were there signs of a further revolution to come. There, on the wide expanse of the Steppe, the herders of wild sheep had recently succeeded in taming a very different animal from the docile creatures that were being domesticated elsewhere. This animal was the horse, and its enrolment in the list of mankind's obedient servants was to have profound consequences.

Continued global warming had opened up new areas for colonization by plants and animals, including human animals. Settled agriculture enabled already occupied lands to support greatly increased numbers. Even the peoples who had not taken up farming had better tools and better weapons with which to harvest and hunt. As human beings improved their ability to exploit and control their environment, their numbers grew. In 6000 BC the population of the world had been about 10 million. By 4000 BC it had risen to around 30 million.

In the years since modern humans had first migrated out of Africa, separation by seas, rivers, forests and mountain ranges had resulted in a diversity of cultures, and an even greater diversity of languages. The boundaries of cultures and the boundaries of languages are seldom the same. If one sees a stranger using a bow and arrow, one does not need to know their word for either *bow* or *arrow* to be able to appreciate the advantages of possessing both. This is how some cultures came to be adopted over wide areas, even though the people adopting them spoke different languages. In 4000 BC, the world's 30 million inhabitants probably spoke around 10,000 languages between them – about twice as many as exist today. This means that the average number of people speaking any one language was about 3000. It is a statistic that brings out with startling clarity the small size and local character of the social universe inhabited by our ancestors of 6000 years ago.

From around 4000 BC, many human societies began to change at a noticeably faster rate, and the organization of those societies became more complex.

To the history of the rise of villages and towns, we now add that of the city. The difference between a village and a town, or between a town and a city, is a difference in what goes on in them, rather than how many people live in them. What characterizes a city is not so much its size, as the role it performs in the administration – political, financial and religious – of the surrounding territory. In a city, there has always been some kind of centre of government: if not a ruler's palace, then at least an important block of government offices. There would also be a superior class of temple, mosque or church, and several fine-looking banks, or, in the days before banks, the homes of rich merchants.

These three – villages, towns and cities – are the significant categories of human settlement. But to talk about the workings of human societies, we need to consider not just physical descriptions of the places where people live, but the particular relationships between human beings in the mass, which means looking at culture, state and civilization.

The concept of a culture has arisen several times already with the meaning of a way of life shared by large numbers of people over considerable distances, but not needing any kind of formal organization. A state is the binding together of large numbers of people under a common government, backed up by force. We will be tracing the development of the first states in this chapter. That leaves civilization. This is a word that arouses strong feelings, but its use in this book is quite specific.

When Mohandas Gandhi, the great campaigner for Indian independence, visited England in the 1930s, a reporter asked him, 'Mr Gandhi, what is your opinion of Western civilization?' His reply was, 'I think it would be a very good thing.' It was a response that nicely pointed up the many possible meanings of the word, and the unthinking way in which it is sometimes used. Many societies – including ancient Rome, eighteenth-century China and nineteenth-century Britain – have employed it with the implied sub-text 'We are civilized; you are barbarians; they are savages.' It is impossible to call oneself 'civilized', in this sense, without implying that someone else is 'uncivilized', which means that any such use of the word necessarily implies abuse of someone. In this book, the word 'civilization' is used with one meaning only: a culture that is spread over a large area and persists for a long time, and finds expression in a particular style of city life.

It is time to return to those towns in and around the Fertile Crescent, and in particular those in Mesopotamia, the region traversed by the rivers Tigris and Euphrates, in what is now Iraq. Mesopotamia has been called 'the cradle of civilization', but that is to go too far. Its claim to special attention lies, not in its uniqueness, but in its having been the earliest such 'cradle'. It also has the advantage for the historian that it was the birthplace of a very durable form of writing, cuneiform, which enables us to trace the development of this form of civilization in a way we cannot do, for example, for the Indian subcontinent or for

China. It was an innovation whose importance rivalled that of the Agricultural Revolution of 6000 years earlier.

Mesopotamia in the period from 4000 BC to 3500 BC was a perfect example of the truth of the saying that 'nothing succeeds like success'. This collection of large towns within easy reach of each other, in such a benign environment, must have constituted a forcing-house for the development of new ideas.

One crucial idea was irrigation. Mesopotamia had an ample supply of water in the form of run-off from the surrounding mountains, but 'run-off' is the operative term. Once the water had found its way into the Tigris and the Euphrates, it effectively by-passed the extensive plains through which they ran, which had little rainfall of their own. The potentially fertile soil was replenished by floodwater from the rivers, but between floods, the ground baked under a fierce sun. Reservoirs and canals solved the problem of water supply during the dry season, and an increased population provided both the labour force and the incentive for their construction. Having been made possible by the increased population, irrigation in turn provided the food to support further increases in population, which required, and made possible, even more ambitious projects.

There has been much argument as to which came first: organized states or large-scale irrigation. It is a futile argument, because it is based on the assumption that one must have been the cause of the other. The only sensible answer is that large-scale irrigation and organized states evolved together, and each was a factor in the other's evolution.

These reservoirs and canals not only ensured a supply of water throughout the growing season, they also helped to control the great rivers. This was a country that had recent experience of devastating floods, the memory of which would later be embodied in one of the world's earliest great folk tales – *The Epic of Gilgamesh* – which inspired the biblical story of Noah and his ark. This story of the heroic deeds of the Mesopotamian King Gilgamesh is told in clay tablets dating from the seventh century BC that were discovered in the ruins of the great library in Nineveh. Fragments found elsewhere suggest that the story was already 2000 years old.

As these projects got larger, the amount of planning and labour management involved also increased. It was this relationship between the size of the project and the organization required that drove the feedback process in which the execution of large projects created habits of co-operation and developed organizational skills, which made it easier to carry out even larger projects. Such projects required not just organizational skills, but organizational structures. Someone had to provide leadership, give orders and see that the orders were carried out. Over time, these command structures began to take a form that we would now recognize as the first stages in the creation of states. We will never know the exact sequence of steps by which the leading towns of Mesopotamia turned into city-states, but there is evidence that by 3500 BC the process was already well advanced.

The development of this assortment of city-states in the area of southern Mesopotamia known as Sumeria was hastened by the invention of writing. It is impossible to organize large projects solely by word of mouth. Around 3500 BC, clay tokens came to be used as forms of authorization for the supply of goods, and accounting information was first recorded on clay tiles. At first, these records were pictographic: two strokes alongside a crude picture of a cow meant 'two cows'. Soon, signs for concepts such as 'next week' and 'urgent' were added.

Busy clerks were always on the look-out for economical ways of recording information. By 3000 BC, the original short list of pictographs had been replaced by a vocabulary of several thousand signs that bore no resemblance to any known object. Many conveyed messages like 'Tell him we want it now' and 'If only it would rain.' And if a scribe wished to write about 'two cows', he no longer had to make two marks to represent 'two'. He now had numerals: simple symbols that allowed him to write down any number he wished. Thus it was that accountancy gave birth to mathematics. And given mathematics, science was just around the corner.

This written language – the world's first – was inscribed on tablets of wet river clay, which were dried to make them permanent. The impressions were made with the cut edge of a reed, which gave them a wedge-shaped appearance, and this form of writing is known as cuneiform, from the Latin word for a wedge. These tablets are one of the most enduring forms of writing ever devised, and the museums of the world house hundreds of thousands of them, most of which have been deciphered, and can be read with ease.

The population of Sumeria, long the world's richest market, continued to expand. By 2700 BC the city of Uruk, on what was then a wide, navigable stretch of the Euphrates, 40 miles from the sea, had 50,000 inhabitants. They lived within a 6-mile circuit of city walls, which were in turn surrounded by canals and palm groves, where there is now merely desert. Uruk may have been the biggest city, but it had many rivals, and that rivalry was anything but friendly. As their populations increased, these cities felt more and more threatened by one another's need for land, water and natural resources of every kind. In the face of these pressures, they gradually evolved into walled city-states, organized, and prepared, to fight to preserve their independence. In the early days, these ready-to-fight-at-any-time societies were governed by 'cabinets' of noblemen, who would elect one of their number to be supreme ruler in time of war. But as time went by, these 'temporary' dictators became more and more difficult to dislodge, until they finally became kings: rulers for life, who exploited their supposed ability to intercede with the gods to bolster their control over their subjects. To administer their kingdoms, they had large numbers of civil servants, but standing armies made up of professional soldiers did not yet exist. Fighting forces were raised as they were required.

The technology and amenities of everyday life had improved since 4000 BC. The invention of the potter's wheel in Mesopotamia around 3500 BC brought an improvement in both quality and productivity to the potter's trade. It did not take long for some bright spark to realize that wheels could be used for other purposes. The earliest surviving representation of a wheeled vehicle – a sledge with four solid wheels – is Sumerian, dating from just after 3500 BC. Pretty soon, hand-carts were a common sight in the streets. These were followed by donkey carts, which could carry loads three times as great as a donkey could carry on its back.

The food surpluses generated by this highly productive system of agriculture were nominally offered to the gods – of which these cities had a multitude – and they were stored in the temple that was the heart of every city. Such surpluses not only enabled the ruling classes to live a life of luxury and ease; they also made it possible for these communities to support large numbers of full-time metal workers, who produced beautiful work in gold, silver and copper. Sumeria had no sources of metal ores, but its food surpluses made it easy to pay for the metals they needed, which were imported by sea and river from far afield.

Accountancy was central to the maintenance of this civilization, but it was not accountancy as we know it. It was concerned solely with physical quantities such as materials received, and work completed. Despite their prosperity, neither the citizens of these states, nor the states themselves, used money. This was a culture without cash. Trade between cities, and with distant countries, was conducted by barter. Work was rewarded in kind by the authorities: in food, drink and accommodation. Such a world without money is difficult for us to comprehend; but our world *with* money would have been even more difficult for them to imagine. Wealth resided in physical objects. The person with lots of cows was rich, because neighbours were happy to accept a cow in payment for landscaping a garden, or a churn of milk in return for mending a plough.

These city-states, comprising the cities and their satellite villages, continued to grow throughout the third millennium BC. By 2500 BC, the two largest, Uruk and Lagash, each had around 200,000 inhabitants. But their days of independence were numbered. In 2350 BC, King Lugalzagesi of the city of Umma established his rule over the whole of Sumeria, This conquest brought him over a million subjects, and it introduced a new dimension to the idea of the state.

While this civilization of the Mesopotamian plain was developing, similar transformations of everyday life were under way elsewhere; some in deliberate imitation of what the Sumerians were doing, some without knowledge of what was going on in Mesopotamia. On the banks of the Nile, the people of Egypt – in contact with the Fertile Crescent, but isolated by expanding deserts to east and west – were engaged in a catch-ing-up exercise. The inexhaustible fertility of the river valley and the increase of population it made possible were powering the development of a civilization that shared many of the char-acteristics of neighbouring cultures, but had features all its own.

The Nile was Egypt's life support system. The country itself had little rain, but the Ethiopian highlands to the south, where most of the river's water originated, had seasonal rains that were more than sufficient. In October, as the flood waters receded, farmers prepared the fields with ox-drawn ploughs, and planted their crops: wheat and barley; peas and beans; onions, leeks and cucumbers; grapes, figs, dates and peaches; melons and pomegranates. They had little grass, but their cows, pigs, sheep, goats, ducks and geese were more than happy, as they tucked into buckets of mash and troughs filled with veg-etable waste. Their owners, too, were happy, or at least the wealthier among them were, as they sat on their verandas, sip-ping home-made grape and pomegranate wines. April was harvest time, when whole families worked from sunrise to sun-set to bring in the river's bounty. After that, it was time to mend the fences and clean out the ditches, in readiness for the next flood, which almost never failed.

As in Mesopotamia, the villages of Egypt had grown into towns, and some of them soon became cities. By 3500 BC, the biggest of them, Nekhen – 50 miles north of Aswan, and bet-ter known by its later Greek name of Hierakonpolis – already had a temple complex, and establishments producing pottery and beer on an industrial scale. It is from Hierakonpolis, around this date, that we have the first evidence of a practice that was to be a central feature of Egyptian culture for the next 3000 years: the mummification of the dead.

We have said that the Nile floods almost never failed. That *almost* contains one of the keys to Egypt's history. About once every ten years, on average, the river withheld its gift: the floods failed, and the crops could not be planted, let alone harvested. When this happened, the country faced famine. Anyone who could provide an answer to the problem would have power for the taking. Thus it was that a collection of powerful personalities – who were soon calling themselves kings – were able to gain power over the cities of the region, in return for their promise to organize the accumulation of food surpluses in the good years, in preparation for the bad.

It is, of course, easier to obtain control over people's bodies if one can obtain mastery over their minds, and this point was not missed by the ruling classes of Egypt. To the promise of physical reserves of food was added the con trick of an alleged 'direct line' to the gods who governed the waters and breathed life into the crops. The same formula – the exploitation of superstitious fear to underpin established religion, which is then used to underpin the power of the state – has occurred throughout history. But nowhere has it been used to more powerful effect than in Ancient Egypt, where the state religion would in due course take the idea to its logical conclusion, by declaring that kings actually *were* gods, to be worshipped as such. The formula was fireproof. In nine years out of ten, the people could be frightened into submission to the authority of their sacred and secular superiors by the threat of divine retribution. In the tenth year, when the floods failed, they learned that it was a punishment for their failings (including ignoring the commandments of those same superiors). For the ruling classes, it was a perfect win/win situation.

As formerly independent cities were brought together in larger units, an army of civil servants was employed to administer them. As in Sumeria, the need to keep records, and communicate instructions, led to the invention of a system of writing. This, too, initially took the form of pictures representing objects, and only later expanded to include ideas and concepts. But thereafter it developed very differently. In Sumeria, the need to write quickly on an unsympathetic surface – clay tiles – led to the simplifying of the symbols, so that they became the economical system of signs known as cuneiform. As the Egyptian system of writing developed, it split into two distinct forms. One became the beautiful pictographic script we call hieroglyphic (Greek for 'sacred carving'). The hieroglyphs were carved on public buildings and painted on walls, especially the walls of tombs, and they remained virtually unchanged for the next 3000 years.

The other, hieratic, was a response to the need to find a speedier way of writing. For this non-monumental writing, the Egyptians had access to what was in effect the world's first writing-paper. On the banks of Nile, an umbrella-like reed called papyrus grew in tall clumps. The lower part of the stem, which was sweet, was chewed, as sugar cane still is today. The higher parts were woven to make baskets and small boats. Around 3000 BC, it was discovered that if overlapping strips of the pith of the stem were dried, the gum they contained caused them to stick together, producing thin sheets that made an ideal writing surface. This material, called papyrus after the plant from which it was made, became their everyday writing medium. For black ink, they used lampblack; for coloured ink, vegetable and mineral dyes. Two thousand years later, papyrus would be adopted in turn by both the Greeks and the Romans.

Like Sumeria, Egypt of the fourth and third millennia BC was a Stone Age society. But with their stone hammers, a virtually unlimited labour force and a mastery of practical mathematics, the Egyptians built monuments of enduring magnificence. The kings, being gods, were immortal and their future had to be catered for. So the practice arose of burying them in stupendous tombs, equipped with everything they would need to lead a kingly existence in the afterlife. In a country of 2 million people, many of whom were not needed for agricultural employment between seedtime and harvest, labour was no problem.

This tradition found its most extravagant expression in the Great Pyramid of Giza, near modern Cairo. This was the tomb of King Khufu (in Greek, Cheops), who died around 2600 BC. The biggest stone structure ever built, it contains over 2 million blocks averaging 2½ tons each, some of which were floated down river from 500 miles away. It was said by the Greek historian Herodotus to have required the labour of 100,000 workers over a period of twenty years. It was the greatest monument of the Age of Stone. It was also one of the last. Unknown to the thousands assembled to witness its capping-out, the first stirrings of a new age – the Age of Bronze – were already being felt elsewhere. The process of ceaseless change begun by the Agricultural Revolution was about to move up a gear.

6

EMPIRES OF BRONZE

Before we get involved in the Age of Bronze, it is worth pausing to consider why the invention of this metal should have had such a dramatic effect on the course of history.

Bronze is an alloy of copper and tin, made by heating the metals together. It is harder than copper, but has a lower melting point, and is easier to cast. Copper itself is obtained from ores such as chalcopyrite (a combination of copper, iron and sulphur), but is occasionally met with in a pure state, for example in meteorites. Many Stone Age societies were familiar with it, and it was much sought after for making ornaments and jewellery. But its rarity and softness were disadvantages when it came to making tools and weapons. In the third millennium BC, people discovered how to produce copper by heating copper ores beyond the metal's melting point. They also learned how to combine copper with tin to give it added strength. The resulting alloy – bronze – revolutionized tool manufacture. It led to an even greater revolution in the making of weapons.

Bronze was first made around 3000 BC, but for hundreds of years it remained a rarity, because tin was hard to come by. It was not until the discovery of rich sources of tin, such as those in Spain and Anatolia, that bronze could be used on a meaningful scale. When it was, bronze weapons transformed warfare. A bronze spear was stronger than a stone one. It was made in one piece, whereas a stone spear was only as strong as its shaft and the binding that tied it to its shaft. The same was true of a bronze dagger. The bronze sword had no Stone Age equivalent at all, its nearest competitor being the stone club.

Bronze weapons and tools were not only more effective, they were easier to make. Stone tools were handcrafted products. They took time, and called for considerable skill. Metal objects could be mass-produced. A single handmade pattern could be used to make hundreds of moulds, batches of which could be filled from one ladle of metal. When the metal cooled, the work involved in finishing off the rough casting was a fraction of that involved in making a stone tool, or a stone weapon.

This change in the technology of peace and war took place against the background of a change in the scale of human society. One of the consequences of recurring wars was a reduction in the number of city-states, as defeated ones were absorbed within the boundaries of their victorious rivals. Some of the victors were conquered in their turn, giving rise to even larger states. In 2334 BC the armies of King Sargon of Akkad, in northern Mesopotamia, conquered the kingdom of Sumeria, which was only in its sixteenth year but already had more than a million people. In doing so he inaugurated the world's first empire. But it was not destined to last for long. The next thousand years in Mesopotamia witnessed a procession of successive empires as peoples in the surrounding regions moved about, and, each in turn, took a fancy to the wealth and amenities of this rich land.

This long contest between competing empires generated a continuous improvement in the technology of war. The effectiveness of bronze weapons, and their ease of manufacture, was only part of the story. What truly changed war was the use of bronze weapons and bronze armour in conjunction with another invention that had appeared in the same part of the world: the war horse.

Horses had been domesticated around 4000 BC by nomads in eastern Europe and Central Asia, but for a long time they were just a food source. They provided meat and milk, but their earliest owners would no more have thought of riding them than they would have thought of riding a cow. It was not until around 2000 BC that horses were first ridden with serious intent, and the place where the practice originated seems to have been northern Iran. Once the skill had been mastered, its usefulness in war quickly became apparent, and the traditional practice of breeding for docility was put into reverse, as the emphasis changed to strength and speed. By 1500 BC, mounted troops were a standard component of armies throughout the Fertile Crescent, and nomad cavalry were inspiring terror in farming communities from eastern Europe to western China. Thus began a pattern of mounted incursions into the settled lands of Europe and Asia that would continue for the next 3000 years. In these conflicts, the wandering nomads of eastern Europe and Central Asia had an unbeatable secret weapon: grass. Grass was one thing the horsemen of the steppes had in abundance. This made it easy for the nomad peoples to maintain large herds of horses, specially bred for speed and stamina. A life in the saddle also meant that every man and young boy was a potential cavalryman, who could be mobilized at a moment's notice.

The combination of horse and metal made the chariot possible. This invention was a development comparable to the twentieth-century deployment of the tank. Once cart builders had a tough, workable material like bronze, its advantages over wood in the construction of military vehicles were obvious.

Between 2000 BC and 1500 BC, many peoples of South-west Asia developed chariots of a sort. But the light, two-man, two-wheeled version developed by the nomads of the steppes was a far more effective fighting weapon than the clumsy four-wheeled carts used by the people of the plains. This light chariot, and mounted archers who could fire arrows while riding at speed, created a new kind of warfare. Armies could now be moved quickly over great distances, and attacks could be launched against unsuspecting cities by forces that were not even known to be in their neighbourhood.

These changes in the technology of war were paralleled by equally dramatic changes in the business of everyday life. The web of trade now extended over thousands of miles. River transport had been transformed by the invention of the sail. Where water transport had once been limited to rafts floating downstream with the current, it was now possible for boats to perform round journeys with the aid of the wind. Nowhere was this more important than in Egypt, a country built on a riverbank. The Egyptians already had boats made of planks, which enabled them to transport heavy loads downstream. But after they invented the sail, around 3500 BC, they could exploit northerly winds to travel up river as easily as they floated down. This ability to transport goods in both directions, and the resources it made available, was perhaps the single most important factor in the catching-up exercise the Egyptians performed between 3000 BC and 2000 BC.

The invention of the sail did not just transform river transportation: it made it possible to cross the seas. Instead of paddling along the shoreline, mariners were now able to face the challenge of open water. The Egyptians' first sailing boats had long, narrow sails attached to two masts. As they ventured

6.1 The Mediterranean in Classical Times

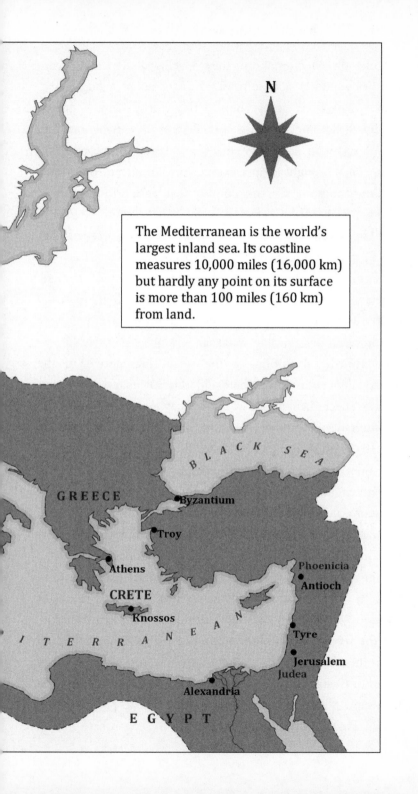

The Mediterranean is the world's largest inland sea. Its coastline measures 10,000 miles (16,000 km) but hardly any point on its surface is more than 100 miles (160 km) from land.

out into the Mediterranean, they developed the large, square sail that would later become the basis of ocean sailing everywhere. These sea-going ships – the world's first – greatly extended the range of Egypt's trade, and they inaugurated an age of Egyptian naval supremacy that lasted for nearly 2000 years. They brought copper from Cyprus, tin from Asia Minor and, most importantly, in a country that had no forest trees of its own, timber from Lebanon.

The development of the sea-going ship was a crucial factor in the speeding up of change that characterized the transition from the Age of Stone to the Age of Bronze. Carrying goods by water was much easier than transporting them overland. This gave a huge advantage to any society within reach of navigable water; an advantage that would persist until the invention of the steam locomotive in the nineteenth century. Nowhere did this advantage operate to greater effect than in the societies that grew up around the Mediterranean. With an area of 1 million square miles, a coastline 10,000 miles long, yet with hardly any part of it more than 100 miles from land, the Mediterranean was a mariner's dream. As settlements and harbours grew up along its shores, it took on more and more of the character of a great inland lake, around which a collection of states sat, in the vivid phrase of the Greek philosopher Plato, 'like frogs around a pool'.

Egypt, ideally situated to benefit from sea-going trade in both the Mediterranean and the Persian Gulf, was the most glittering and powerful of these maritime civilizations. But during the second millennium BC, a number of others appeared upon the scene. One of these, the Minoan, arose on the rocky island of Crete. Here, in what was at first sight an inhospitable landscape, a race of hardy farmers grew wheat, planted olives and vines, and raised sheep. For 500 years, they conducted an export trade in wool, wine and oil with other countries and with their own colonies around the Aegean. The remains of their palaces testify to the prosperity that resulted. In the ruins of one of these palaces, a gamesboard was found, inlaid with ivory and the beautiful blue gemstone lapis lazuli. The ivory would have come from the tusks of African elephants, the lapis lazuli from its only source, the mines above Faizabad, in Afghanistan. It was a find that encapsulated both the luxury enjoyed by the ruling classes in Bronze Age civilizations, and the trading networks on which that luxury was based.

In 1628 BC, the Minoans' coastal settlements were inundated by an enormous tsunami, and their fields buried in ash, as a result of a volcanic eruption on the island of Thera (Santorini), 100 miles to the north. Their civilization survived, despite famine and social disruption, but in 1450 BC it finally succumbed to an attack by invaders from Mycenae, on the Greek mainland, in the course of which most of its palaces and towns were razed to the ground.

The fall of the Minoan civilization coincided with the appearance of a new sea-going culture in the eastern Mediterranean – that of the Phoenicians. The Phoenicians, who spoke a language related to Hebrew, lived in the coastal areas of what is now Syria and Lebanon. This region is blessed with some of the finest natural harbours in the world. In 1500 BC, there was already a busy sea-going trade with Egypt and Mesopotamia. Three products in particular formed the basis of this: pine and cedar wood; cloth dyed with the famous 'royal' or 'Tyrian' purple dye, obtained from the *murex* shellfish; and ivory from African elephants, which was transhipped to Mesopotamia and elsewhere.

At first, the Phoenicians had been subject to Egyptian sovereignty, but the Egyptian empire was unravelling in the face of attacks from both north and south. By 1000 BC, with the weakening of Egyptian influence in the region, the leading Phoenician cities – Tyre, Sidon, Byblos, Berytus (Beirut) and Ugarit – had developed into independent city-states. They were home to thousands of craftsmen producing highly sought-after metalwork, fine linen and embroidery. As their sea-borne trade prospered, the Phoenicians established trading posts the length and breadth of the Mediterranean. One of these, Carthage, in modern-day Tunisia, would later become the greatest Phoenician city of all.

A vivid picture of the trading activities of the Phoenicians at this time is provided by the account left by an Egyptian merchant named Weinamun, who was sent to Byblos by the ruling Pharaoh in 1075 BC to obtain shipbuilding timber. He was sent home with a flea in his ear, by Zeker Ba'l, the ruler of Byblos, who resented the suggestion that he should deliver the timber as a tribute as his forebears had been expected to do. When Weinamun returned with 5 jars of silver, 4 jars of gold, 500 ox hides, a large quantity of ropes and cloth, and 30 baskets of fish, Zeker Ba'l mellowed, and 300 men and 3000 oxen were set to work to fell the great cedar trees, and transport them to the harbour.

The trading empire of the Phoenicians left one supreme legacy in the form of the alphabet, the most economical writing system of all. It was not actually their invention; they had adapted it from one used by their predecessors in that part of the world, the Canaanites. Where, and when, that alphabet was invented is unknown. All we know for sure is that there were a number of similar scripts in use around the eastern

Mediterranean in 1500 BC, one of which, the North Semitic, became the parent of hundreds of alphabets in Europe, west and Central Asia and Africa. It was the use of this North Semitic alphabet by the Phoenicians around 1100 BC that led to a version of it being adopted by the Greeks, and through them, by all the peoples of Europe. The Phoenician alphabet had only consonants and comprised twenty-two letters. It was the Greeks who added five signs to represent vowels, and gave Europeans, and people who speak languages of European origin, the alphabets in use today.

The invention of the alphabet was a landmark. Cuneiform, hieroglyphics and Chinese pictographic writing were crucial to the development of their respective civilizations. But all these early writing systems involved a long apprenticeship, and they could only ever be in the possession of a small, leisured elite. Alphabetic writing offered the prospect of literacy to many more people, and the part it would later play in making it possible to print cheap books with movable type puts it firmly in that super-league of inventions that includes wheeled vehicles, the steam engine and the computer.

The great mass of written material we have inherited from the Bronze Age civilizations of the Mediterranean and the Fertile Crescent has had a distorting effect on the writing of history. To go by some historians' accounts of the period, one would think that Europe north of the Alps was at this time a kind of 'black hole', either uninhabited, or peopled exclusively by savage tribes. Nothing could be further from the truth. Because many of them were illiterate, their stories have not come down to us. And if we stick to a definition of civilization that insists on the existence of cities, we cannot call them civilized. But the spread of Bronze Age culture did not end at the foothills of the Alps, or the entrance to the Black Sea. In the centuries after 1500 BC, from Spain to Ukraine, a highly developed farming culture evolved. It was based on villages rather than towns, but it supported a substantial population. The wealth it generated for its tribal rulers is demonstrated by the tombs in which they were buried. Their swords and their chariots, their drinking vessels and their gold jewellery, and their faithful retainers were buried with them, to serve them on their travels beyond the grave.

7
THE WORLD IN 1000 BC

In 4000 BC the population of the world was around 30 million. Had a census of world population been taken in 1000 BC, it would probably have shown a total nearer 120 million. More than half lived in four regions of long-established agricultural settlement. These four, each with a population of or approaching 20 million, were:

1 China

2 the Indian subcontinent

3 Egypt, the Fertile Crescent and Iran

4 Europe.

The emphasis of the previous two chapters on the early history of South-west Asia and the Mediterranean is justified, because of the worldwide influence of many of the developments there. But it also reflects the quantity of information available. Archaeological digs in South-west Asia have uncovered a vast store of written records, on clay, stone and papyrus, that enable us to read what the peoples of these civilizations were doing and saying.

We are less well informed about the early history of South and South-east Asia. We know that the Indus Valley, in present-day Pakistan, was the home of a civilization that was already ancient in the third millennium BC. Unfortunately,

much of the physical evidence of this civilization has been carried away by floods. Its written language has not been
deciphered, and a lot of this writing was done on perishable
materials such as palm leaves, leaving little to be deciphered.
Agriculture had spread to this region from the Fertile Crescent,
and, as in the Fertile Crescent, it was at first confined to upland
regions. But mastery of irrigation techniques later enabled it to
spread across the plains. Like the Nile, the Indus flooded every
year, and spread rich alluvial soil over a wide area growing
wheat, barley, rice and cotton. Humped cattle, buffaloes, sheep,
goats, pigs, elephants and camels had all been domesticated.

By 2500 bc, this system of mixed farming was supporting
a population of around 5 million, spread over a vast area.
Whether this was a unitary state, or a collection of city-states,
is unknown. It contained two great redbrick cities – Harappa
and Mohenjo-Daro – whose civic amenities would not have
shamed the finest cities of Mesopotamia. They had wide
streets, laid out in a grid pattern; fine houses with central court-
yards and individual wells; public baths; and sewerage systems
unmatched anywhere. The houses were constructed of mud
brick, but the drains and public buildings were made of high-
quality kiln-fired brick. While these two cities were the most
important settlements, hundreds of smaller towns and villages
filled the land, covering most of what is now Pakistan and as
much again of present-day India. But starting around 1900 bc,
this civilization went into decline, and its cities were abandoned. Floods were undoubtedly partly to blame. Some of the
excavations around Harappa have involved the removal of 30
feet of alluvial mud. In other places, desiccation seems to have
been the principal explanation, as rivers dried up completely.
Whatever the combination of factors that led to the

disappearance of this sophisticated civilization, by 1000 BC it was just a folk memory for the inhabitants of the villages that remained.

Our knowledge of early Chinese history is equally fragmentary, because we have no contemporary records, and we are forced to rely on semi-mythical accounts written down much later. The oldest surviving specimens of Chinese writing take us no further back than about 1500 BC. They indicate the existence of a mature writing system, with a long history behind it; but of that history we know nothing. This script is composed of characters that resemble those in use today, to the extent that some can be read by present-day Chinese without specialist knowledge. The family resemblance between these 4000-year-old characters and the modern written language is symbolic of something unique to Chinese civilization: a continuity over enormous periods of time, something we meet repeatedly in the history of that civilization.

China was a long way from western Asia and the Mediterranean. But there was no insuperable barrier north of the mountains of Tibet, and trading contacts – via third parties in the regions in-between – existed from an early date. Even more important was the sea-borne trade around the shores of the Indian Ocean. The technologies that China imported from peoples further west included the cultivation of wheat and barley, the manufacture of bronze, the idea of the chariot and those two supreme inventions of the people of the steppes, the ridable horse and the stirrup. In return, Europe and western Asia received benefits too numerous to list. Porcelain (first century AD), paper (first century AD) and gunpowder (ninth century AD) and the magnetic compass (around AD 900) are just a few of the Chinese inventions that would later find their way along these two great arteries of trade: the coastal route around the Indian Ocean, and the Silk Road across Central Asia.

In China, as in countries to the west, history had taken a new course with the invention of bronze. This transformation is vividly illustrated by a discovery made in 1976, close to the city of Anyang, 300 miles south of Beijing: an undisturbed tomb containing an astounding collection. Inscriptions in the tomb identified it as the last resting-place of the Lady Fu Hao, wife of a king named Wu Ding. Alongside thousands of other objects, and amid the usual collection of faithful retainers' skeletons, the tomb contained hundreds of magnificent bronze vessels and jade carvings, of extraordinary beauty and quality of workmanship.

Modern Anyang is a pleasant, modest-sized town, but the ancient city of the same name covered an area of 25 square miles. Excavations elsewhere in the region have confirmed the existence of other hitherto unsuspected cities, all of which were built around royal palaces and ritual centres. These excavations have yielded large number of 'oracle bones': ox shoulder-blades and turtle shells used for divination. Decipherment of the inscriptions on these bones has revealed the ancient roots of the reverence for the past, and in particular reverence for one's ancestors, that still counts for so much.

The use of the words 'China' and 'Chinese' should not be taken to imply political unity. In 1000 BC, what we call 'China' was what it had been for hundreds of years, and what it would remain for hundreds of years to come: a collection of independent feudal states, each with its own army, and each ever ready to go to war with the others.

Across the sea in Japan no comparable civilization had yet arisen. This was a settled Stone Age culture of hunting, fishing and food gathering. Food was plentiful, but as with hunter-gatherer societies everywhere, numbers remained small, and the largest settlements were no more than collections of wigwam-shaped thatched huts.

Far away to the south, similarly undisturbed by contact with the outside world, and scattered thinly across their inhospitable continent, the native peoples of Australia practised a mobile hunting and gathering lifestyle little changed from that of their ancestors of 3000 years before.

To the north and east of Australia, hundreds of islands that in 4000 BC had not yet received their first human footprint were now home to permanent settlements. Over a period of 2000 years, beginning around 3000 BC, the Pacific Ocean had been the scene of an astonishing succession of voyages by the ancestors of the peoples who are nowadays classified as Micronesians and Polynesians. Starting from South-east Asia, they had colonized the whole of Indonesia and the Philippines by 2000 BC. By 1500 BC, guided by the stars, and aided by their profound knowledge of the behaviour of ocean currents, they had traversed the whole of Micronesia and Melanesia, and settled just about every island in 4 million square miles of ocean. In 1000 BC, their fishing and farming villages covered almost the entire western Pacific, south of the Tropic of Cancer and north of New Zealand.

On the other side of the Pacific, the descendants of the original settlers of the Americas had prospered and multiplied. Most of them still followed a hunter-gatherer style of life, but in the tropical zones of both continents, independent Agricultural Revolutions had occurred that owed nothing to the examples of the Fertile Crescent or China. One of these, in Central America, was unique. Almost everywhere else, settled agriculture was based on the dual domestication of wild animals and plants. But this corner of the world contained no animals suitable for domestication. It did, however, possess several wild food plants with a potential for improvement, including maize, squash and beans. Starting around 3000 BC, these people had engineered an Agricultural Revolution that owed nothing at all to the labour of beasts, or to the meat they might have provided. In spite of these disadvantages, they had created a farming culture that was able to support a sizeable population. Their most striking achievement was the transformation of maize from an insignificant wild cereal into a source of nourishment that would eventually provide something like 90 per cent of the food requirements of the peoples of Central America. The wild ancestor of maize was a grass called teosinte, which still grows in Mexico. Fossilized remains of tiny cobs of primitive maize from the early days of domestication show just what an impressive achievement the transformation of this crop was, and what a long time it took.

The most notable culture in Central America in 1000 BC was that of the Olmecs, who lived around the southern shores of the Gulf of Mexico. This region had the benefit of plentiful rain and a rich soil, which enabled it to support a style of agriculture that would have been impossible in the more arid regions to the north and west. Like mature agricultural societies everywhere, these people engaged in long-distance trade. The merchants who carried on this trade – which included precious goods such as jade, obsidian and cacao beans – lived in towns. But population densities were much lower than in the civilizations of Eurasia, and none of these towns were big enough to count as cities. Nevertheless, they contained impressive ceremonial centres and temples, which were adorned with magnificent stone sculptures. The great age of the Olmec culture lasted for 500 years, from 1300 BC to around 800 BC, but their art and their religion, including their cult of the jaguar, and their building of pyramids, exercised a powerful influence on later civilizations, right up to the Aztecs of the sixteenth century.

Two thousand miles to the south, in present-day Peru, another highly individual system of agriculture had developed in the Andean highlands, where nature had assembled a rich assortment of plants and animals crying out for domestication. We still have a lot to learn about the emergence of agriculture in this high-altitude environment, but it is clear that by 1000 BC, a farming culture based on terraced fields on the valley sides was already a thousand years old. The plants involved included a cereal – quinua – and the potato, which was to become one of the world's most important food crops. Their animals included the guinea-pig and three members of the camel family, the alpaca, the guanaco and the llama, that provided milk, meat and wool, and performed a vital role as pack animals.

Despite the difficulties of travel in this punishing terrain, these hardy creatures made it possible for the farmers of the High Andes to trade with fishing communities of the Pacific coast, 500 miles to the north. Among the plants these fishing peoples had domesticated were gourds, which provided the floats for their nets, and cotton, which they wove into both fishing nets and cloth. Like most of the peoples of the Americas, they lived in villages. Apart from the handful of small towns the Olmecs had built, villages were the only settlements in the whole of the Americas. The first American city was still a thousand years away.

Our final destination in this worldwide round-up is the continent of Africa, where our story began. Its most densely populated region in 1000 BC was still the Nile Valley area of Egypt. It represented only 1 per cent of the area of the continent, but it contained 50 per cent of its people. Further west, 4000 years of drought had created the Sahara Desert. Camel caravans occasionally made their way across it, but in terms of human settlement it was emptier than it had been for 20,000 years. In the eastern highlands, where humanity had first evolved, pastoral nomads travelled with their flocks and herds, as their ancestors had done for hundreds of years before them. Elsewhere, the scourge of sleeping sickness, carried by the tsetse fly, rendered some parts of the continent virtually uninhabitable, and desperately weakened the populations of many others.

In the belt of open savannah south of the Sahara, and north of the tropical rain forest, an Agricultural Revolution had occurred that owed little or nothing to similar developments elsewhere. The population involved in this farming culture was small, as were the settlements, and evidence of its extent and timing is hard to come by. Cattle were important, and the crop plants included sorghum and millet, two plants that are today the staple food of millions. But as far as technology was concerned, the peoples of sub-Saharan Africa still lived in the Age of Stone. The Bronze Age, which had created such turmoil elsewhere, had passed them by.

The invention of bronze had a dramatic effect on the scale and style of warfare, and initiated a thousand-year period of upheaval, as state fought state and empire succeeded empire. Around 1200 BC, another metal – iron – appeared upon the scene, and the business of war was transformed yet again.

Iron is one of the commonest materials in the earth's crust, and though rare in its pure form iron ores are widely distributed around the world, with substantial deposits accessible at surface level. The problem with iron is not its availability, but its usability. Even if you can achieve the high temperature needed to extract the metal from its ore, you will be left with a mass of cinders containing a few lumps of a metal too brittle to make tools, weapons or anything else of the slightest use.

The metal content of iron ore was probably discovered by accident, when lumps of ore found their way into very hot fires. The metal-workers who produced bronze would have recognized the similarity between copper ores and iron ores long before they were able to do anything about it. A summary of what they ultimately learned to do will show what a remarkable achievement theirs was. To produce weapons-quality iron they had to:

1 heat the ore to at least 1450°C (compared with only 1000°C in the case of copper)

2 repeatedly reheat the resulting ingot on a bed of burning charcoal (to introduce carbon into the mix)

3 hammer it after each heating (to get rid of the cinders and form it into the desired shape)

4 give it a final heating, before quenching it in a bath of cold water.

When one considers that this solution could have been arrived at only by trial and error, one has to marvel at the determination of the mechanical geniuses who solved the problem.

Iron ore seems to have been successfully smelted for the first time in the copper-producing region stretching from Anatolia (Turkey) to Persia (modern Iran) soon after 2000 BC. Thereafter, it took several hundred years for the technology to be fully mastered, and to become known over a wider area. The product that resulted was wrought iron, or more correctly, steeled wrought iron. The manufacture of cast iron, for constructional purposes, was a Chinese discovery that did not become widely known elsewhere until the fourteenth century AD.

This new metal, cheaper and more plentiful than bronze, transformed the arts of peace and war. From around 1200 BC, itinerant blacksmiths spread out in all directions, making sickles and ploughshares for farmers, and swords and spears for soldiers. Iron ploughs made ploughing easier and faster, and made it possible to bring into cultivation lands that had hitherto been too difficult to work.

The new swords had even more dramatic consequences. The first to take advantage of them were the pastoral nomads of the steppes, who lived near the lands where the iron was first made. But they were not the only ones to benefit from the new weapons. In countries further south, the Bronze Age had been the age of the aristocratic charioteer. Now, with the introduction of the cheap iron sword, the cheap iron spear and the cheap iron shield, the balance of advantage swung decisively in favour of well-drilled foot soldiers.

One group that took enthusiastically to this new technology of war were the Greek-speaking peoples who lived around the Aegean. The origin of these peoples is shrouded in mystery, but they seem to have entered Greece from the north in a series of migrations between 2000 BC and 1500 BC. By 800 BC, with their iron swords and their superior military tactics, they had conquered the whole of the Greek mainland, and occupied much of the coast of Asia Minor.

If these invaders had ever had a writing system of their own, they seem to have lost it during the period known as the 'Greek Dark Age'. It was not until they developed their own version of the Phoenician alphabet around 800 BC that they began to leave written records from which their later history can be pieced together. From these records, we can identify many features that appear to be quintessentially Greek. The most striking of these was a fierce, self-conscious pride. This was very much a product of their physical situation. They typically lived in small territories comprising a town and its agricultural hinterland, in a narrow valley running down to the sea, shut off from their neighbours by mountain ranges. Such a situation encouraged a sense of separateness, which was embodied in the word – *polis* – they used to describe the communities of which they were citizens. *Polis* (plural *poleis*) is usually translated as 'city-state', but the translation misses the essence of what the Greek word implied. For its citizens, the *polis* was not the town and its surroundings. It was the body of citizens who collectively decided how their communities should be governed. During the Dark Age, the *poleis* seem to have been ruled by kings. But by 800 BC, most were run by small groups of aristocratic landowners, governing with the acquiescence of the citizens.

The prickly civic pride of these citizens was a guarantee that there would never be a unitary Greek state. It also created a state of mind in which a *polis* was ready to fight with another at any time to safeguard its independence. But in spite of their highly developed sense of separateness, and their readiness to fight one another, these communities were united in their consciousness of being Greek, though this was not the word they applied to themselves. 'Greek' was the name the Romans later gave them. They called themselves *Hellenes*. And they drew a clear line between Hellenes and non-Hellenes. They called the latter 'barbarians', in imitation of the 'bar, bar' sounds made by people who did not speak Greek. Their sense of a common heritage was reinforced by two elements of their culture that both dated from the eighth century BC: the Homeric epics and the Olympic Games.

There may not actually have been a poet called Homer, but even if there was, the two stupendous poems that bear his name – the *Iliad* and the *Odyssey* – are clearly not the work of just one man. The mythical or semi-mythical events to which they refer – the siege of Troy and the journey home from Troy – were located in the late Bronze Age, and Greek children had been hearing them at their mothers' knees for centuries before they were first written down.

The Olympic Games were the most important of a number of similar athletic festivals, in which young men competed for the glory of their *poleis*. They were held at Olympia, a wealthy religious centre near the western coast of the Peloponnese, the great near-island that forms the southern part of the Greek mainland. This festival loomed so large in the Greek consciousness that it became the basis of their reckoning of time. In the Greek calendar, years were counted from the supposed date of the first holding of the games, which was put at 776 BC. The four-yearly intervals between successive games were referred to as the First Olympiad, the Second Olympiad, and so on. At first, the competition had occupied just one day, and had involved only one event, a 180-metre running event. During the next three or four centuries the programme was extended to include jumping, throwing, wrestling and chariot-racing, until it ultimately occupied a total of five days. The winners received only an olive wreath as their reward, but the fame they won, in their own cities and throughout the Greek-speaking world, puts one in mind of the hero-worship that in our own age follows a Pelé or a Maradona. As one would expect, with so much at stake, professionalism soon reared its head. Like football clubs in our own day, some of the *poleis* would later recruit professional athletes from far afield.

The growth and survival of this collection of mini-states were greatly helped by a historical fluke. At the time when they were creating their traditions, and fighting their private wars, there was no major power in the eastern Mediterranean able to take advantage of their weakness, and reduce them to subservience. The Minoans had left the stage. Egypt was pre-occupied with threats to its own borders, and had no energy to spare for Mediterranean adventures. The once-powerful Hittite kingdom in Anatolia had collapsed. Persia, the power that would later constitute a threat to their survival, was far distant,

and a long way in time from the great empire it was to become.
The power vacuum thus created not only protected this collection of little states from outside interference, but also opened
up rich opportunities for trade and colonization.

'Little states' is an exact description of what these communities were. In 400 BC, when this experiment in civilization was
about to enter upon its most brilliant period, only three of
them had more than 20,000 citizens. These were Athens – the
most populous city on the Greek mainland – and Syracuse and
Acragas, two settlements on the island of Sicily that had been
set up by mainland Greeks several hundred years earlier.

'Citizen' in this context did not mean what it means today.
A citizen was someone who had the right to participate in public discussions of the community's affairs, and to record a vote
on such matters. First and foremost, a citizen was a man. So far
as speaking, voting or even appearing in the public assemblies
were concerned, women were non-persons: they existed in a
political limbo, along with resident aliens, children and slaves.
The 60,000-odd citizens who were entitled to participate in
the discussion of public affairs in the Athens of 400 BC were the
politically visible portion of a population of half a million.
Slaves and resident aliens outnumbered them four to one.

It might be thought that a collection of small communities,
many of them in cramped valley situations with no easy means
of overland communication, must of necessity have been poor
in material goods, but that would be to overlook the significance of the sea at their doorsteps. Chains of islands made for
easy navigation, and hundreds of Greek settlements dotted the
coastlines, not only of the Greek mainland itself, but of Asia
Minor and the Black Sea. The whole eastern Mediterranean
was one enormous market-place, and these Greek settlements,

along with cities of the Phoenicians and the great city of Alexandria, at the mouth of the Nile, were its market stalls.

Nowhere was there anything remotely like it. Ships by the hundred plied back and forth. The Greek city-states, seemingly so insignificant as individual entities, had the best of both worlds: the free air of the city, and the benefits of a world wide web of trade and learning. They had control of their own affairs, free of imperial bureaucracy, yet they were able to benefit from a vast network of trade. Their situation was unique, and it produced a civilization that was unique: a civilization more brilliant than any that had gone before, and as brilliant as any that would come after.

One reason for the amazing achievements of this civilization was what one might reasonably call its rootlessness. These Greeks were recent arrivals in their new homelands. Compared with the Egyptians, or the Chinese, they carried much less cultural baggage from the past. They honoured their ancestors, and they had their ancient heroes; but they had no inhibitions about doing and thinking what had not been done or thought before. And they had no conspiracies of god-kings and priests to tell them what they should think. They had gods – plenty of them – but gods who devoted so much time to the pursuit of their own illicit love-affairs were hardly the kind to intimidate free-thinking citizens.

In a 300-year blaze of creativity, between 500 BC and 200 BC, these Greek cities around the Mediterranean created immortal works of art, architecture and literature that still make hearts sing and pulses race. They produced a string of geniuses – Archimedes, Aristotle, Pythagoras, and a host of others – whose work in mechanics, mathematics, astronomy and natural history laid the foundations of modern science. And they invented an approach to logical argument and philosophical enquiry that has become so dominant that most of us are not even aware that it *was* invented, and think it is just the natural way of going about things.

As might be expected, it was in the most populous of these city-states – Athens – that the light of this civilization shone most brightly. And it was in Athens that a remarkable experiment in communal living – the practice of democracy – was first conducted. In 507 BC, the chief magistrate, Cleisthenes, determined to limit the influence of noble families on the conduct of public life, 'took the people into partnership'. Public rights and duties were henceforth no longer based on family or clan, but on membership of a *deme*, or township, which maintained its own register of citizens; and elected not only its own officials, but a proportion of the 500-member council that supervised the affairs of the *polis*. Every citizen (that is, every free male) also had the automatic right to attend, and vote in, the assembly that met in the city itself.

An aggrieved nobility called in the aid of the rival city-state of Sparta, in an attempt to frustrate this new constitution, but the outrage of the Athenian citizenry was such that the Spartans were compelled to withdraw. This appeal to an outside power was neither forgotten nor forgiven, and the episode intensified the Athenians' determination to hang on to, and make the most of, the system of democratic government they had invented.

Many people assume that modern parliamentary democracy has its origin in this Athenian model, but that is a misconception. Modern democracy does not derive from the practices of these Athenian slave-owners 2000 years ago. The idea that it does has its source in the vanity of slave-owning and slave-trading politicians in Britain and America in the eighteenth and nineteenth centuries, who lived in houses that imitated Athenian models, and who saw themselves as reincarnations of the orators and statesmen of that glittering age.

The true roots of present-day democracy are to be found in economic and political developments in Europe – particularly in England and France – between the sixteenth and eighteenth centuries. What we got from Athens was not the practice of democracy, but their way of talking and thinking about it. We gained access to this when the writings of Greek political philosophers were rediscovered in the fifteenth and sixteenth centuries.

The independence of these city-states was snuffed out when a Macedonian prince – the future Alexander the Great – inherited his father's crown in 326 BC, and set off to conquer the known world. He naturally started off by incorporating the Greek states in his embryonic empire. This brought to an end the political independence that had provided the soil in which Hellenic civilization had been nurtured. But it also brought to an end the perpetual fighting between them, and gave them sixty years of domestic peace during which their civilization recorded some of its greatest achievements.

Alexander the Great's conquests spread Greek influence around the eastern Mediterranean and across South-west and Central Asia, as far as northern India, where his soldiers finally forced him to turn back. He died in Babylon, on his way home. After his death, his short-lived empire split into a number of large fragments, governed by his generals. Four hundred years later, these fragments were reunited in an even greater empire, based on Rome.

In the eighth century BC, around the time when the Homeric epics were first written down and the Olympic Games were first held, Rome was just a little market town at the lowest crossing point on the River Tiber, 15 miles from the sea. By 500 BC, it had grown into a prosperous city-state of some 50,000 people, with a republican form of government.

Somewhere around 380 BC, the city suffered a severe setback when it was subjected to a seven-month siege by an invading army of Gauls from northern Italy. At one stage only the Capitoline Hill remained in Roman hands. The Gauls were eventually bought off, but only after they had reduced the entire city to ruins. When the attackers had dispersed, the Romans rebuilt their city behind new defensive walls.

Between 380 BC and 300 BC, the Romans were involved in a series of bloody wars with neighbouring states that resulted in their gaining control of the whole of Italy. This led to a confrontation with Carthage, the great Phoenician city on the north coast of Africa. The population of Rome by this time was close to 100,000, but that of Carthage was around 250,000. Its prosperity, and its trading empire, excited the envy and resentment of the merchants of Rome. The result was a series of wars that started in 264 BC and lasted over a hundred years, to determine who was to be 'top dog' in the Mediterranean. The matter was settled in 146 BC, when a Roman army captured Carthage, slaughtered 200,000 of its inhabitants and sold the remaining 50,000 into slavery.

A century and a half of war, in Italy and beyond, had left the Roman state with a first-class army and navy. With Carthage out of the way, Rome was the undisputed ruler of Italy, Spain and North Africa. War was by now a habit, and each conquest fed the appetite for more. Southern France came next; then it was the turn of mainland Greece and the Greek cities of Asia Minor. The momentum of conquest was unstoppable. In the first century BC, Roman armies overran the whole of mainland Europe west of the Rhine and south of the Danube. Next came Syria, Palestine and Egypt. By the end of the first century AD, the empire extended from southern Scotland to the Persian Gulf.

This was an empire built on war. But while wars continued to push its frontiers outwards, within those frontiers war became a thing of the past. The *Pax Romana* – the 'Roman peace' – provided an environment in which trade flourished and city life prospered. Thousands of miles of magnificent roads provided fast and safe movement between cities. Aqueducts brought water from the mountains, and household water meters recorded the quantity consumed. Splendid public buildings lined the city streets. Artificial harbours and lighthouses were built in great ports such as Ostia and Alexandria, where ships up to a thousand tons in weight could be built and repaired.

As far as civil engineering was concerned, it was the most inventive and creative civilization the world had seen. But strangely, in matters of science, it was one of the most sterile. This huge empire, with its enormous wealth, with the privileged leisure that this made possible, and with access to the accumulated learning of the Egyptians, the Babylonians and the Greeks, in half a dozen centuries added hardly anything of note to the world's stock of mathematical or scientific knowledge. On the other side of the world, the Chinese were making breakthrough after breakthrough. But the Romans knew little of these advances, and might not have been excited had they known more. The Roman mind-set had been formed around the waging of war, and the administration of a far-flung empire. It was not the sort of mind-set that leads to a Scientific or an Industrial Revolution.

Up to the time of the Carthaginian Wars, Rome had been a fairly equal society. The soldiers who went to fight those wars were free farmers, with a stake in a society with no real extremes of wealth. But long years of conscript war service, during which they were unable to care for their farms, left their families burdened with debt. When they returned to civilian life, they discovered that they were the new poor, and that their city was run by, and for, a class of wealthy aristocrats who owned great estates worked by slave labour. During the course of the next two centuries, the resentment of this ground-down peasantry resulted in a series of unsuccessful uprisings, all of which were brutally put down.

In 73 BC, it was the turn of the slaves to rise up against their masters. A former soldier named Spartacus, who had been sold into slavery, escaped with seventy other slaves and went into hiding. This was the beginning of a great revolt that ultimately involved 90,000 slaves, who fought a two-year campaign. When they were finally defeated, 6000 were crucified along the roads leading to Rome.

Between AD 100 and AD 200, the Roman empire reached a pinnacle of wealth and power. To control the population of almost 50 million, the imperial authority was able to call upon a regular army of 300,000 men. Rome itself, with more than half a million inhabitants, was the most populous city in the world. Despite this, it was not a powerhouse of commerce or industry. Its life revolved around the administration of a great empire and the consumption of the products of that empire. For the rich and well connected among its citizens, this was a golden age. 'The universe has become a single city', wrote a teacher of rhetoric, Aelius Aristides, in his *Eulogy of Rome*, around 150. 'The whole world is in festive mood. It has abandoned its weapons of war to give itself up to the joy of living.' His contemporary, the historian Appian of Alexandria, spoke of 'A sure and lasting peace, instituted to create permanent happiness.'

But the empire was living on borrowed time. As well-to-do Romans reclined on their couches in their Chinese silks and their Arabian perfumes, playing with their pet monkeys while their slaves cooled them with fans made from the feathers of ostriches, a rising tide was lapping their walls. All along their northern frontiers, the barbarians they so despised – the Franks, the Goths and the rest – were increasing in numbers. Attracted by the wealth of the empire, but also driven by pressures generated by other tribes behind them in eastern Europe and Central Asia, they were demanding to be allowed to settle within the empire's margins. In 251 the Goths crossed the Danube. In 256 the Franks crossed the Rhine. Before long, the Alemanni were making raids as far south as Milan. Towns-people whose defensive walls had been allowed to fall into disrepair during the long period of peace were now hastening to restore them.

While the empire was struggling to repel these attacks from outside, it was beginning to disintegrate within, undermined by civil wars and rampant inflation. At the same time, a split had begun to open up between the empire's Greek-speaking eastern half and the Latin-speaking west. The leading city of the Eastern empire was the ancient Greek city of Byzantium in Asia Minor (modern Istanbul), which had grown in wealth and population until it rivalled Rome itself. In 324, the Emperor Constantine I (Constantine the Great) made it his capital, calling it a 'New Rome' and renaming it Constantinople.

Constantine, the son of an army officer who had himself achieved the status of deputy emperor, had fought his way to the imperial throne via a succession of civil wars, after being proclaimed emperor by his troops while campaigning in Britain. Being superstitious, like most Romans of his day, he attributed his success to divine intervention by the God of the Christian religion to which he had converted (although he was careful to mention the part played by his own genius).

At the time Constantine converted, Christianity was already more than two and a half centuries old. It had originated in the Roman province of Judea, at the eastern end of the Mediterranean. It was rooted in the teachings of a wandering Jewish preacher named Jesus, who was born around 4–6 BC. Most of what we know about him is contained in records compiled at least forty years after his death. In his early thirties, he spent two or three years preaching. Around the year 30, when he would have been in his mid- to late-thirties, he incurred the wrath of the religious authorities in Jerusalem, who had him charged with blasphemy, in a trial that resulted in his crucifixion.

Jesus's disciples, and a group of later converts of whom the most notable was a Hellenized Jew from Tarsus, in south-central Turkey, who was later canonized as St Paul, succeeded in perpetuating his memory, and spreading his message, far beyond any reasonable expectation. Although Jesus was an orthodox Jew, his teaching – of personal salvation in an afterlife, as the reward of faith – was cast by his followers in inclusive terms that made it attractive to the hopeless and downtrodden of all beliefs and of none. His message of universal love and disregard for the vanity of worldly goods and worldly power operated across class boundaries, to Jew and non-Jew alike. By the time Constantine himself became a convert, there were already hundreds of Christian congregations scattered throughout the empire.

This new religion, founded by a Jew and initially mainly confined to Jews, had its roots in the Jews' own religion, Judaism, which was some two millennia old when Jesus was born. The early Christians took from Judaism two fundamental ideas. The first of these was a belief in a single, all-powerful God. The Jews had originally worshipped a multitude of gods. Over the centuries, one of these, Yahweh (Jehovah), had gradually assumed pre-eminence in their worship, until a stage was reached when they abandoned other gods and worshipped only Him. (*Him*, rather than *Her*, because Judaism, like all religions that worship only one god, was invented by men, who naturally thought of their God as being male.) This mindset – monolatry – in which they accepted the existence of other gods, but no longer worshipped them, was later rejected in favour of monotheism, the belief that there was only one God. Jesus's followers – Jew and non-Jew alike – adhered to this belief, and were quite clear in their minds that they were worshipping the Jewish Jehovah.

Where Christianity parted company with the religion from which it had sprung was in its second fundamental proposition, which, ironically, also ultimately derived from Judaism. Through centuries of exile and persecution, the Jews had clung to the belief that they were God's chosen people, and that one day God would send them a redeemer – a messiah ('anointed one') – who would rescue His people from bondage. The early Christians persuaded themselves that this promise had been fulfilled, and that Jesus was the messiah. The word 'Christian' was derived from *christos*, the Greek form of messiah.

It is hard to know whether Jesus saw himself as anything more than a prophet, but it is safe to say that the guide to conduct contained in his teaching could never by itself have fuelled the triumphant spread of Christianity. The required fuel was provided by the 'extras' added by his followers, especially by Paul. This more systematic expression of belief contained three major elements. The first of these was that Jesus was not a mere mortal, but the 'Son of God', a sort of incarnation of Jehovah himself. The second was that he had risen from the dead, three days after his crucifixion, and now 'reigned' for ever in heaven. The third – Paul's own master-stroke – was, that by his death on the cross, Jesus had obtained forgiveness of sin and the promise of eternal life in heaven for all who believed in him. It was a package of which any salesman would have been proud. Once it had been put together, Rome's traditional gods were never in with a chance.

Most of the new religion's early adherents were Jews, and its spread had been greatly assisted by the widespread dispersal of this element of the empire's population. By the first century, there were some 7 million Jews within the empire's boundaries, the vast majority of whom lived outside Palestine. (Almost half the population of Alexandria was Jewish, for example.) During the second century, the Jewish element in the Christian community was diluted into insignificance, as more and more non-Jews responded to missionary activity. This was in spite of continuing persecution, which at times saw the feeding of Christians to lions, to provide holiday entertainment in the sports stadiums of the empire.

This fast-growing religion was given a boost in 313, when Constantine issued a decree – the Edict of Milan – that granted toleration to all religions but made Christianity a favoured state religion, and restored all Church property confiscated during the earlier persecution. For the remainder of his reign, he lavished wealth on Christian churches, and took an active part in Church affairs. By his example, he turned Christianity into a fashion statement for the ruling class. By the time he died in 337, he could reasonably have claimed that his unwavering devotion had opened up the possibility that the Jewish preacher's teachings might one day form the basis of a worldwide religion. In 380, when another emperor, Theodosius I, refused to acknowledge the old Roman gods and made Christianity the official religion of the empire, this possibility became a probability.

One thing that neither Constantine nor his successors could hope to turn was the tide lapping at the empire's borders. After his death, the pressure from the northern barbarians became more insistent. In 376, the Goths crossed the Danube.

In December 406, the Vandals and the Suevi crossed the frozen Rhine, overrunning much of Gaul. Finally, in 410, the Visigoths penetrated to the heart of the empire, and sacked Rome itself. For three days and three nights they pillaged the city, while those of its citizens who were able to do so fled.

In 455, Rome was sacked even more thoroughly, this time by the Vandals. In 476, it was the turn of another group of raiders from the north, the Goths. On this occasion, the visitors stayed. Their general, Odoacer, with the blessing of the imperial authorities in Constantinople, proclaimed himself 'King of Italy'. When he did so, the Western empire, which had already fallen apart, ceased to exist.

Constantine's Eastern empire lasted until its conquest by the Turks in 1453. But the bringing down of the curtain on the Western empire in 476 makes a convenient marker for the boundary between the classical age of Greece and Rome and the world of medieval Europe.

10
THE BIRTH OF INDIA

There are times when the phrase 'Indian subcontinent' comes in useful. But it is rather a cumbersome expression, so for the remainder of this book, until we reach 1947, we will instead use the term 'India' to denote the entire subcontinent, south of the mountains of the Himalaya and the Hindu Kush.

Around 1500 BC, an invading people entered India from the north-west. They were pastoral nomads with light skins, and they called themselves Aryans. They spoke a language belonging to the Indo-European language family to which present-day European languages such as English, French and Russian belong, along with Asian languages such as Persian and Hindi. For several centuries after their arrival, these Aryans continued with a nomadic way of life based on cattle breeding, and it was not until around 1000 BC that they adopted settled agriculture. They left no written records, so the only information we have concerning their lives is contained in the later, largely mythical, epic poems that embody their tradition of oral story-telling. These contain accounts of heroic adventures and wars with the aboriginal inhabitants, which in many ways resemble the epics of ancient Greece.

The closest parallels to Homer's *Iliad* and *Odyssey* are the two great collections of stories known as the *Mahabharata* and the *Ramayana*. The *Mahabharata* – the world's longest poem – recounts a mythic tale of the early stages of the conquest of

India. The *Ramayana* tells the story of a god-like hero (Rama), and an Indian Helen of Troy (Sita), who is abducted by Ravana, the demon king of Sri Lanka. Both date from the same era as the Greek epics, and have retained much of their resonance. For most Europeans outside Greece, Homer's stories are something they know of, rather than something they know. For Hindus, and for most other inhabitants of the subcontinent, the characters in these ancient stories are a living presence and the inspiration for an endless stream of film spectaculars.

The other great monuments of early Indian literature are the liturgical texts known as the Vedas. These are the most sacred of the holy books of Hinduism, the most ancient of the world's great religions. The oldest of the Vedas is the *Rig Veda*, a collection of hymns to the gods, which appears to date back to a Bronze Age culture, sometime before 1000 BC. All the Vedas were composed in Sanskrit, a classical language that bears the same relationship to modern Hindi and Bengali that Latin does to French and Spanish. In the nineteenth century, Sanskrit and Latin were themselves shown to be cousins, sharing a common (Indo-European) ancestry, with a homeland somewhere in the Steppe country where eastern Europe meets Central Asia.

As the Aryan invaders settled in these new lands, the development of their culture echoed that of the Greeks. They began to make iron tools and weapons around 1000 BC, though not on a significant scale until about 500 BC. They established themselves first in the Ganges Valley, but by 400 BC their settlements extended as far south as the River Godavari. The Ganges Valley had a wetter climate than that of the Indus, and the staple crop was therefore rice, rather than wheat or barley. Settled agriculture and iron technology made possible a substantial increase in population. By around 500 BC, conflict between rival tribal kingdoms had resulted in consolidation into about half a dozen states, each centred on a small capital city defended by mud-brick walls.

It was during this period of warring states that the holy books of the Hindu religion took written form. Until then, they had been handed down through generations of Brahmins, a hereditary priestly class that constituted one of the topmost levels of the system of caste. Caste was a strict, layer-cake division of society that had its origin in the earliest days of the Aryan invasion, but which crystallized in the period from 800 BC to 500 BC. Alongside the Brahmins were the Kshatriyas (warriors); below them were the Vaishias (merchants) and the Shudras (farmers). Contact between the members of different castes was limited, and strictly controlled by social custom. Marriage between people of different castes was rare. It was possible, if the woman was of lower caste than her prospective husband, but it was virtually impossible if the man was of lower caste than his prospective wife. Outside the four main castes there was a multitude of people of no caste at all, whose status would, over the succeeding centuries, harden into that of 'untouchable'.

Concern with caste has remained a persistent feature of Indian life, and it is a powerful factor in political, as well as social life. The original classification based on four principal castes has long since proliferated into a multitude of castes and sub-castes. Just as it had its birth in the period when the Hindu religion itself was being created, it is still intimately tied up with it. But Hinduism and caste can, and do, exist apart. For example, caste is alive and well as a social institution in the central highlands of Sri Lanka, among people of Indian ancestry, but Buddhist faith. By contrast, on the island of Bali, in Indonesia, there are devout Hindus for whom caste is a matter of minor concern.

Hinduism is a complex and subtle religion. Even its most erudite practitioners have been known to disagree as to just what its essence is. This is partly a consequence of its age. Having been around longer than other religions, it has had more time to develop complexity. But it also reflects the two very different aspects that Hinduism presents to the world. In its immediately visible aspect, it is a complicated collection of rituals and celebrations, allowing for the worship of a host of local gods. But Hinduism has another face, which is not seen by the casual onlooker. This is the 3000-year-old philosophical tradition, originating in the Upanishads, a collection of commentaries on the Vedas, whose subject is the search for ultimate truth and a basis for morality. For many Hindus it is this search that is the essence of their religion, not any particular set of observances.

Around the fifth century BC another religion arose in north-east India that became one of the great religions of the world. This was Buddhism. It had its origin in the teachings of a north Indian prince with the family surname of Gautama. He was born in the foothills of the Himalaya, sometime between 550 BC and 420 BC – probably nearer to the latter. The uncertainty attaching to his birth is an indication of how little we know about his life. We also know little about the early history of the religious movement he inspired. What is certain is the colossal impact his teaching had on his early followers, and the power his thinking still has today.

Gautama's outlook and teaching were a product of the time and place in which he grew up. He was born into a society in which the concept of reincarnation – the rebirth of a soul in another body – was a fundamental aspect of religious belief. (Pythagoras, the great Greek mathematician, who lived around the same time, also believed in it.) This was an age when it was fashionable for thoughtful young men to take time out to live a simple life, while they contemplated the sorrows of the world. (Thoughtful young women were too busy having babies and raising children to be able to indulge themselves in this way.)

Legend has it that when he was about thirty, Gautama walked out on his wife and his new-born son, and rode off into the night. It is also said that he travelled for seven years, living an austerely simple life, in the hope of finding an answer to the problem of suffering, through the medium of meditation. The enlightenment he finally claimed to have experienced led to his being called the Buddha ('the awakened one').

Gautama had at first accepted the idea that an individual human life was just one stage in an unending cycle, involving rebirth in different forms. But he came to believe that suffering and disappointment were the consequence of unsatisfied desires, and that the human spirit could escape from the perpetual cycle of rebirth by overcoming desire (in the widest sense of yearnings of an earthly kind). Another already-existing idea that was incorporated into Buddhist doctrine was that of karma. This was a cause-and-effect relationship between past actions and future experience, whereby good conduct was rewarded both by a happy state of mind and a tendency to further good conduct – either in this life, or in a later one.

Central to Gautama's teaching was the pursuit of the Middle Way: a path between the extremes of out-and-out worldliness and harsh self-denial. He preached the importance of meditation in the pursuit of *nirvana*, a state of peace and blessedness, in which the spirit is able to rise above the pain and disappointments of everyday life. *Nirvana* was not a celebratory condition, like the Christian heaven, with its angels and trumpets, or the Muslim paradise, with its gardens and beautiful maidens. It was a state of peace, in which the soul was no longer troubled by earthly longings and frustrations. The conquest of desire that led to *nirvana* was to be achieved by pursuing the noble eightfold path: right views, right intention, right speech, right action, right livelihood, right effort, right awareness and right concentration.

Buddhism was basically a godless religion, but the need that many human beings have for someone, or something, to worship, would later cause its founder to be venerated as a kind of god. In the centuries after his death, the faith based on his teaching split into fiercely disputing sects, as happened with both Christianity and Islam. These sects went on to develop their own versions of Buddhism, which were spread far and wide by the missionary activities of monks and nuns, supported by the sponsorship of Buddhist merchants who settled in places like northern China.

Nothing promotes a religion like the conversion of a powerful ruler. In the case of Buddhism, the required shot in the arm was provided by the apparent conversion of one of the greatest rulers in Indian – or any other – history: the Emperor Asoka (pronounced Ashoka). Asoka was the last major emperor of the Maurya dynasty, which had come to power in north-east India as the result of a military coup in 321 BC. The leader of this coup, Chandragupta Maurya, Asoka's grandfather, had created an empire stretching from the Hindu Kush to the Ganges delta. This was further extended to include the great central plateau of the Deccan by his son, Bindusara. It was this enlarged empire, covering most of present-day India and Pakistan, that Bindusara's son, Asoka, inherited when he ascended the throne in around 268 BC (there is some uncertainty about his dates).

Asoka began his reign with more conquests. But in the eighth year of his reign, after a bloody war against the state of Kalinga (present-day Orissa), he seems to have developed a revulsion at his own bloodthirstiness. Thereafter, he adopted a Buddhist approach to his role. The most striking feature of his reign was his untiring endeavour to persuade people of all faiths to work together in tolerance for the good of everyone (and for the easier management of an enormous and disparate empire). For the remainder of his thirty-five-year rule, he devoted himself to the peace of his realm and the welfare of his people.

Asoka's sympathy towards Buddhism did not result in its becoming a state religion, an idea as foreign to Indian thought then as it is now. Nor would it succeed in displacing the much more ancient Hindu religion. But the prestige associated with an emperor's encouragement, and the active support he gave to its missionaries, resulted in the hundreds of millions of followers it has today in Central Asia, South-East Asia and China.

The empire of Asoka's grandfather, Chandragupta Maurya, had been a powerful and prosperous state with a huge standing army. Its roads, and its elegant capital, Pataliputra (present-day Patna), had made a profound impression on a Greek ambassador, Megasthenes, who sent home a breathless description of his first visit. Given the tendency of all Greek accounts of India to mix fact with downright fiction, one should not take his report at face value. But to have so excited a cultured Greek diplomat and historian, the empire and its capital even in 300 BC, must have been pretty impressive. But this empire of Chandragupta Maurya had a dark side. It was what we would call a police state, with a draconian penal code, overseen by an emperor who took care never to sleep in the same bed twice and had his food tasted in his presence, for possible poison.

The state that Asoka set about creating was as different from his grandfather's model as it was possible to be. The Buddhism to which he now apparently subscribed (but which he never publicly espoused) preached a political morality that included an obligation to fight poverty and insecurity. Asoka tried hard to fulfil this obligation. Instead of military conquest, he substituted the principle of 'conquest by *dharma*' (the principles of right life). He greatly reduced the size of his army, and he devoted the resources released to a great programme of public works: wells and bathing tanks; hospitals (for both people and animals); rest houses for travellers; and drinking places for cattle. He promoted female education. He enforced a regime of tolerance for all religions, and travelled widely in his dominions, to see for himself the lives of his subjects and to ensure the carrying out of his policies. He appointed regional commissioners, whose duties were to listen to complaints and to pay special attention to the needs of women and minority groups. He arranged for his ambitions, and his guiding principles, to be engraved on stone columns throughout the empire. One typical announcement read: 'All men are my children. As I desire all the welfare and happiness of this world, and the next, for my own children, so do I desire for all men.'

How far these broadcast sentiments reflected deep conviction and how far they represented what we would now call 'spin' we cannot now say. But there can be no argument about the beneficent effect of Asoka's long reign on the welfare and prosperity of the people of his far-flung empire.

It was an attitude, and a programme, that could not be expected to survive his death, and it didn't. Even during his reign, his tolerant attitude to many competing faiths and sects did as much to encourage dissension as to discourage it. After he died, around 238 BC, his empire disintegrated. But more than 2000 years later his memory still serves as an inspiration to those who strive to make a better life for the people of the nation he served with such wise endeavour.

The Maurya dynasty, which ended with Asoka, ruled over the most populous, and one of the most prosperous, empires the world had ever known. At the time of his death, the population of India was around 50 million. This was half as big again as the population of China, and a quarter of the population of the entire globe.

There now followed several centuries of India's 'Dark Age'. What historians mean when they label any period a Dark Age is 'This came before a brilliant, well-documented era, and we don't know much about it, so we will assume that nothing of much importance happened.' What we do know is that during these centuries, the population fell precipitously. How much of this was due to war, how much to famine and how much to pestilence, we do not know. But whatever the cause, between 238 BC and AD 320 the population of India declined from more than 50 million to less than 40 million.

In the year 320, much of India was reunited under a new dynasty, the Guptas. The two centuries that followed were a period of busy trade with far-distant countries, which delivered wealth and luxury for those at the top of the social pile. It was also a golden age of artistic achievement, resulting in works of art that bear comparison with the products of any civilization in history. These include magnificent stone carvings and exquisite modelling in copper and bronze. In literature, this was the time when the great epics, the *Mahabharata* and the *Ramayana*, were put into their definitive Sanskrit form. It was also the period in which Kalidasa – the Sanskrit Shakespeare – wrote his great love poem *Meghaduta* ('The Cloud Messenger'), and the play *Shakuntala*, which is one of the sublime masterpieces of world drama.

The Gupta dynasty was not only notable for its artistic achievements; it was also an important staging post in the history of science. It witnessed a revival of the universities that had graced the reign of Asoka. Out of these came a stream of writing that would later inspire the scientific culture of Islam, and through Islam the Scientific Revolution in Europe. Preeminent among the scientific innovations introduced by the gifted mathematicians of this period was the system of notation we call Arabic numerals. It was an Indian mathematician, Aryabhata, who, in 499, published the first book employing a system of numbers with place values and a decimal point. His work found its way, via ninth-century Baghdad, to thirteenth-century Europe, and it would be difficult to overstate the importance of this Indian contribution to the development of modern commercial and scientific civilization.

11

THE MAKING OF CHINA

The sense of superiority displayed by the Greeks and Romans had its mirror image in China, where people looked out at the world and saw only barbarians. Educated Chinese knew of the existence of the Mediterranean civilizations, and the Greeks and Romans knew something of China, but not enough to undermine their self-esteem. The Chinese world-view was summed-up in the name – *Zhongguo* – by which they referred to their own country. Literally translated, it meant 'the middle kingdom', but the underlying sense was 'the centre of the world'.

The Chinese fascination with jade had created a long-distance trade with the peoples of Central Asia, where the stone was found. These Central Asian peoples also had trading links with the inhabitants of Mesopotamia, who had a similar love affair with the blue stone lapis lazuli, found only in Afghanistan. These east–west routes eventually joined up to form the 4000-mile-long Silk Road. Along this route, from around 100 BC, camel caravans carried cloth destined for the silk-mad ladies of Rome, on the first stage of a land and sea journey of 9000 miles. When it reached Rome, the cloth was picked apart and rewoven to make the semi-transparent fabric that Roman taste preferred. It was sometimes, literally, worth its weight in gold.

The Silk Road became a conduit, not just for textiles from the east, but for wool, silver and gold from the west, and for the transfer of ideas in both directions. But it was a trade conducted through intermediaries, leaving the civilizations at both ends of the route in a state of ignorance about one another's achievements.

Just as the Agricultural Revolution in China occurred later than that in the Fertile Crescent, so did the rise of towns and cities. When they did arise, it was as a result of the introduction of large-scale irrigation. The millet-based farming culture of the Yellow River region had originated on valley slopes, where natural rainfall could be retained in terraced fields. During the first millennium BC, increased population and large-scale land ownership made possible the construction of a system of dykes and canals across the floodplain of the river, bringing a huge expanse of fertile land into production for the first time.

While this transformation of the economy of the Yellow River region was in progress, a change occurred in the agricultural basis of life in the Yangtze Valley, 400 miles to the south. The process resembled the opening up of the Nile Valley. Here, too, dense, marshy woodland – in this case, steaming-hot jungle – was cleared to reveal a fertile, flood-replenished soil. But to exploit its potential to the full, a new kind of farming had to be invented. The staple crop of the region, rice, had hitherto been grown either dry, on rain-watered uplands, or in the shallow man-made pools called paddies. From about 500 BC, a new method of rice farming was developed, using varieties that thrived in deep-water paddies.

The birth of this new culture of deep-water rice farming coincided with the onset of China's Iron Age. The change to a society based on iron impacted first on the tools and equipment used in everyday life. War continued to be a matter of personal combat between aristocratic charioteers, but as new iron weapons were invented, the balance of advantage swung in favour of armies of disciplined foot soldiers, as it had around the Mediterranean.

From 481 BC to 221 BC, in what is known as the Warring States period, war was a permanent feature of Chinese life. At the beginning of this period, seventeen more or less equally matched states were competing for mastery. By 318 BC, their number had been reduced to seven. At this stage, the western-most state – Quin (pronounced Chin) – which had managed to avoid most of the earlier fighting, embarked upon a campaign of conquest, which ended in 221 BC. It is from this date that we can at last use the term 'China' as the signifier of a political and cultural unity, rather than a mere geographical label.

The country did not long remain unified, and its history for the next 2000 years would be a story of break-up, followed by chaos, followed by reunification. The civil wars that inter-rupted the periods of settled rule were usually initiated by a rebellion of a hungry and oppressed peasantry. But throughout these upheavals, the consciousness of a shared culture, and a shared history, would remain, giving China a sense of continu-ity with a distant past that is still a potent force.

A central element in this sense of historical continuity was supplied by the teachings of a great philosopher who was born in 551 BC, and who died, at the age of seventy-three, at the outset of the Warring States period. His name was K'ung Fu-Tzu, or, as he is known to people outside China, Confucius. He may have been the child of impoverished nobility; he cer-tainly grew up poor. Inspired by his widowed mother, he became an indefatigable learner and a brilliant teacher. In his forties and early fifties he was a successful career politician, but finding his rather strait-laced attitudes unwelcome in official circles, he went into voluntary exile for twelve years, devoting himself to the education of a band of disciples. At the age of sixty-seven, he returned home to teach, and to put his political and social theories into written form.

Although Confucius was a reformer, he was no revolutionary. The driving principle of his thought was the search for what was good in the traditions and practices of the past, in order that they might be enshrined in guidelines for action in the present. His main concern was the right ordering of society, and the qualities required of those who aspired to govern it. He insisted that only those who had been appropriately educated were fit to exercise authority over their fellow men. It was a proposition that would later form the basis of one of the most enduring features of Chinese society: the mandarin class of career civil servants, selected by competitive examination and responsible directly to the emperor, rather than serving the interests of a local aristocracy. These highly paid mandarins were, however, largely recruited from the land-owning classes, and in social terms they and the aristocracy represented a single class, physically and mentally far removed from the peasant masses whose taxes they collected. They were at once officials, scholars and gentlemen, a combination that European societies of the same period would not have recognized. Their power would later be enhanced by the fact that in China there was no established religion to challenge the authority of the state.

These mandarins were technocrats, their outlook summed up in a famous passage from the influential philosopher Meng-Tzu (Mencius). Writing in the fourth century BC, he said:

> The pursuits of men of quality are not those of the poor. The former work with their brains, the latter with their bodies.

Those who work with their brains govern the others; those
who work with their bodies are governed by them . . .
Those who are governed support the others: those who
govern are supported by the rest.

Or, as a popular saying of the time had it, 'If a man becomes
an official, all his dogs and chickens will be promoted.'

This system of administration by highly educated career
civil servants had enormous strengths, but contained its own
weaknesses. It was a highly effective machine for carrying on
the day-to-day business of a great empire. But the penalties for
non-performance were severe, and the inevitable consequence
was a 'play safe' attitude that not only dominated public administration, but infected thinking about life in general. The
conservatism that resulted from a constant referring back to
the past was no obstacle to progress in practical matters, but sti-
fled the sort of speculative thinking that was essential for
scientific progress. The Confucian respect for the clan, the
family and seniority in general was another factor discouraging
dissent. It was this combination of a centrally administered
empire and conservative patterns of thought that prevented this
brilliantly inventive civilization from generating the restless
questioning of accepted ideas that made possible the kind of
scientific advances made in classical Greece or seventeenth-
century England.

At the time of Confucius's death in 479 BC, China was on
the brink of a technological revolution. By the time the country was united in 221 BC, the tide of innovation was in full
flow. In the centuries that followed, the country experienced
an Industrial Revolution not unlike that experienced by
England in the eighteenth century. Some of the inventions

brought into industrial use at this time would not be introduced into Europe for another thousand years.

There was a parallel revolution in agricultural practice. By the sixth century BC, Chinese farmers were sowing their crops in rows. This resulted in a far higher yield than scattering the seed by hand, and it made weeds easier to control. (It would be advocated as an innovation by an English agricultural manual published in 1731.) A century later, the weeds were being kept down by the use of cast-iron hoes. As early as 85 BC, the Chinese were using multi-row drill ploughs, with seed hoppers that automatically fed the seed to rows as they were drilled, something that would not appear in Europe until the eighteenth century.

A development of huge importance, with no counterpart anywhere else in the world, was the introduction, around 200 BC, of the trace harness with a breast strap. This made it possible for horses to perform with ease tasks that might otherwise have killed them. The Roman empire at this time was almost totally dependent on water transport for the movement of heavy materials. Its wonderful road system was virtually useless for the transport of goods, because the only harness available would have strangled any horse forced to pull a heavy load. A load of hay that had to be carried 30 miles cost twice as much as it did at the farm gate. By contrast, a shipload of Egyptian wheat could be sold in the markets of Rome for only a quarter more than it would have fetched in the markets of Alexandria.

In the first century BC, the Chinese further increased the working capacity of their horses by devising the collar harness that is still used on working horses today. This was another device that would not be seen in Europe for a thousand years. Its development did not just revolutionize overland transport;

it gave a further huge boost to the productivity of Chinese agriculture. A horse needs more food than an ox, but can perform much heavier work, more quickly.

This period saw, too, the invention of paper manufacture, with consequences for the entire world. Neither the Egyptians, nor the Greeks nor the Romans had any knowledge of paper. Their nearest equivalent was papyrus, made from the stems of the Egyptian reed of the same name. Nor did the later scribes of medieval Europe know of it. They wrote on parchment made from animal skins.

Chinese paper was made by mixing cloth fibres with water and size. The mixture was run into tanks containing a cloth or wire screen, where the surplus liquid was drained off. The residue was dried, and the resulting sheet of paper was then peeled off the screen. This is essentially how paper is still made, although most everyday paper is made from wood pulp. As far as we know, the process has only been discovered once in the history of the world – and that was in China around 100 BC. The oldest surviving piece of paper with writing on dates from about AD 100. It took 700 years for Chinese paper to reach Europe (via the Arabs), and a thousand years for Europeans to discover the secret of its manufacture.

Some of the industrial activities undertaken in China at this time are breathtaking. An example that illustrates the scale and ambition of early Chinese industry was the practice of deep drilling for brine and natural gas. By the first century BC, the Chinese were able to sink foot-wide boreholes, lined with bamboo tubing, to depths of nearly 5000 feet. The method used was to attach a cast-iron drill bit to the end of a 100-foot length of bamboo cable, which was suspended from a tall derrick. A team of men would press down on, and then release, a lever, which would cause the drill bit to drop suddenly to the bottom of the hole. As the hole got deeper, another length of tubing would be attached, and so on. The process was repeated, if necessary, for months on end, until an artesian, salt-bearing spring was hit. When it was, the naturally pressurized brine would be distributed, sometimes over many miles, through another system of bamboo tubes. Other wells were sunk to exploit underground reservoirs of natural gas, which was similarly distributed to where it could be used as fuel to heat the cast-iron pans in which brine was evaporated to yield salt. The gas from shallow wells could be burned as it came from the pipe, but that from deeper reservoirs had first to be mixed with air in giant cast-iron carburettors. There must have been a lot of accidents before a safe method of operation was worked out.

These advances in industry and agriculture both contributed to, and were driven by, a population explosion. Between AD 1 and 2 the imperial government conducted a census that revealed a population of 60 million, which equalled that of the entire Roman empire. The most densely populated region was still the area around the Yellow River. Here, where there had once been only villages, and the occasional town, there were now fine cities, the equal of any to be found elsewhere. In these cities, the land-owning nobility and an army of civil servants lived in luxury. The amenities of the capital city of Changan in the first century were not very different from those of fifteenth-century London or Paris, and its population was greater than both combined.

For the mass of the peasantry, living close to subsistence, the increase in numbers was not matched by a corresponding improvement in their standard of living. Crop failure and famine were ever-present threats. When the crops did fail, desperation would produce uprisings. Most were ruthlessly put down, but some were so expensive that they overthrew a dynasty. After a period of chaos, a new leader would appear, and a new dynasty would be created. It was a process that would be repeated many times during the next 2000 years.

The disaffection of an oppressed peasantry was not the only problem that China's rulers had to contend with. There was also the ever-present threat from enemies beyond their frontiers. To the east, these were protected by the ocean. To the south and west, mountains provided a barrier against invasion. But in the north and north-west, their borders were open to attack from the horse-riding nomads whose herds wandered the grasslands of Central Asia. One of the first acts of the Quin Emperor Shih Huang Ti, in 221 BC, had been to disarm the empire – apart from his own personal army – and to melt the confiscated weapons down for bells and statues. Having thus neutered any potential internal opposition, he turned his attention to the external threat, and ordered the construction of a 'Long Wall'. This was the precursor of what non-Chinese know today as the Great Wall of China, or as it has been called, 'the longest cemetery in the world' (from the number of people who died during its construction). Completed in 214 BC, it was both a chain of watch-towers looking out across the steppes whence an attack might come, and a statement to outsiders of where the new empire's boundaries lay.

With each new dynasty, the Confucian system of public administration would resume more or less unchanged. And Confucian theory had a formula to explain what had happened. A successful uprising was, by definition, proof that the previous emperor had ceased to govern his people in a proper way, and had therefore lost the 'Mandate of Heaven' that gave him his right to rule. The subsequent establishment of a new dynasty was evidence that the new emperor had received the Mandate of Heaven. This is an elusive concept, but one that has exercised a hold on the Chinese imagination for 2000 years and still has force today. It is intimately connected with a view of history that sees human events as a series of repeated cycles of prosperity, moral decline, dynastic collapse, chaos and dynastic renewal, leading to prosperity once again.

Confucianism is not a religion, in the sense that Christianity or Islam are. Confucius had no time for superstition, and the ethical system he espoused had no supernatural element. It contained no heaven or hell, and, strictly speaking, it required no priesthood. But in practice, the more senior Confucian officials gradually assumed responsibility for the performance of rituals dedicated to traditional gods. So as well as organizing water supplies when the rains failed, it became part of a city magistrate's duty to lead prayers for rain. This religious role supplied a further strengthening of the power of the mandarin class, and a further enhancement of their status.

The veneration in which Confucius was held would in due course lead to his being worshipped as a kind of god. But the earth-bound nature of his teachings left his followers free to seek the 'consolations of religion' elsewhere, and China – and its poor, in particular – continued to provide a fertile soil for the growth of foreign religions.

Of all the religions that would later offer the peoples of China the consolations that Confucianism could not, the first, and the most important, was Buddhism. During the Later Han dynasty (AD 45–220) there was a great expansion of foreign trade, and a considerable number of Central Asian merchants took up residence in the northern cities. It was from these communities that Buddhism spread to the Chinese population. In the period of dislocation that followed the fall of the Later Han, it acquired many adherents, including the barbarian invaders who had taken control of the frontier regions. In a striking parallel with the experience of Christianity in the Roman empire, this imported religion would later survive periods of persecution to become the faith of choice, not only of a downtrodden peasantry, but of a significant proportion of the upper classes, whose pious donations financed the building, and swelled the coffers, of the monasteries and nunneries.

Peasant rebellions and nomad invasions were not the only misfortunes endured by this great civilization during these centuries. The huge increase in population – from a mere 20 million in 400 BC to more than 60 million in the year 100 – was reflected in the increase of large towns, in the populations of those towns, and in the amount of travel between them. The consequence was a series of devastating epidemics, as Chinese armies ventured into frontier regions and a succession of new viruses and bacteria found their way into urban concentrations of people without acquired immunities. In 208, an epidemic killed two-thirds of the troops in the army in Hupeh. In 275, tens of thousands died in an outbreak in Honan. In 312, pestilence attacked a population already weakened by famine and plagues of locusts, and much of north and central China became, in a contemporary description, 'a great wasteland'. On this occasion, according to official records, only two in a hundred taxpayers in Shensi province survived. In 322, and again in 423, disease is recorded as having wiped out 30 per cent of the population of unnamed provinces. And these were only a few of scores of major epidemics, for most of which we have no record of the numbers who died. What we do know is that by the fifth century the population of China, which in the year 100 had exceeded 60 million, was less than half that figure. Some of this was attributable to war and famine, but much more was due to pestilence. In China, as elsewhere, the domestication of animals and the invention of urban living had turned out to have another, much darker side.

1 2

THE WORLD IN 500

By the year 500, the culture of wet rice farming with iron tools developed in China was also firmly established in the two countries – Korea and Japan – most exposed to Chinese influences. Wet rice farming had reached Japan, via Korea, by about 300 BC, but it was not until AD 250 that it was sufficiently widespread to open up the possibility of a civilization of the kind that agricultural settlement had created elsewhere. Historical records of this period are virtually non-existent, and such information as we have comes from Chinese and Korean archives. But it is clear that Japan was united under a single government and already a power to be reckoned with in 391, when it despatched a military force that succeeded in conquering three kingdoms in the south of the Korean peninsula. By 500, the wealth extracted from these dominions, and Japan's own rapidly improving technology, had fuelled a huge increase in its population, and created a luxurious lifestyle for its ruling classes. From a mere million in 250 BC, when wet rice farming was first introduced, Japan's population had risen to 5 million. In addition to tribute, the Korean connection provided a steady stream of craftsmen – irrigation experts, weavers, blacksmiths and so on. It was also the vehicle for a host of cultural innovations originating in China, of which the most notable were Confucian philosophy and the Chinese system of writing, later adapted to create a purely Japanese script.

This period of Japanese history is known as the Yamato, from the name of the imperial family, which claimed descent from the sun goddess, Amaterasu, and which would provide Japan with its emperors for the next 1500 years.

A key element of Japanese culture at this time was respect for the *uji* – the family. This did not just mean family in the sense of blood relations. It also meant family in the sense of the clan, and the largest family of all, the whole people, of which family the emperor was the head. Each family had its own deity, and it was the responsibility of the head of the family to ensure the proper worship of the family deity. This family worship existed within a wider context, Shinto – or more correctly, Ancient Shinto – a religion with many gods, some connected with natural forces or objects, such as the sea or mountains, and some concerned with processes, such as growth or creation.

To the south and east of Japan, the colonization of the islands of the Pacific was by now almost complete. The adventurous Polynesians, in their double-hulled sailing canoes, had just arrived in Hawaii, after a centuries-long, island-hopping migration of 2500 miles from the Marquesas Islands. Other Polynesians had got as far as Easter Island, after an equally long journey – in both miles and years – from Tahiti. These settlements were not the outcome of chance discoveries. They were the result of systematic exploration, by superb navigators, who took with them the dogs and pigs, and the breadfruit, coconuts, bananas and yams, they would need to re-establish themselves in their new homes. Only New Zealand remained to be discovered. Amid its lush vegetation, flocks of giant flightless birds wandered, ignorant of the human nemesis that threatened them just over the horizon.

The people of Australia were still isolated from the rest of the world. A thinly spread population in an unrewarding environment, they lacked the means to embark upon the urban/agricultural adventure that had transformed the lives of people elsewhere. For them, change could come only slowly, and their way of life continued in the pattern of gathering and hunting that had characterized it for thousands of years, and would continue largely unchanged for another thousand.

On the other side of the Pacific, 13,000 feet up in the Andes of South America, there was a lake – Lake Titicaca – that extended for 3000 square miles. Along its shores, an ancient civilization, with centuries of prosperity still ahead of it, was enjoying a golden age. Archaeologists know it as Tiahuanaco (or Tiwanacu), from the name of the great city at its heart. The foundation of its wealth and power was a unique system of agriculture, in which crops were grown in raised fields, capable of producing tens of thousands of tons of potatoes a year. They were watered by a network of irrigation canals, constructed to retain the heat of the midday sun through the cold mountain nights, protecting crops from the mountain frosts. The bountiful harvests supported an empire that embraced large areas of present-day Argentina, Bolivia, Peru and northern Chile. Tiahuanaco city was a ceremonial capital with perhaps 50,000 inhabitants, adorned with temple complexes whose magnificent ruins still impress today. Some of the stones used in its construction weigh 100 tons, and their nearest source was 3 miles away. The people of this mysterious civilization produced elegant jewellery and pots, but they had not discovered the secret of smelting iron. Their impressive architecture was the product of Stone Age technology, using axes made of flint.

In the Valley of Mexico, 5000 miles to the north, another Stone Age civilization was also at its height. Its chief city, Teotihuacán ('City of the Gods'), was even larger than Tiahuanaco. In 500, it was already four centuries old, and with a population of around 150,000, it was one of the biggest cities in the world. In area, if not in population, it was bigger than Rome. It covered 8 square miles, and was laid out in a grid pattern, with palaces, squares, hundreds of temples and two great pyramids, the Pyramid of the Sun and the Pyramid of the Moon. At 210 feet high, and with a base measuring 760 feet by 720 feet, the Pyramid of the Sun was the largest building in the Americas, and the third largest pyramid in the world. Such art and architecture, and such a large population, could only have been possible with a highly productive system of intensive agriculture. But without written records, there is little that can be said about the life of its people, or the extent of its empire, if empire it was. It remains a tantalizing mystery.

Several hundred miles to the east of Teotihuacán, on the Yucatan peninsula, the civilization of the Maya was in full flower. This civilization, which occupied an area about 500 miles by 300 miles, resembled no other, before or since. It had been created in almost impenetrable jungle, where nothing could be built, and no crops could be sown, until space had been cleared (with stone axes). And this in a hot, steamy climate, where annual rainfall was 120 inches, and the dry season lasted just a few months. Despite these difficulties, hundreds of temples, ritual enclosures and pyramids were constructed, which even in their ruined state inspire awe at their monumental quality, and the expenditure of labour they represent.

The Mayan was not really an urban civilization. What were assumed to be cities by their nineteenth-century discoverers are now considered ceremonial centres: religious and administrative capitals of districts in which the basic unit was the farming village. Nor was it an empire, with a central administration. It seems to have been more in the nature of a collection of city-states, with the ceremonial centres fulfilling the role of the city, and with religious observation, and the propitiation of the gods, occupying a central role in the community's life. The Maya had a highly developed system of hieroglyphic writing, but most of their literature was destroyed, in an act of barbarism, by sixteenth-century Spanish priests who considered it to be 'the work of the devil' (a description that better fits their own behaviour). As a result, we know almost nothing about everyday Mayan life. We do know that maize and beans were their staple food, that avocados were an important crop and that they drank chocolate. And we know that they had their own ideas of what constituted personal attractiveness. The skulls of newly born babies were squashed between boards to produce an elongated head. Squints were particularly prized, and to achieve them, babies had wooden balls hung between their eyes.

The few Mayan writings we do possess are mostly astronomical and priestly records. The calculations they contain are of a quality unsurpassed by any Stone Age civilization. But for all their intellectual achievements, the Maya made no great advances in technology. Given the terrain they lived in, it is understandable that they never developed wheeled vehicles. But neither did they have pack animals. Everything in this civilization, including their massive masonry, was either carried or manhandled.

North of the present-day Mexican border, no urban civilization had yet appeared. In and around the Valley of the

Ohio, the people of the Hopewell culture had an economy based on the growing of maize, squash and beans, as well as hunting, but their settlements were villages, not towns. Elsewhere on the continent, hunting and gathering cultures remained largely unchanged. This general absence of settled agriculture is reflected in the size of the population, compared with other parts of the Americas. The population of North America at this time, north of present-day Mexico, was possibly no more than about 2 million. Central and South America, by contrast, had a population of around 13 million.

In Europe, the cultures of the Stone Age had long since been left behind. Few Europeans lived by hunting or foraging. Almost everywhere, either pastoralism or settled agriculture provided the framework of everyday life. Within the boundaries of the former Western empire, many cities still maintained the traditions of Roman civic life, but many others had been abandoned.

Both inside and outside the former empire's boundaries, the technology of iron tools and iron weapons was universal. A feature of European life at this time was movement from the insistent pressure of mounted nomads coming out of Asia. As they forced their way into eastern Europe, earlier arrivals were compelled to keep moving west. Celtic peoples made way for Germanic peoples, who had themselves been forced to make way for Slavs, and so on. In the fifth and sixth centuries, with the Roman legions gone, every country in western Europe experienced waves of invasion. At first these tended to be opportunistic: sudden raids in search of loot, wives and slaves. But as time went by, they became expeditions in search of a permanent home. When a promising place was found, the raiders would settle down, and start farming. The peoples they displaced were forced to eke out a living in less fertile places, in the hills or on the seacoast.

Around the Mediterranean, especially in the Eastern empire, city life continued much as before. But in northern Europe, from Britain to the shores of the Black Sea, the farming village was the basic unit of human settlement. Many of the Roman towns were half-ruined: quarries for building materials, rather than machines for living in. In Britain, the native noble families had endeavoured to maintain the old Roman way of life, but during the fifth century, they had been increasingly beset by invaders from across the North Sea – Angles, Saxons and Jutes.

At the other end of Eurasia, on the borders of India, the relentless pressure of attacks from the nomads of the steppes seemed finally to be easing. In 475, the Huns had crossed the mountain passes of Afghanistan, and advanced on Peshawar. In the years that followed, aided by the disintegration of the Gupta empire, they had reached the Indus and ravaged Kashmir, leaving a trail of massacre and destruction. For a generation afterwards, they ruled over the north-western corner of the country, but then they were driven back to the hills. They would remain a threat for another hundred years, but it would be many centuries before a nomad host again descended into the plains.

In Africa, south of the Sahara, the discovery of the secrets of iron working, and the development of indigenous systems of agriculture, had enabled many peoples to make up for the time they had lost when the Bronze Age had passed them by. In the interior of the continent, where diseases such as yellow fever, malaria and sleeping sickness were endemic, and insect-borne diseases prevented the use of horse, ox or camel, the development of a settled civilization was not to be expected.

Life there continued to follow ancient ways of gathering and hunting, and population remained sparse. But elsewhere, the developing skills of both pastoralists and farmers had yielded increases in food production, and brought about new technologies, that had made possible a rapid growth in population.

One of Africa's most dynamic civilizations was located 7000 feet up in the Ethiopian highlands, where forest-dwelling insects could not live and plough-pulling animals therefore could. This was the Christian kingdom of Aksum. It had been expanding since the first century, and its busy Red Sea port of Adulis was the centre of a trading network that extended from southern Italy to south India.

On the opposite side of the continent, on the River Niger, there was another centuries-old culture based on dry rice farming and iron working, which engaged in long-distance water-borne trade in copper, gold and luxury ceramics, and could boast at least one town – Jenno Jene – with 10,000 inhabitants.

From Kenya almost as far as the Cape, lands that had once been the preserve of scattered bands of Stone Age hunter-gatherers were now home to a great family of iron-using farmers and pastoralists. These were the Bantu-speaking peoples, who in 3000 BC had migrated in two streams – one to the east, and one to the south – out of what is now Nigeria. By 1000 BC, the eastern stream had crossed the continent as far as Lake Victoria. Following the highlands where the tsetse fly could not live, their descendants had continued onwards, and by 500, they were settled in the Northern Transvaal and in Natal. The descendants of the western branch had meanwhile reached the western fringes of the Kalahari desert. As they had settled in new territories, their numbers had increased substantially.

12.1 Estimated Total World Population at Selected Dates

Year	Global Population *(millions)*
30,000 BC	0.5
6000 BC	10
4000 BC	30
1000 BC	120
500	200
1095	300
1455	400
1763	800
1913	1600
2007	6500

The growth of population in sub-Saharan Africa between AD 100 and AD 500 – from around 12 million to something like 18 million – was spectacular. It was also exceptional. In most parts of the world, the growth in numbers that had continued non-stop since the emergence of agriculture had ground to a halt. In some places, it had gone sharply into reverse. From a mere 10 million in 6000 BC, the world's population had grown hugely, until by the beginning of the first century it had reached 250 million. But over the next 400 years, it dropped to 200 million. War and famine were part of the explanation, but the principal reason was disease.

When human beings moved out of Africa, they left behind the insects that were unable to follow them into cooler regions. In doing so, they also left behind the diseases these insects carried. The result had been a 'holiday' from insect-borne diseases that had lasted for thousands of years. But when they created settlements and domesticated wild animals they became exposed to new diseases harboured by these animals, and these diseases evolved in ways that enabled them to exploit human hosts.

By the time the Chinese were using wheelbarrows, and the ladies of Rome and Cleopatra, queen of Egypt, were wearing silk, human beings had been exchanging microbes with their invited guests – pigs, chickens, cows – and with their uninvited guests – mice, rats, flies and fleas – for thousands of years. But the resulting infections were for a long time confined to specific corners of the world, and deserts, seas and mountain ranges had been effective barriers. Even where such barriers did not exist, urban populations were often too small to sustain prolonged epidemics. But the Indian Ocean and the Mediterranean were now crowded with shipping, and the Silk Road, and routes like it, were busy highways. Saddlebags and ships' holds made ideal mobile homes for rodents and insects, and the disease-carrying parasites they harboured. Crowded cities awaited them at their journey's end. Humanity had invented the global village, and the bugs were having a ball.

The regions that suffered most were those at the ends of the Eurasian web – Europe and China – which had had less time to evolve resistance than the ancient civilizations at its heart. We have seen in the previous chapter how China endured one epidemic after another in the 300 years after AD 100. By the end of these three centuries of torment, the population had fallen from more than 60 million to a mere 25 million. Rome's experience had been no less horrific. In the year 165, soldiers returning from Mesopotamia brought a new disease – possibly smallpox – that wrought havoc across the empire for the next fifteen years. In the years 251 to 266 another pestilence of equal virulence struck. When the infection was at its height, the city of Rome was said to have

12.2 Changes in Human Populations
AD100 – AD500

Regions experiencing an increase in population

Population (millions)	Sub-Saharan Africa	Japan	Central and South America
Year			
100	13	2	9
500	20	5	13
Change	+50%	+150%	+40%

Regions experiencing a fall in population

Population (millions)	China	India	S.W. Asia	Europe	Other*	World*
Year						
100	65	45	46	37	38	255
500	32	33	41	30	31	205
Change	-50%	-25%	-10%	-20%	-20%	-20%

* excl. North America

Source: D. Christian, *Maps of Time* (University of California Press, 2004) p.344

(No figures are given for North America, as estimates for the continent at these dates are a matter of considerable dispute.)

suffered 5000 deaths a day. This, too, could have been small-pox, but it could equally well have been measles, presenting its visiting card to a Europe hitherto unacquainted with it.

In this new situation, increased food production and improved technology no longer led inevitably to increased numbers. All the ingenuity that human beings could muster could not prevent their numbers from falling. In Japan, in Central and South America, and in the healthier parts of sub-Saharan Africa – regions isolated from Eurasian plagues – numbers had continued to rise. By contrast, during these 400 years, the population of Eurasia had fallen by about a quarter. Humanity was no longer a species on the march. Over most of its range, it was a species under siege.

1 3

THE TRIUMPH OF ISLAM

It had taken 300 years from Jesus's first outdoor sermon for Christianity to become the official religion of a great empire. The next religion to arise in the same corner of the world – Islam – achieved an identical result in half the time. Whereas Christianity had to wait for the conversion of an emperor, Islam acquired its empire at the point of a sword.

The founder of Islam was an Arab merchant named Muhammad, who was born in the town of Mecca, in Arabia, in around 570. Mecca was a prosperous oasis some 20 miles from the Red Sea coast, and a staging post on trading routes from southern Arabia to the Mediterranean lands. As the home of the Ka'bah sanctuary it was also a destination for long-distance pilgrimages. The Ka'bah was a black meteoritic stone that played an important part in Arab religion, which at that time had many gods. Once a year, people flocked to Mecca to visit this important shrine, to do business, negotiate marriages and generally have a good time.

Muhammad's father and mother died before he was six, and he was brought up by his grandfather and later his uncle. When he was about twenty-five, he was entrusted with the trading goods of Khadijah, a rich widow who was so impressed with his abilities that she accepted his proposal of marriage. This marriage enabled him to carry on business on his own account.

Muhammad was a serious-minded young man, and he got into the habit of spending nights in a cave outside the town, reflecting on the life he saw about him, and in particular on the greed and selfishness of the merchants of his native town. One night, when he was about forty, he had a vision of the Angel Gabriel, who told him that he (Muhammad) was the 'Messenger of God'. Over the next twenty years, he experienced a succession of what he took to be divine revelations concerning the conduct of men towards God (Allah) and their fellow men.

Muhammad gathered a group of like-minded friends, and began to preach in public. His preaching was resented by the merchant class in his native town, especially when he began to acquire a following among the poorer classes. His message was subversive. It preached the worship of one God in a town that was a polytheistic religious centre, to the likely detriment of the pilgrim trade. It also raised the ties that bound together fellow believers above the ties of family and clan that were the foundation of Arab culture. So long as he enjoyed the protection of his clan, his enemies were unable to touch him. But on the death of his uncle, the new head of the clan disowned him, leaving him exposed. In July 622, when he was about fifty-two, he made his escape to Medina, a large oasis some 250 miles north of Mecca. This flight, which is known as the Hegira (Arabic *hijra*), is the date from which the Muslim era is reckoned.

In Medina, Muhammad joined up with a group of sympathizers with whom he had previously made contact. Having no power base in the town, they supported themselves by robbing passing camel trains. It was in these piratical escapades that Muhammad first revealed the organizational gifts that would form the basis of his later success. In his personal dealings, he seems to have been the essence of gentleness (as single-minded empire builders often are). But in his pursuit of religious and political power, he was as ruthless as he was gifted. He remained in Medina for seven years, during which time he honed his military skills, and built up his financial resources, by continued acts of piracy against passing caravans. All this time he was systematically strengthening his power base by individual conversions, and by the negotiation of military alliances. He was so successful that in January 630 he was able to march on Mecca at the head of a force of 10,000 troops, and take possession of the town with the loss of only two men. Having established his authority, he won over his former enemies by making the pilgrimage that was the basis of the town's prosperity a sacred obligation for his followers.

He confirmed his position as the most powerful man in Arabia by a further series of alliances. He was aided in this endeavour by some very fortunate timing. The Persian empire, one of the great powers of the day, had two years earlier been defeated by the Byzantine empire (the Eastern Roman empire based on Constantinople), and many tribes that had formerly enjoyed the support of the Persians against Byzantium now turned to Muhammad for protection. In 630, in his last major campaign before his death, he led a 30,000-strong force as far as the Syrian border, forming further alliances, and preparing the way for a later invasion of that country.

Muhammad died in Medina in 632, when he was about sixty-two. He left behind a united Arabia. He also left behind the makings of a magnificent fighting machine, equipped with a weapon that was to prove irresistible after his death. This was the concept of jihad – 'holy conflict' – in which military struggle was a missionary endeavour, and death in battle was a direct route to eternal bliss. What he did not leave was a nominated successor, an oversight that would later cause a split in the religion he had created: the dispute between Sunni and Shia. The Sunni were those who believed that the Prophet had chosen his comrade-in-arms Abu Bakr as his successor (caliph) before he died, and that Abu Bakr had designated his own successor, and so on. The Shia, or Shi-ites, believed that his choice had fallen on his cousin Ali, his daughter Fatima's husband. They further believed that the legitimate succession had descended through a line of spiritual leaders (imams), each descended from Ali and Fatima, each of whom had designated his own successor. It was a dispute that would persist down the centuries, and it still haunts Islam today.

Muhammad's disciples wrote down his revelations in his lifetime. Twenty years after his death, these were gathered together to form the basis of the holy book of the Muslim faith – the Qur'an. Qur'an means 'recitation', and the act of reciting its verses, in the beautiful cadences of the Arabic in which it is written, has a significance, and a power, that is impossible to convey to anyone to whom its language is inaccessible.

The revolutionary message of the Qur'an was embodied in its basic proposition: 'There is no God but God (Allah), and Muhammad is his Prophet.' Islam means 'surrender to God', and it is a word that embraces both the religion prescribed in the Qur'an and the attitude of mind it enjoins. Like Jesus, Muhammad preached the necessity of right conduct in preparation for a day of judgement, after which the faithful would spend eternity in paradise, while the infidels – those who denied the faith – suffered unending torment. It was this promise that fuelled the stupendous success of Islam's first century and a half.

There is no force in human affairs that can match the devotion of people who are happy to die for a cause, and who know in their hearts that their reward will be eternal bliss. It was the calm way in which Christians faced death in the arena that persuaded so many Romans that theirs was a faith worth having. The way in which the soldiers of Islam faced death in battle may seem on the surface to have been utterly different. But deep down, the joyous assurance was the same. Both attitudes to death had the power to change the world – and both did.

Muhammad's God, like Jesus's God, was the God of the Jews, and both religions honoured the Hebrew Prophets. But one crucial difference would always distinguish Islam from Christianity. In the eyes of the faithful, Muhammad was mortal. He was the messenger of God, not a god himself. The concept of the divinity of Jesus, which ultimately became the central tenet of Christianity, had no counterpart in Islam.

After Muhammad's death, one of his companions, Abu Bakr, was recognized by some as the first caliph, or successor. Under him, and his successor, Umar, the tribes were fashioned into a formidable fighting force, driven by religious zeal (and the prospect of plunder), and also by the pressure of over-population in the barren Arabian peninsula. According to Muslim tradition, Muhammad had before his death sent messages to the emperors of the Eastern Roman empire and of Persia, calling upon them to accept his teaching. When the required submission was (understandably) not forthcoming, his successors embarked upon jihad. Ctesiphon, the Persian capital, was captured in 637, Jerusalem in 638. Having next conquered Egypt, they used Egyptian ships to invade Cyprus in 649. By 664, they had taken Kabul. By 711, they had crossed the Straits of

Gibraltar and were advancing into Spain. Wherever they went, the Arab troops were kept separate in garrisons, to ensure that they did not settle down to comfortable city life, as victorious nomads elsewhere had been known to do.

As time went by, and the teachings of the Qur'an were codified, 'people of the book' were allowed to keep their own religion – and avoid military service – provided that they paid tribute, that is to say, an annual tax. People of the book meant Jews, Christians and any others who had a holy book that was revealed by God before the final holy hook, the Qur'an. For 'pagans', however, it was a different matter. For some, the consequence of conquest was enslavement. (The prospect of acquiring slaves was another strong incentive for those embarking on jihad.) But for many, the choice was instant conversion or instant death.

With the expansion of the empire of Islam, the incentive for Jews and Christians to convert increased. In prosperous Islamic cities, conversion opened doors to the young and ambitious, and it was a point that was not lost on bright young people of the book.

The momentum of conquest swept all before it. By 780, under the eastern caliph, Harun al-Rashid, and a separate caliphate in Spain and Morocco, the territory of Islam stretched from Lisbon, taking in most of Spain, the whole of North Africa, through Mesopotamia and Persia, all the way to Samarkand in Central Asia.

It was near Samarkand, at the battle of Talas in 751, that the army of Islam acquired a group of prisoners with a secret that changed the course of European history. They were Chinese papermakers, and it was as a result of their capture that knowledge of papermaking found its way to Europe. Arabic manuscripts written on paper survive from the ninth century. It was through the Muslim peoples of southern Spain that the secret of papermaking passed to Christian communities in Spain and Italy, and thence to northern Europe. Books already existed in Europe, having been invented by first-century Christians who wanted a way of collecting many texts in one volume, rather than on a long roll of papyrus. But before paper, books were costly things to make. Using parchment, a 200-page volume of a modest size required the skins of twelve sheep, and a huge amount of labour. Paper reduced the cost to a fraction of what it had been. As an unintended consequence of Islamic conquest, Christian Bibles and the works of pagan writers became much cheaper to produce.

The security of a wide-ranging empire encouraged trade, which was made easier still by a common language (Arabic), a common law and a single currency. Chinese jade, silk and porcelain were imported, via middlemen in Java or Sumatra. From Africa came gold, slaves and ivory; and from Russia, furs and amber. On the back of this trade, a brilliant civilization arose, unmatched outside China. Great cities were founded, like Cordoba in Spain, which housed half a million people and had a library with 100,000 catalogued manuscripts. At al-Rashid's court in Baghdad, music and literature blossomed. Under his patronage, the writing of a particularly pleasing poem could earn the gift of a bag of gold, or even a country estate.

An important element of Islam was the obligation to pursue knowledge. This imperative, and the resources of the empire, created an environment in which science flourished. In the early years of conquest, in the belief that the Qur'an was the only book necessary, the armies of Islam had burned every book they came across. But fortunately for the generations that came after, saner counsels later prevailed, and a great gathering in of knowledge followed. From Toledo in Spain to Isfahan in Persia, under a succession of rulers sympathetic to science, ancient texts were translated from Greek, Sanskrit, Syriac and Pahlavi. In 830, al-Rashid's son, al-Ma'mun, founded the House of Wisdom in Baghdad, where scholars worked on translations of works by Aristotle, Archimedes, Ptolemy and others that had been recovered from the far corners of the empire. At the same time, trading contacts with India and China introduced ideas and mathematical techniques unknown to the Greeks. Islamic scholars of this time were in possession of a greater body of scientific knowledge than had ever before been assembled. It was this store of knowledge that would later kick-start Europe's Scientific Revolution, when Arabic texts were translated into Latin.

One of Islam's great gifts to science was the system we call Arabic numerals. The sort of pencil-and-paper calculations that scientists like Isaac Newton had to perform would have been impossible if they had only Roman numerals, in which the number 1767 is represented by the letters MDCCLXVII. Strictly speaking, we should call Arabic numerals Indian numerals, since they were developed in India in the first millennium BC. But they came to us via the writings of the Arab mathematician al-Khwarismi, who was one of the many fine scientists who graced al-Ma'mun's House of Wisdom.

The period from the ninth to the twelfth century was the golden age of Islam. As a religion, its greatest days lay in the future. It would go on to make converts by the hundred million: in south-east Europe; in Africa; and across Asia, all the way to China and Indonesia. But as a secular power, its influence was beginning to fade by the tenth century. It was still a force to be reckoned with, but, weakened by internal dissension and confronted by countries with substantial resources of their own, it was no longer irresistible.

1 4

EUROPE AFTER ROME

In Europe, the centuries before and after the fall of the Western empire were a period of turmoil, as wave after wave of invaders, themselves driven on by other waves of peoples entering Europe out of Asia, made their way across the continent in search of a permanent home.

One consequence of the fragmentation of the Western empire, and the settlement of northern regions by newcomers, was the appearance of new languages. Though different from that spoken in its youth, the Latin spoken in the empire's twilight years was recognizably the same language. As the empire gave way to a collection of independent chiefdoms, language was set free. In regions separated by natural barriers such as the Pyrenees and the Alps, distinct Latin dialects arose. Over the next eight or nine centuries, these mutated into the 'Romance' languages, Italian, Spanish, Portuguese, French and Romanian. This happened in spite of conquest by peoples speaking Germanic languages. The descendants of the Franks, who conquered what is now France, finished up speaking the Latin dialect of the original inhabitants, not the Germanic language of their ancestors. Further north, however, where invaders found themselves in sparsely populated territories, there was no pressure to adopt the speech habits of a local population, and their descendants, separated by rivers, seas and mountains, gradually developed the dialects that became Dutch, German and Swedish.

In lowland Britain, where a Roman culture had flourished for four centuries, the newcomers might have been expected to adopt Latin, as the invaders of Gaul (modern France) did. But they didn't. Instead they kept their Germanic speech, which eventually became the language we know as English. The native British, who were not Latinized to the extent that the inhabitants of Gaul were, had kept their own language, and in the mountain fastnesses to which the invading Angles and Saxons did not penetrate, this gradually mutated into modern Welsh.

Both language groups – Germanic and Latin – were members of the Indo-European family, which had its origins somewhere in the Steppe regions where Europe meets Asia. To the east of the lands occupied by the Germanic-speaking peoples, the Slavs spoke a third group of Indo-European dialects, the forerunners of Czech, Polish, Serbo-Croat and Russian. Although they lived to the east of the Latin and Germanic speakers, the Slavs, descendants of nomads who had entered Europe from Asia around 2000 BC, had been established in Europe for much longer. When the ancestors of the Celtic speakers who now occupied the western fringes of the continent had travelled the same route, around 500 BC, they had passed through the Slavs' homelands without displacing them. But the passage of the Germanic-speaking peoples (also on their way out of Asia) had acted like a wedge, splitting the Slavs into two linguistic groups. The more southerly developed dialects that would later become Czech and Serbo-Croat; the more northerly would become Polish and Russian.

A succession of epidemics, which probably included smallpox, measles, influenza and plague, assailed the densely populated lands around the Mediterranean from the second to the seventh century. They undoubtedly played a part in the weakening of the Western empire. During these centuries, waves of settlement washed into the thinly populated regions to the north. As elsewhere, settlement implied agriculture. But there was no steep learning curve to be climbed. These settlers had the accumulated knowledge of the existing populations of the north and the civilized peoples of the south to draw on, and their new lands had fertile soil and plentiful rainfall. The cool climate suited wheat, barley, oats and rye. In addition, steady rain meant vigorous grass, and vigorous grass made happy cows. Admittedly there were trees to clear, but the newcomers had the tools to do it, and they had sufficient numbers. As they cleared the forests and brought new land into cultivation, food production increased and numbers grew still further. By the end of the eighth century, the population of these once half-empty lands had overtaken that of the formerly crowded old imperial territories. It was a change of fortune that would never be reversed.

There was a difficulty to be overcome before the newly cleared lands could be fully exploited. These potentially fertile soils were heavy. They consisted of alluvial deposits washed down from the mountains, or sticky clays left behind by ancient glaciers. Tackling them with hand-drawn ploughs and deer-antler ploughshares would have been a quick way to a broken heart. Drainage, too, was a problem. In the hot south, the overriding priority was to preserve the moisture in the soil. In the north, the challenge was how to get rid of it.

The system of agriculture that arose in response to these challenges was the most important development in the history of Europe in the six centuries that followed the fall of the Western empire, and it laid the foundations for all that came after. Between the sixth and eighth centuries, increased food output was largely the result of the clearing of forests. But from the beginning of the ninth century, new technologies played an increasingly important role. By the end of the tenth century, north European farming had been utterly transformed, and measured by output per man, it had become the most productive system of agriculture the world had ever known.

The most important new technology was the heavy two-wheeled plough, with an iron blade that cut the sod, an iron ploughshare, and a mouldboard that turned the furrow over. This could handle the heaviest of soils. Most importantly, it buried and killed weeds. By creating furrows, it also created channels for surface water to drain away. With its aid, the task of bringing new land into production was transformed, so that far more was now available to support a growing population.

But the consequences of the introduction of the heavy plough went much further. On heavy soils, it needed up to eight oxen, compared with the team of two that had hitherto sufficed. This meant that peasant farmers were forced to pool their resources in order to acquire both ploughs and the beasts to pull them. They also had to work as a co-operative, taking turns to use their ploughs, in new kinds of fields that were divided into individually owned strips that were long enough to avoid wasteful turning before the beasts needed to stop for a rest. But this new arrangement meant that sowing, harrowing and harvesting also had to be organized co-operatively, which could only be done under the auspices of a village council. The new plough therefore had huge consequences for both property rights and for social relationships. It introduced people to the idea that customs and institutions were not immutable; it accustomed them to the idea, and the practice, of self-government; and it provided a dramatic illustration of the benefits of technological change. Nine hundred years before the invention of the steam engine, it opened up people's minds to the possibility of the process of continual reinvention that created our modern world. It was a revolution that puts in perspective the historian's traditional preoccupation with the small change of dynastic successions and the scoreboard of battles won and lost.

The number of important innovations that occurred during Europe's so-called Dark Ages is too great for detailed examination here. Among those that left a permanent impression on agriculture and the economy were:

1 The substitution of three-course rotation of crops for the previous two-course rotation. This consisted of two fields under different crops and one fallow, rather than the previous one fallow and one cropped. This increased output per worker by 50 per cent, as well as providing insurance against crop failure.

2 The introduction of the Chinese-invented collar harness, which made it possible for the first time for European horses to pull heavy loads. A horse could do twice as much work in a day as an ox, implying a doubling of output ploughing or harrowing.

3 The introduction of the horseshoe and the whipple tree (a hinged rod attached to the harness), which respectively protected the horse's foot and made possible the pulling of large wagons.

But it was not only in agriculture that these centuries displayed enthusiasm for innovation. In 1044 we find the first tidal mill in Venice. Domesday Book, a survey carried out on the orders of William I, king of England in 1086, revealed that there were 5000 water mills in England alone. If that does not impress, consider the case of the monk called Eilmer, of the English Benedictine abbey of Malmesbury, who took off from the abbey tower one day in 1010 (900 years before the Wright Brothers flew their first aeroplane) in a glider of his own design. He flew 600 feet, but broke both his legs, because (as he later observed) he omitted to insert a tail in the rear end ('caudam in posteriore parte'). The Dark Ages clearly had a few bright sparks.

While technology was transforming people's lives, changes were taking place in the social framework. In the chaotic conditions created by the end of Roman rule and waves of migration, people sought protection for their lives and property. At the same time, ambitious individuals took advantage of these conditions to increase their wealth and influence. Out of this meeting of a desire for security and a lust for power, there gradually arose a new set of social arrangements: the institution known as feudalism. In its fully developed form this consisted of a hierarchy of mutual guarantees and obligations. At the lowest level was the peasant, who had a right to work, keep, and bequeath his land, in return for an obligation of service to his superior, who might be a lord of the manor, or the abbot of a monastery. This service took the form of a certain number of days' work on his superior's land, but it also involved an obligation to fight in any conflict in which his superior might get embroiled. The peasant's superior stood in a similar relationship to his own superior, and so on up to the person – duke, king or prince of the church – who stood at the summit of the pyramid of power. But the obligation worked both ways. The peasant's right to protection from his lord created a reciprocal obligation upon his lord to assure him of that protection.

While the system of feudalism was taking shape, a power struggle of a different kind was being played out: a struggle for mastery between Church and State. By the eighth century, many small kingdoms had formed larger units. The largest of these was the Holy Roman Empire, so named from the aspiration of its successive rulers to recreate in their own persons the glory of the defunct Western empire. The first and most famous of these was the Emperor Charlemagne, who became king of the Franks in 768. By a series of conquests, he made himself the ruler of an empire that stretched from the Pyrenees to the Danube, and from the Baltic Sea to Rome. The 'Holy' element reflected his achievement in converting to Christianity the subjects of many small kingdoms.

For the Church of Rome, Charlemagne's conquests were both good and bad news: they increased the Church's influence and wealth, but also represented a rival power and a rival claimant for the loyalty of the millions who now subscribed to the Christian faith. The centuries that followed witnessed a continual jockeying for power between emperors and popes. This struggle for supremacy was neatly symbolized by the scuffle at Charlemagne's coronation in Rome on Christmas Day in the year 800, when Pope Leo III, catching him unawares, produced a crown and placed it on his head, hailing him as 'Caesar' and 'Augustus'. Charlemagne was not amused, and left instructions to his successor not to allow such a thing to happen to him. The symbolism of a pope supplying an emperor's legitimacy was powerful in a superstitious and chaotic age. When Napoleon Bonaparte assumed the title of 'emperor' a thousand years later, he took the precaution of crowning himself.

The popes were not only engaged in a continuous struggle for supremacy with the secular rulers of the continent; they were also engaged in a struggle for primacy with the Eastern Church based in Constantinople, the capital of the Eastern, or

Byzantine, empire. The year 1054 witnessed a final rupture between the two, after a prolonged theological dispute. Thereafter, Rome was on the look-out for a chance to put one over on its eastern rival.

Forty years later, the opportunity presented itself. The Seljuqs – a group of Sunni Muslim Turkish tribes – had earlier appeared out of Asia, and taken control of Persia (Iran), Mesopatamia (Iraq) and northern Syria. They were nominally subject to the spiritual rule of the caliph of Baghdad, but their emperor, or sultan, was effectively ruler of the entire region. After conquering Armenia, they had turned on the Byzantine empire, and inflicted a bloody defeat on its armies at the battle of Manzikert (present-day Malazgirt) in Turkey. In the following year, they swept through Palestine and occupied Jerusalem. There they massacred thousands of Shi'ite Muslims. Less tolerant than their Arab predecessors, they also closed the city to Christian pilgrimages. By 1092, they stood on the shores of the Bosphorus, in a position to attack Constantinople itself. In the extremity of his need, the Byzantine emperor appealed for help not to his opposite number in the West, but to the pope in Rome.

The pope, Urban II, knew an opportunity when he saw one. If he could arrange a rescue of the remnant of the Eastern empire, he would be able to establish once and for all the primacy of the head of the Church of Rome, not only over the Western emperor, but over the Eastern Church as well. There were other benefits from a military campaign against the Turks. The increasing prosperity and growing population of western and northern Europe had created a class of restless young men of good breeding, with time on their hands, who needed an outlet for their youthful aggression. Their restlessness had found expression in petty wars and squabbles that had become a serious concern for the Church authorities. If they could be persuaded to fight the Turks instead, the people left behind could hope for a more peaceful existence. It had worked for Islam, 400 years earlier. The first wave of holy war under Muhammad's leadership had been partly inspired by the need to find an outlet for the warlike instincts of the young tribesmen whose feuds had made the lives of the people of Arabia miserable.

For the young men in question, the opportunity to kill with a clear conscience, and acquire loot in the process, did not need much promotion. And a now prosperous western Christendom had the resources to mount the kind of expedition the pope had in mind.

On 18 November 1095, Urban convened a council in the city of Clermont, in southern France. At a crowded outdoor assembly, he made one of the most momentous speeches in European history. He called upon his listeners to declare a truce in their own disputes, to turn their warlike energies against the Turks, to go to the aid of their fellow Christians in the east, and to reopen the holy city of Jerusalem to Christian pilgrims. The response to his speech was enthusiastic. Four hundred years after Muhammad, jihad – sacred conflict – was being preached again. But this time its warriors were marching to a different tune.

The Christian Europe that Pope Urban called to arms in November 1095 was very different from the empire over which Constantine had ruled 700 years earlier. One striking difference was the absence of large cities. It was not just that there was no great city like Rome to provide a focus and model. There were few towns anywhere deserving of the name of city. The population of the more northerly regions had increased as the descendants of earlier invaders had cleared new lands with their heavy ploughs. But in the southern lands, numbers had still not recovered from centuries of famine, disease and warfare. Only one Christian settlement – Constantinople, with a population of around 100,000 – retained a semblance of the Roman empire's glory. Two others, Toledo in Spain and Palermo in Sicily – both former Muslim cities – had around 20,000 inhabitants, and Venice had maybe 10,000. No other Christian settlement approached this size. Both Christendom and 'pagan' northern Europe were lands of villages and small towns. And despite the continued influx of new peoples from the east, such had been the depredations of famine, war and plague that Europe's population was smaller than it had been a thousand years before.

Sad though this comparison may seem, this is not how things appeared to educated Europeans of the time, who were chiefly conscious of the progress they had made over two or three centuries. New land had been brought into cultivation, and agricultural practices improved, in the tenth and eleventh centuries. For those looking back on these changes, the conquest of the wilderness and the huge increase in agricultural productivity were sources of wonder, and more than a little pride.

It was not only their technological progress that made these eleventh-century Christians feel more secure than their great-grandfathers. For nearly six centuries, Europe had been assailed by wave after wave of invasion: Germanic tribes from the east in the fifth century, and again in the sixth and seventh; Viking sea-raiders and Magyar and Muslim horsemen in the ninth and tenth. But by the end of the eleventh century, not only had the pressure of such attacks abated, Europe now had a formidable defence in the form of the heavily armoured knight, equipped with sword and battleaxe. The continent was more secure within its frontiers than it had been for 500 years, and if fighting had to be done, it was now as likely to be taken to Europe's enemies as to take place on European soil.

One European country – England – had just experienced an invasion that would have a profound effect. In 1066, a dispute over the succession to the English throne had brought an army under William, Duke of Normandy across from France. After a victory at Hastings, on the south coast, he was enthroned as King William I. The country was parcelled out among his comrades in arms, whose descendants gave England a French-speaking aristocracy for the next 300 years. By 1095, under William's rule, England, despite its still modest population of around a million, had been transformed from a European backwater into a power of the first rank.

'Christendom' was a religious entity, not a political one. It was the name given to the collection of European states whose rulers subscribed to the Christian faith. Western or Catholic Christendom, which looked for guidance to the pope in Rome, extended from Ireland and northern Spain to the eastern borders of Poland and Hungary, and from northern Norway to the Mediterranean island of Sardinia. Eastern or Orthodox Christendom, which owed religious allegiance to the Patriarch of Constantinople, comprised the rump of the former Byzantine empire (Greece and Constantinople, and part of Anatolia), plus the recently converted principalities of western Russia.

The 'empire of Islam' was in many ways Christendom's mirror image. It, too, was a community of faith, not a political entity. Its boundaries extended from southern Spain all the way to Central Asia. Like Christendom, it included a large number of sovereign states of various sizes, of which the most vibrant and powerful was the Turkish Seljuk empire, which stretched from the eastern Mediterranean to Afghanistan. The territory of Islam contained many great cities, such as Cordoba, Alexandria and Baghdad, whose opulence Christendom could only dream of, and in which science was pursued at a level unmatched anywhere.

At the other end of Eurasia, China was enjoying a peaceful and prosperous period, once again united under a strong dynasty, the Sung. The country had at last made good the population losses of the second, third and fourth centuries. Having fallen from some 65 million in the first century to barely 30 million at the end of the fifth, the population had stuck at that level, the imperial census still registering a population of 30 million as late as 845. Now, just 250 years later, it exceeded 80 million. Most of the increase had occurred in the south, particularly around the valley of the River Yangtze, which had hitherto been regarded as the poor relation of the more prosperous north.

Despite this massive increase in population, living standards had not fallen. On the contrary, they had continued to rise. This was probably the first time in the history of the world that a sustained increase in population over such a wide area had been accompanied by a continuing rise in the general standard of living.

An important element in the creation of this prosperity was the invention of paper money, or as the Chinese called it 'flying money' (because it flew in the wind). The government had originally authorized sixteen private banks to issue the new currency, but in 1023 it had rescinded this authority, and set up its own agency to issue banknotes, backed by cash deposits. Paper money allowed taxes to be collected in cash rather than in goods or services. But a consequence was to force a large part of the economy on to a cash basis, as merchants and peasants alike had to sell goods and services for cash to obtain the money to pay their taxes. The creation of a paper-money economy – the world's first – not only provided a lubricant that eased commercial transactions, it also acted as an incentive to put idle hours to productive use.

Another significant factor was the low cost of transport over much of the country. Sailing barges on China's great rivers could be correspondingly large, and wind cost nothing. The resulting carriage costs were a fraction of what they were in countries forced to rely on land transport. The east–west river routes were linked together by the north–south Grand Canal, completed in 611. This unique network of wide, navigable waters gave easy access to something like 50 million of the country's 80 million people. It offered economies of scale to merchants and manufacturers alike, and provided a strong incentive towards specialization and the division of labour. The result was a commercialized pattern of output and exchange and a volume of production and consumption such as the world had never known. Travellers returning to other lands had difficulty in obtaining a hearing for their tales of the wonders they had seen, in what was beyond question the wealthiest and most cultured country in the world.

The innovations that had driven China's first Industrial Revolution a thousand years earlier had not been forgotten, and now provided the basis of a commercial and industrial renaissance. To give just one example, according to government tax returns, the country's coke-fired furnaces in the year 1078 produced 125,000 tons of iron. This was almost as much as would be produced in the whole of Europe 600 years later.

None of this economic growth could have happened without a matching increase in food production. This was made possible by the introduction of a new variety of rice that could be grown on land that received little summer rain. Even more importantly, it enabled farmers to harvest two crops a year from irrigated land that had formerly yielded only one.

Across the sea in Japan, no such transformation of the economy had occurred. The authorities there had, as a matter of policy, restricted contact with China two centuries earlier, and life had continued on largely traditional lines. Nor had there been a comparable increase in numbers. The country's population in 1095 was much as it had been in the year 500, around 4 to 5 million. But although these centuries had brought no dramatic changes on the economic front, in cultural terms, they had been the most fruitful in the country's history. A century and a half of peace, and reduced exposure to

Chinese influences, had created space for a cultural flowering of extraordinary proportions. The most important element of this was the development of purely Japanese scripts. Hitherto, the Japanese had made use of Chinese characters, a clumsy vehicle for the expression of their own language. Now, with more suitable scripts at its disposal, written Japanese, like a bird let out of a cage, soared and sang. Outstanding among the works produced at this time were those written by daughters of the Fujiwara, a quasi-royal family that traditionally supplied ladies-in-waiting to the imperial household. Two of their books – *The Tale of Genji*, by the Lady Murasaki Shikibu and *The Pillow Book of Sei Shonagon*, by the Lady Sei Shonagon – still stand as masterpieces, not just of Japanese, but of world literature, 900 years after they were written.

Unknown to these peoples of Asia, and cut off from their wealth and diseases, the native peoples of Australia continued in their traditional way of life. Dependent upon gathering and hunting in an ungenerous environment, their numbers remained small. They travelled in small bands, consisting of two or more families. Although they practised a nomadic lifestyle, they had a close attachment to places that were socially and religiously significant, to which they returned for purposes of celebration. Even in the most densely populated coastal regions, there were, on average, only twenty or thirty people to 100 square miles of territory. In the almost empty interior, such a band might have 1000 square miles of country to itself. The population of the entire continent probably numbered no more than a million. But long separation had resulted in those million speaking more than 200 languages. They had no books, and few possessions, but they had a rich culture of song and dance and story-telling.

Further east, the north and south islands of New Zealand at last had a human population. Just when, and from where, they were first settled, is not known. The settlers spoke a Polynesian language – Maori – and they probably reached the north island around the year 800. Wherever they came from, their journey must rank as one of the most impressive ever made. The nearest island group to the north-east is the Kermadecs. To have come from there would imply a dangerous ocean crossing to an unknown destination, by double-hulled canoe, of around 750 miles. The crossing from any other island group would have been even longer. Such a journey could not have been made by accident. It must have been a planned, and carefully provisioned, voyage by people looking for a new home. Whether the Maori of today are descended from just one boatload, or from several, is unknown. But however many there were, they were forebears to be proud of. When they made their first landfall they must hardly have been able to believe their luck. They had behind them a 2000-year-old tradition of intensive agriculture, and they brought with them the yams and the pigs they would need to recreate the smallholdings that had supported them in their previous homeland. As it turned out, these new lands were too cool to support the mix of crops they were accustomed to, but an unexpected bonus awaited them, in the shape of a dozen different species of flightless birds called moas. Some of these were merely the size of turkeys; others stood 10 feet tall and laid eggs nearly a foot long. Few explorers have been rewarded with a more gratifying landfall.

On the other side of the Pacific, human numbers continued to grow. The settled regions of Central and South America were now home to something like 20 million people; half as many again as there had been in the year 500. In the central Andean region around Lake Titicaca, the Tiahaucan civilization still survived. But in central Mexico, the glory days of the great city of Teotihuacán were a fading memory. In the tenth century a people called the Toltec had sacked and burned Teotihuacán, and established an empire based on their own capital of Tollan, 50 miles north of present-day Mexico City. Their influence extended into the lowlands of Guatemala, where the ancient urban civilization of the Maya had collapsed for unknown reasons. Only in the highland regions of the Yucatan peninsula did Mayan cities such as Chichén Itzá and Mayapán continue to prosper.

North of central Mexico, most people still lived by gathering and hunting. But they had a new weapon – the bow and arrow – that had been unknown to their ancestors. Introduced to North America by the Inuit, it had made its appearance in central North America in the eighth century. It had transformed the lives of the millions of native Americans whose standard of living depended on their ability to bring down fast-moving prey, and their numbers had increased accordingly.

Nowhere in North America had city dwelling developed on the scale it had further south. But here and there, settled agriculture had given rise to permanent village life, with some settlements big enough to deserve the name of towns. In the heart of the continent, where the boundaries of present-day Utah, Colorado, Arizona and New Mexico meet, the farming people of the Anasazi culture lived in communal apartment houses with up to 1000 rooms. The first settlers there had lived in caves or adobe (dried mud) huts, and supplemented a hunting lifestyle by cultivating maize and pumpkins. Over the centuries, farming had gradually assumed a greater importance in their lives. They had added beans to their farming repertoire, and had domesticated the turkey. Later still they had learned to cultivate cotton, and by 1095 they were producing pottery and textiles of outstanding quality.

In the woodland areas where the Ohio and Mississippi rivers met, another complex of cultures – the Mississippian – had spread across the valley floors. Based on the cultivation of a superior variety of maize, this culture had given rise to a collection of towns – North America's first – which featured central mounds, almost 100 feet high, some of which carried temples and some the palaces of local rulers. These rulers were buried in graves reminiscent of the tombs of Bronze Age China or Middle Kingdom Egypt. One that has been excavated contained the remains of a high-status male, who had been buried on a platform made of 1000 shell beads, alongside seventy young females who had been sacrificed to accompany him in death. At the close of the eleventh century, the largest of these Mississippian towns, Cahokia, just east of present-day St Louis, was home to around 20,000 people.

In sub-Saharan Africa, the population had been increasing for the best part of a thousand years. Starting from around 15 million in the first century, numbers had risen steadily until they now stood at around 30 million. This sizeable population was scattered, and this part of Africa had few towns, even small ones, and no cities.

Much of the increase in Africa's population came about from the adoption of settled agriculture, but some was the result of the occupation of new lands by pastoral nomads. It must have been around this time that the great migration of the Bantu-speaking farmers, which had begun on the borders of present-day Nigeria and Cameroon a thousand years earlier, finally reached the Cape.

Humanity had negotiated a dangerous corner. For nearly a thousand years, plague, war and famine had wrought havoc across the length and breadth of Eurasia. From a low point of around 200 million around the year 500, numbers had at last begun to recover. Only in South-west Asia were numbers still substantially lower than they had been a thousand years before. In Europe and India, the population was almost back to first-century levels. In China, in southern Africa and in the Americas, people were thicker on the ground than ever. The future was looking good for the human species. The population of the world, at 300 million, was at record levels. Technology had already delivered much, and could no doubt deliver more. As they contemplated their situation, the more fortunate members of this extravagantly successful species could have been forgiven for thinking they really were masters of the universe.

16
RIDING THE ROLLER-COASTER: THE EUROPEAN EXPERIENCE

Pope Urban's call for a holy war against Islam was well timed. The eleventh century was a period of disunity and lack of confidence in the Islamic communities around the Mediterranean. Christian advances in Spain had led to the loss of Toledo in 1085. In 1087, a joint Pisan-Genoese fleet had destroyed Mahdia, the commercial capital of North Africa. Sicily had succumbed to a Norman invasion in 1092. At the same time, the Muslim cities in Syria and Palestine, on the frontier between the Islamic Fatimid empire and the Byzantine empire, had grown accustomed to a degree of self-rule that made it difficult to present a united front to an invader.

After a few self-appointed crusades had come to grief, the first 'official' contingent set off from the German city of Mainz in August 1096. With few Muslims in the European countries they had to pass through, they made do with killing Jews wherever they found them. The Christian king of Hungary refused them passage, but other rulers proved more supportive (or more frightened), and by May 1097, this first group, and two others that had originated elsewhere, were camped outside the walls of Constantinople in a combined force some 100,000 strong. In the absence of a united resistance, the campaign that followed went from success to success. On 15 July 1099, they entered Jerusalem itself. In a two-day orgy of killing, they massacred virtually its entire population: men, women and children. When it was all over, they marched in solemn procession to the Church of the Holy Sepulchre, to thank God for His support in their endeavours.

This First Crusade initiated a series of bloody assaults on the people of Islam, and other unfortunates elsewhere, that went on for the next 300 years. Whenever a pope had a problem at home, or felt the need of a bit of favourable publicity, he would call for a crusade: against Islam; or against 'pagan' countries in eastern Europe; or sometimes even against dissident groups within Christianity itself. And the burning and the bloodletting would begin all over again. The massacres were not, of course, all on one side. Over the next 300 years, Muslim armies gave as good as they got, and it would be a bold person who would hazard a guess as to which side slit the greater number of throats in the service of the same God. The details are too tedious and depressing to go into. The consequences, unfortunately, are with us still.

These conflicts, although they involved some memorable massacres, had no visible effect on population levels in the countries concerned. In Europe in particular, human numbers continued to race ahead. From a level of around 35 million in 1096, by 1300 the continent's population had doubled to some 70 million.

This increase in population partly reflected an increase in the amount of land available for food production. Above the tree level, huge tracts of previously empty land were converted to sheep pasture. An important factor in this extension and improvement of crop and livestock farming was the work of the religious orders, who applied both economies of scale and a scientific attitude to the business of agricultural improvement. In the short span of forty years in the early thirteenth century, the Cistercians alone created 328 new monastic houses, many of which ran huge flocks of sheep on lands where no domesticated animal had previously been seen.

In regions where village life already had a long history, the increase in numbers led to the creation of new towns. In Flanders and Brabant (modern Belgium) half the population now lived in an urban environment. Across the continent, some of the enormous wealth accruing to the Church was being employed in the construction of magnificent cathedrals, eighty of which were built in France alone between 1150 and 1280. In villages and lesser towns, thousands of smaller, but still beautiful, churches were being built, lovingly decorated with stained glass, paintings and sculpture. The ability of these communities to support the armies of skilled and unskilled workers thus employed was a vivid illustration of the scale of food surpluses that new technologies were generating. It was also a measure of the enormous wealth the Church had at its disposal, both from its own resources and from the gifts of rich benefactors.

The most striking evidence of the growth of the European economy between 1100 and 1300 was the increase in the size of cities, among which those of Italy were pre-eminent. In 1100, few had had more than 5000 inhabitants. By 1300, Florence, Genoa, Naples and Palermo each held around 100,000 people. Venice, the greatest city of all and the centre of a maritime empire that extended all the way to Constantinople, held nearer 200,000.

This increase in the urban element was a reflection of a continuing improvement in agricultural productivity. A more efficient agricultural sector yielded two benefits. By increasing output per acre, it made it possible to support a greater population. By increasing output per farm worker, a smaller proportion of the workforce was needed in agriculture. This in turn made it possible for more people to live in towns, and to work in occupations other than farming.

In northern Europe, the improved efficiency of agriculture was the product of new technologies: horses, heavy ploughs and three-course rotation. A simultaneous revolution of a different kind was engineered in southern Europe, and in northern Italy in particular. The wide valley of the River Po had fertile soil and ample sunshine. What it lacked was summer rainfall. In 1177 and 1229 respectively, the Milan city authorities constructed two great canals, the Naviglio Grande and the Muzza, which are still the largest in northern Italy. These provided the basis of a network of irrigation channels, which spread a film of life-giving water across the landscape. It was now possible to grow a new suite of introduced crops. Sorghum, a crop that does not need much water, had already been introduced from Africa in the ninth century. By the late tenth century, two of China's best-kept secrets, mulberries and the silkworms that fed on them, were being cultivated near Brescia. Soon afterwards, durum wheat, rich in protein, was introduced from the Islamic world. By the beginning of the fourteenth century, it was being used to make pasta.

The cities that arose on the back of these revolutions in agriculture were involved in a wide network of trade. Even more so than in Roman times, transport by river and sea was the basis of Europe's prosperity, and access to navigable water was the determining factor in the growth of cities. Florentine merchants sailed to England, where they mingled with market-day crowds in the wool towns of the Cotswolds. The ships of north German cities brought Swedish copper to the quays of Genoa. Venetian galleys carried German silver to Constantinople and Alexandria, and returned with Egyptian cotton and Indian Ocean spices. To those who enjoyed the benefits of this trade, it must have seemed that they were living in a golden age. But within half a century, this glorious pageant had dissolved in a nightmare of disease-induced terror.

Even before 1300, there had been signs of trouble. An important factor in the previous increase in food output had been the marked improvement in the continent's climate between 950 and 1250. But after 1250, climate change went sharply into reverse. Alpine glaciers advanced, and rainfall became heavier. Winters became longer and more severe, and summers became shorter, cooler and wetter. Wheat-growing was abandoned in upland areas, and vineyards in fringe areas such as England were decimated. These opposing trends of a still-growing population and falling food production generated famines of increasing severity. England, whose population had trebled to over 3 million in two centuries, endured half a dozen famines between 1270 and 1311. Between 1315 and 1332 famine struck repeatedly, in country after country. The four years from 1345 to 1348 saw crop failures and malnutrition on an unprecedented scale. By then, it must have seemed that things could not possibly get any worse. But the worst was still to come.

Early in 1346, stories began to circulate in the trading cities of Europe of disasters far away in East Asia. The reports had grown with the telling. It seemed that there was no calamity – flood, famine, earthquake or plague – that had not struck the crowded cities of China. All had been accompanied by loss of life on a horrific scale. The merchant classes of Italy and Flanders were used to travellers' tales, and knew enough to

16.1 The Black Death in Europe, 1347–52

The infection undoubtedly reached Europe by sea from Caffa, but not in a single voyage. It reached Genoa in the same month that it reached Dubrovnik – three months after it had devastated Messina. It took until 1352 to reach Moscow because overland transport was virtually non-existent, and the rats had to travel via the Baltic. Source: P. Ziegler, *The Black Death* (The Folio Society, 1997).

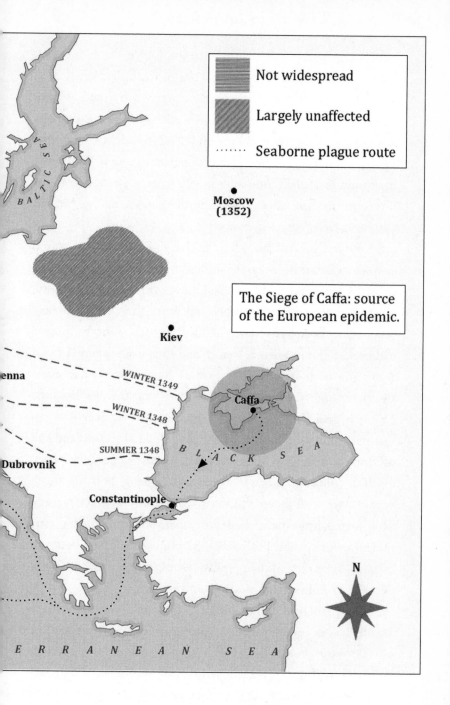

Not widespread

Largely unaffected

.... Seaborne plague route

Moscow
(1352)

The Siege of Caffa: source
of the European epidemic.

Kiev

enna

WINTER 1349

WINTER 1348

SUMMER 1348

Dubrovnik

Caffa

B L A C K   S E A

Constantinople

BALTIC SEA

N

ERRANEAN   SEA

discount them by a substantial margin. But even discounted, these stories seemed to possess a core of truth that left hearers profoundly grateful that they were separated by thousands of miles of land and ocean from the scene of whatever disasters were really taking place. By the end of 1346, it was known that a plague of unprecedented proportions was raging in China and India, and had killed thousands in countries as far west as Syria. It was still an exotic story, blood-curdling in the telling, but too remote to be of any real concern.

One day in October 1347, twelve ships homeward bound from the eastern Mediterranean docked in the port of Messina in Sicily. Within days, plague had the city in its grip. Those still unaffected turned on the sailors, and drove them from the harbour, to seek shelter elsewhere. Within three months, plague had broken out in Genoa, Venice and Pisa, from where it raced across northern Italy. By the end of June 1348, it had cut a swath through the populations of Paris and Seville. By June 1349, it had laid waste to London and advanced across Germany. Six months later, it had the whole of Ireland and half of Norway in its grip. Everywhere it was the same story. Some of those infected survived, but most died a horrible death within days of displaying the first symptoms. We have no way of knowing how many died altogether, but a reasonable estimate is that between 1347 and 1352 plague carried off between 30 and 40 per cent of the population of Europe, west of Russia: perhaps 25 million out of a total of some 75 million.

This pestilence, which medieval Europe knew as the Black Death, was bubonic plague, revisiting Europe after an absence of 600 years. Compared with some infections – such as influenza – plague is a comparatively slow mover. This four-teenth-century wave took five years to work its way across

Europe. Once established in a region, the disease has a habit of recurring at irregular intervals over a century or more. After its previous visitation in 542, when it had been similarly spread by ship, it had ricocheted around the continent for two centuries. The source of that earlier pandemic seems to have been one or other of two long-established reservoirs of infection among burrowing rodents and their fleas: one in Africa, the other in the foothills of the Himalayas. This fourteenth-century outbreak, however, almost certainly originated in the grasslands that stretch from southern Russia to the borders of China.

The agent of this latest pandemic was a Mongol army that, in 1346, laid siege to the Genoese trading city of Caffa (modern Feodosiya) in the Crimea. The siege had been frustrated by an outbreak of plague in their ranks. Before they had departed, they had left a souvenir of their stay in the form of plague-ridden corpses, which they had fired over the city walls. When plague broke out in the city, the survivors had beaten a quick retreat to their ships, and sailed for home. It was these ships that sailed into the harbour in Messina in that fateful October of 1347.

It is not possible now to fully appreciate the sense of despair and dislocation that spread across medieval Europe in the wake of this devastating assault. We are still, as they were, exposed to the threat of major pandemics. But if such a plague were to visit us, we would at least have some idea of what was happening. The people of the fourteenth century had no such understanding. In a superstitious age, with no knowledge of the mechanics of infection, people turned to social or supernatural explanations. Many interpreted it as the act of a vengeful God, heaping punishment on a sinful world. Some looked for scapegoats, and turned on minority groups such as Jews and lepers. In the French city of Strasbourg, on 14 February 1349, even before the infection arrived, 2000 Jews were murdered by a mob; and several thousand more met a similar fate in the weeks that followed.

Even where superstition was disdained, the bright confidence generated by two centuries of increasing prosperity evaporated. For those who survived, it was the end of an age, and it seemed inconceivable that good times could ever return. But looking back now, what is striking is the strength of the recovery that Europe made from the greatest disaster its peoples have ever experienced. It took a long time. It would not be until around 1550, a full 200 years after the plague first struck, that the population would again reach 75 million. But the technological advances of the preceding centuries had not been lost, and within a generation fine minds were once again taking up the challenge of innovation. And by the mid-fifteenth century, a new generation of entrepreneurs and adventurers had arisen, who knew only economic growth and social progress, and who looked forward to new discoveries and increased prosperity.

Socially and psychologically, mid-fifteenth century Europe was a very different place from the Europe of a hundred years earlier. Old beliefs had been shaken, and long-established social relationships ripped apart. One of the chief victims had been the system of land tenure that had formed the framework of European society for 300 years. With fewer mouths to feed, marginal land went out of cultivation. On the good land, the problem was to find people to work it. Competition between landowners for the available work-force increased the bargaining power of those who remained. The outcome was a permanent shift from a feudal relationship, in which land was held in return for service on a superior's estate, to a cash economy, in which work was paid for, and tenants paid rent for land that was then worked as the tenant thought fit. With labour at a premium, farm hands who worked for wages were no longer tied to their native village. Fit young workers who did not like the terms they were offered could move elsewhere, and many did.

This post-Black Death society was not just physically foot-loose, it was also psychologically footloose. Workers who travelled were more open to new ideas than people who had spent their whole lives in the same small village, bound to the same lord. People who had seen their priests powerless to prevent or adequately explain the wiping out of whole families, were much more open to the preaching of those who suggested that all was not well with the existing religious order.

Perhaps the most important factor contributing to the changed atmosphere was the wealth and self-confidence of cities. In political terms, they created a third force, separate from the land-owning aristocracy and the Church. In cultural terms they constituted a new source of patronage for artists, architects, writers and musicians. And in intellectual terms, they were a forcing house for new ideas and a shelter for independent thinkers. It is striking that in the half century between 1400 and 1450, a new European university was founded on average every other year, all of them in cities.

Although no one in Europe or Asia could have known it, a significant milestone was passed somewhere around 1450 to 1500. It was about then that Europe's expertise in science and technology at long last drew abreast of China's. The date cannot be fixed precisely, because we are talking about a complex of achievements and expertise, not a single event. But if China was still ahead of Europe in science and technology in the second half of the fifteenth century, its lead was shrinking fast. In terms of sheer volume, whether of manufacturing output or scholarly activity, Europe was still a long way behind, and it would be many, many years before it would catch up. But in terms of potential, as measured by the best practice of its most skilled mechanics, and the knowledge and speculations of its leading scientists, Europe was at last in the same league.

Something we can be precise about is the date of the event that launched Europe on the trajectory that would leave every conceivable scientific rival trailing in its wake. The date was 1455, and the event was the publication of the first Bible to be printed with movable type. The place was the city of Mainz, on the Rhine, and the person responsible was a metalworker and printer named Johannes Gutenberg.

In fifteenth-century Europe there was a huge unsatisfied demand for the written word. The new universities were one element of this demand. The churches and the monasteries, with their need for bibles and prayer books, were another. An enlarged leisured class, many of whom could now read, represented a third. The pool of potential readers was further enlarged by the development of clear optical glass in fourteenth-century Italy, which led to the invention of spectacles (also in Italy), so that only the cost of books now prevented short-sighted people from reading. In the early fifteenth century, books were still hand-written by trained copyists. The entire annual salary of a professor at the University of Pavia at this time would have purchased just two books on law, or ten on medicine. We talk much today about information technology, but the transformation wrought by the successive invention of spectacles and printing constituted an IT revolution as signifi-cant as anything we have witnessed in our lifetimes.

Gutenberg's solution to the problem of how to print quickly and cheaply was to prepare a block by assembling reusable metal characters – 'moveable type' – in a frame that was fitted into a press in which the paper and the inked block were brought into close contact. None of the elements in the process was new. Paper was a Chinese invention that had been in use in Europe for over a century. The Koreans had been using movable type for 200 years, and the idea had already been taken up in both China and Japan. But those countries did not have the advantage of languages that used an alphabetic system of only twenty or so letters. Presses had been used in Europe for grapes and olives since Roman times. Gutenberg's achievement lay in bringing these elements together. It would seem that he was printing from movable type as early as 1439, but none of this work survives. It was the Bible he published in 1455 that now stands as the memorial to his world-changing invention.

In May 1453, while Gutenberg's two-dozen-strong team was quietly working away on the three-year project that would become the Great Bible, an event occurred that had as great an influence as the invention of printing. This was the fall of Constantinople to the Ottoman Turks.

Constantinople (Istanbul) occupies one of the least stable stretches of land of any capital city in the world. In its 3000-year history, it has experienced more than fifty major earthquakes. But its geophysical disadvantages have for most of that time been outweighed by the commercial advantages of its location. Originally known as Byzantium, it was renamed and greatly enlarged in 324 by the Roman emperor Constantine, who made it the capital of his Eastern empire. After the Western empire disintegrated in the fourth century, the city continued as the Greek-speaking capital of Eastern Christianity and the hugely wealthy heart of the shrunken Byzantine empire that the Eastern empire became. In 1054, after a decisive break with the Church of Rome, it became the administrative centre and spiritual home of the Greek Orthodox Church. By 1453, it had been a merchant city of the first rank for more than a thousand years: the most important node in the web of exchange – of goods and ideas – between Europe, Central Asia, India and China.

The city's defences had withstood the forces of the Seljuk Turks, those followers of Muhammad whose appearance on the opposite shore of the Bosphorus in 1092 had sparked off the First Crusade. But during the Fourth Crusade in 1204, this Eastern Christian city had, with almost unbelievable irony, been sacked by a Western Christian army. These crusaders had conducted a massacre of the population, and had afterwards spent several years stripping the city of its treasures, which were either melted down or shipped back home. (Present-day Venetians, whose forebears promoted this atrocity, still proudly display the golden horses looted on that occasion.) The city was recaptured by Eastern Christian forces in 1261, but the hugely profitable trade between Europe and Asia thereafter passed through the Genoese-controlled suburb of Galata, on the opposite shore of the Golden Horn, the great natural harbour that forms the city's northern boundary.

For the next 200 years, Constantinople itself, although still nominally the capital of what remained of the Byzantine empire, was a poverty-stricken shadow of its former greatness. Given its condition, it might seem strange that its final fall in 1453 should have come as such a shock. But the event was more than symbolic. These Ottoman Turks, who had emerged from lands on the eastern shores of the Mediterranean, were already in control of Serbia, Greece and Bulgaria, which they had conquered in the late fourteenth century, and of Anatolia, which they had occupied in the early fifteenth. When Turkish cannon demolished the triple defensive walls of Constantinople, Europe woke up to two unpalatable facts. First, that a new power of phenomenal strength was encamped on its doorstep. Second, that this power had a stranglehold on the trade route that supplied a large part of its comfort and prosperity. For the time being, it suited the Ottoman rulers to allow this trade to continue, but entirely at their discretion, and on their terms.

17

THE SCOURGE OF ASIA

The expanse of open grassland called the Steppe that stretches from the northern shores of the Black Sea, across Asia and all the way to China, has exercised a potent influence on the course of world history. The nomadic peoples who lived in this region affected the lives of their settled neighbours for over 3000 years, and it was only around 300 years ago that modern technology enabled those neighbours to neutralize the threat these nomads posed.

The history of these peoples was determined by their relationship to the horse. The small, hardy wild horse of Central Asia was first domesticated around 4000 BC, but for 2000 years it remained a herd animal, kept for its meat and its milk. It was not until around 2000 BC that peoples living around the southern shores of the Caspian Sea, in what is now northern Iran, invented riding. Riding made it possible to manage much larger flocks and herds, which in turn could support a larger population. It also led to a change in breeding strategy. Whereas docility and a high milk yield had formerly been the attributes most valued, the desirable qualities in a horse now became stamina, speed and manoeuvrability. With these qualities, new options were opened up, including the acquisition of wealth and captives by highly mobile forms of warfare.

The huge extent of their lands and the long period during which their ancestors had lived in them explains much about the impact of these nomads on neighbouring countries. From the western borders of Ukraine to the eastern edge of Manchuria is more than 5000 miles: as great as the distance from Seattle to southern Spain. The grasslands that occupy this range are interrupted in places by mountains and deserts, but they contain an area of wild pasture greater than all the grasslands of the United States and Canada combined. By the twelfth century these lands had been the home of wandering tribes for more than 15,000 years, during which time they had evolved a wide range of ethnic characteristics and several distinct language families.

In the accounts left by those with whom they came in contact, these peoples appear under many names. There were the Aryans, who invaded northern India during the Bronze Age. Then there were the Hsiung-nu, who built up a great empire to the north-west of China around the second century BC, and fought wars against the newly united Chinese for a couple of hundred years. Related to them were the Huns, who invaded Europe in the dying years of the Roman empire. Later came the Seljuq Turks, who created an empire in South-west Asia in the twelfth century.

The Mongols, who conquered China in the thirteenth century, had their homeland in the region still known as Mongolia. They were nomads who moved in wagon trains, in the company of their flocks and herds. When they were not on the move, they lived in small cities. But these were cities of tents, not brick or stone. Although their wagon trains carried all their worldly goods, they were not looking for a home. Wherever they went, they were always at home, and their worldly goods consisted of much more than a few pots and pans. Their prowess in war supplied them with plenty of loot, and in later centuries their wagons were often laden with jewels, silk, perfumes and fine carpets. When they were at peace, their wealth was augmented by tribute of goods and treasure exacted from settled peoples, as the price of *their* peace. And their tents, at least the tents of their rulers, were not mere mobile homes: some were more like portable palaces.

Considered collectively, the males of these nomad nations were beyond dispute the finest horsemen ever known. From the time that they were able to walk, they spent their lives in the saddle. And those lives were not spent ambling behind sleepy herds of sheep. This was an energetic culture, and a fiercely competitive one. These wandering tribes owed allegiance to khans – emperors – who might at any moment summon them to war, and their readiness to fight was ensured by the mounted games and contests in which they continually engaged.

During the 3000 years these nomads ruled the Steppe, their warlike character and their speed of movement inspired terror from the Danube to the Yangtze. They were equipped from an early date with powerful bows, and they were the inventors of the stirrup. With its aid, they developed a phenomenal ability to fire arrows while riding at speed. But their most important weapon was surprise. They were highly mobile, and by the twelfth century they were able to maintain lines of communication over huge distances. As a result, their commanders were able to co-ordinate the movements of widely separated units, sometimes hundreds of miles apart, and bring them to bear against unsuspecting cities with devastating effect. If they found themselves faced with a strong opposing force, they had a trick that almost never failed, one with which they were still able to deceive their adversaries 2000 years after it was first tried out. This was the pretended rout, in which their troops would ride away in the heat of battle, tempting the opposing cavalry to pursue them. When they reached the place where their massed archers lay waiting to release a storm of arrows, they would turn and cut their enemies to ribbons.

Another pattern that often repeated itself was the behaviour of these fierce, hard-living nomads on the rare occasions when they stayed behind after conquering a rich, settled empire. Before such conquests, they usually harboured a profound contempt for the soft ways of civilized society and an aversion to settled living. Their traditional course of action was to loot and desecrate the cities they had taken, kill a sizeable number of their citizens, and then leave, subject to the promise of future tribute. But sometimes a nomad aristocracy would linger in cities whose rulers they had deposed, and succumb to the delights of civilized living. After a century or two had passed, either their subject peoples would rebel and send them packing, or another lean and hungry band of nomad cavalry would appear over the hill, and treat the now effete descendants of the original conquerors to a dose of their forefathers' medicine.

Of all the assaults that these extraordinary warriors made on the settled empires of Europe and Asia, none matched the campaign initiated by the Mongol emperor Genghis Khan in the early years of the thirteenth century. It earned him the right to be regarded as one of the most gifted military strategists of all time. He created the most powerful military machine the world had ever seen, and his methods were still being studied in military academies 700 years after his death. Two outstanding military commanders in the Second World War – the American General George S. Patton and the German Field

Marshal Erwin Rommel – were self-confessed admirers and students of his tactics.

Genghis Khan's given name was Temujin, and he was born near Lake Baikal, in Central Asia, around 1160. He was what adherents of monotheistic religions call a pagan, that is to say, he did not subscribe to any faith. This is an important fact in trying to make sense of his later career. Unlike many men who have waded through blood to build an empire, he was not driven by religion. He seems to have been superstitious, and he was capable of being impressed by learned men of any faith. In later life he welcomed many of them to his court. But he was unprejudiced when it came to killing: belief and unbelief were alike irrelevant when there was a massacre to be attended to. He started off as the leader of an impoverished clan, and it is conceivable that his murderous career – and his apparent lust for world domination – had its roots in humiliations we know his family suffered after his father's death. We know little about his early life, but it seems reasonably certain that when he was nine years old his father was poisoned in a continuation of an ancient feud.

Temujin's rise to power began when he was given command of a force about 20,000 strong, contributed by neighbouring tribes for the purpose of settling a feud between rival clans. By 1206, when he was between forty and fifty years of age, he had overcome all his potential rivals, and was acknowledged as Chingiz Khan ('universal monarch') of all the Mongolian peoples, a title that was rendered in European languages as Genghis Khan.

Genghis's rise to power coincided with a period of Chinese weakness, and in 1215 he succeeded in capturing Peking (modern Beijing), the capital of the empire of Kin, which at that time occupied that part of China north of the Yangtze River. His victory was welcomed by the mandarin class, who considered that their rulers had lost the Mandate of Heaven, and he recruited a number of them as advisers, doctors and administrators to accompany him on his travels. His appetite for conquest now fully aroused, he turned west, and in the course of a seven-year campaign, he subjugated – and devastated – the Muslim empire of Khwarizm (modern Uzbekistan), while one of his generals invaded Persia and another moved against Russia.

By this time, Genghis had moulded the numerous Mongol clans into a nation that was organized for perpetual war. Its early victories had been won with the traditional combination of mounted archers and sturdy, grass-fed ponies. But attacks on cities required other methods. From the peoples they vanquished, the Mongol armies acquired new technologies: siege ladders, heavy catapults, giant crossbows, smoke screens, burning oil. Throughout these years of virtually non-stop warfare, the same pattern of conquest prevailed. A Mongol army would appear and demand the surrender of a city. If its citizens surrendered, they were carried into slavery and their city razed to the ground. If a city attempted to defend itself, the entire population would be put to the sword and their city likewise razed to the ground. Sometimes the population of a city would be slaughtered just to put fear into the next one on the list. It was a full twenty years after Genghis had begun his campaigns before his Muslim and Chinese advisers were able to persuade him that leaving cities standing and extracting tribute might be a better way of running an empire. Even then, the point did not register with some of his generals. When they later attacked the lush and civilized land of Iraq, they wantonly destroyed irrigation works that had taken thousands of years to perfect, and initiated the process of desertification from which that country still suffers.

In 1226, when he was about seventy years of age, Genghis drew up plans for the subjugation of the whole of China, where his generals had been meeting with problems. But on his way there in the summer of 1227, he fell while hunting and suffered a stomach haemorrhage. Knowing that he was dying, he called his advisers to his tent and gave precise orders for the completion of the campaign and the division of his empire. After his death, his army accompanied his body slowly and silently back to his capital on the steppes. Everyone they met on the way was killed, to ensure that news of his death did not arrive before his corpse did.

When he died, Genghis was master of an empire that stretched from eastern Persia to the shores of the Pacific. His son, Ogodei, who succeeded him, built a great new capital, Karakorum, in central Mongolia, and continued with the programme of conquest. His armies were maintained at a peak of efficiency in order to continue the strategy of simultaneous campaigns on widely separated fronts. These were based on intelligence provided by the finest network of secret agents in the world, and informed by a messenger system that extended across most of Asia. His forces were also equipped with a new invention – gunpowder – that the Chinese had developed but not exploited. In 1233, in alliance with the Sung dynasty of southern China, Ogodei captured the north Chinese city of Kaifeng, and placed northern China under subjection. In a reversal of previous Mongol attitudes, he accepted the suggestion of his Chinese adviser, Yeh-lu Ch'u-ts'ai, that preserving the prosperity of a conquered people was more advantageous than mindless devastation. Instead of destroying the city, he made it his provincial capital and encouraged its already very considerable trade. Chinese history might have been very different, had that Chinese adviser not succeeded in persuading his Mongol master to make this exception to the policy of systematic devastation.

In the autumn of 1236, Ogodei despatched a 150,000-strong army to conquer Europe. In 1238 and 1239, his generals captured and destroyed the principal cities of Russia. They then annihilated a combined Polish-German force, and advanced into Hungary, burning, pillaging and massacring whole populations. In December 1241, when they crossed the frozen Danube, western Europe was wide open to them. Nowhere, in a continent divided by its own petty squabbles, was there a force that could hope to halt their progress. Those troops of heavily armoured knights, whose cavalry charges had seemed such a potent weapon a century earlier, were outclassed in this new, highly mobile style of warfare. It could surely only to be a matter of time before these fierce invaders would be looking out on the Atlantic.

Western Europe was saved, not by its own efforts, but by the contents of a wine jug. At the very moment when his generals were assembling their forces on the banks of the Danube, Ogodei died as the result of a drinking bout. Whether he had overindulged, or been poisoned, we will never know. But when news of his death reached his troops, they turned for home, never to return. It was not grief or shock that caused them to abandon their campaign. A dispute had arisen as to who should be the next khan, and Mongol custom required that the leaders of the clans throughout the empire assemble in their capital to elect a new emperor.

1 8

RIDING THE ROLLER-COASTER: THE ASIAN EXPERIENCE

The journey through disaster and recovery travelled by the peoples of Europe between 1096 and 1456 had a parallel in Asia. The peaks and troughs did not coincide, but they were equally extreme.

In China, the expansion of population that had begun with the founding of the Sung dynasty in 960 continued unabated. A 50 per cent increase in numbers between 1000 and 1100 was followed by similar increase between 1100 and 1200, by which time the population was around 120 million. These increases reflected a continuation of the agricultural and industrial progress described in Chapter 15. But advances in the amenities of everyday life were also having their effect. A feature of this was the growth of tea drinking. Since tea was made with boiled water it must have significantly reduced the incidence of water-borne diseases.

China under the Sung was an inward-looking civilization, but it was a brilliant one. One reason for its prosperity was its greater tolerance of commercial activity. Under previous dynasties, the mandarins, with their disdain for commerce, had always been a drag on business. Now, although the administrative classes still did not involve themselves in the sordid business of buying and selling, they were much less concerned with controlling those who did. And in this atmosphere of increasing wealth and civic peace, the arts flourished. Music, drama, poetry and painting attained levels of distinction surpassing anything this ancient civilization had previously known. Literature, in particular, flourished. (The world's oldest surviving printed work, a Chinese Buddhist text, the *Diamond Sutra*, was printed in 868.) Now, with the adoption of a Korean invention – printing with movable type – a publishing industry, in the modern sense, came into existence. Its products included works of devotion and entertainment, as well as a host of instruction manuals in subjects such as textile technology and agricultural practice.

But then disaster – or rather, a series of disasters – struck this glittering civilization. By 1300, the population had fallen to less than 80 million, a decline of more than 30 per cent in a single century. Some of this fall was the result of famines similar to those occurring in Europe, as a deteriorating climate collided with an expanding population. But the loss of numbers in China was greater, because the country suffered a calamity that Europe escaped: a Mongol invasion.

When the armies of Ogodei captured Kaifeng in 1233, the Sung were rewarded for their support with part of the province of Honan. But greed got the better of them, and while the attention of the Mongol commanders was engaged elsewhere, they set out to conquer the rest of the province. This rash decision cost them their empire. In 1236 three Mongol armies invaded the territory of the Sung and laid waste the provinces of Hopei and Szechwan as a prelude to overrunning the whole empire. But the centuries-old cavalry warfare of the steppes was no use in the country to the south, with its mountains and wide rivers, its paddy fields and lakes. The invaders had to master a new strategy, fighting on foot, and taking cities one at a time after long sieges fought with heavy artillery, while some of their armies were engaged elsewhere.

The struggle continued on and off for the next thirteen years. But in 1259, something happened that sealed the fate of the Sung. In that year a new khan, a grandson of Genghis named Kublai, succeeded to the Mongol throne. Forty-three years of age, and a gifted politician and soldier, Kublai had been governor of Honan province since 1251. Ardently interested in Chinese civilization, he had spent the previous eight years restoring his province to prosperity after the damage wrought by the earlier invasion. In 1260, he affirmed his Chinese identity by inaugurating a new dynasty – the Yuan – and moving his capital from Karakorum in Mongolia to a new city he named Ta'tu, on the site we now know as Beijing.

For four years, the southern Chinese were spared his attentions, while he fought a civil war in Mongolia with a brother who disputed the succession. In 1264, with that war won, he set himself to complete unfinished business in China. The Sung generals and their soldiers fought with skill and courage, and at one stage Kublai's enterprise came close to failure, when, in his new incarnation as a Chinese emperor, he also had to wage a war against a wave of nomad warriors in Turkestan. It was not until 13 April 1279, after nearly fifteen years of war, that his conquest was completed, in a naval battle off Canton. The dream of nomad rulers for centuries – the subjugation of the whole of China –had been realized at last.

Kublai's ambitions did not stop at the frontiers of China. In 1274, and again in 1281, he prepared invasions of Japan, but they were both disasters. His first invasion force included 900 ships, 40,000 men and 15,000 horses. A great storm blew up while his army was retreating to their ships: 300 ships were lost and 20,000 of his troops were killed or drowned. Unable to admit defeat, he spent seven years creating an even greater armada. In 1281, a stupendous fleet, carrying 150,000 men, left Korea in settled weather. Again, a typhoon blew up and 4000 of his 4500 ships were turned to matchwood on the rocks, leaving 130,000 Chinese dead. The Japanese from then on believed that their islands were protected by 'divine winds' (*kamikaze*).

It is sometimes said that after the conquest of China, the Mongol 'empire' was the most extensive the world has ever known. In one sense this is true, in that it was ruled by members of the same family. But in the eyes of his brothers, Kublai, in his role as emperor of China, had 'gone native', and they refused to recognize his sovereignty over the territories that they themselves controlled.

Kublai was not the wanton destroyer of cities and enemy of civilization that his grandfather Genghis had been. But his years of conquest had none the less wrought devastation and caused the deaths of perhaps 30 million people. For the rest of his reign, he devoted himself to making good the damage his own ambition had caused. He repaired the roads and lined them with trees to provide shade. He created the world's greatest postal service, employing a reputed 200,000 horses. He constructed a new canal, linked to the Grand Canal, which brought food to the capital, along a course most of which is still in use today. And he built up stores of surplus grain, for free distribution when crops failed.

In warfare Kublai was a Mongol through and through. But his empire-building seems to have been driven by an idea that was wholly Chinese: the desire to demonstrate that China really was 'the middle kingdom' – the centre of the world. And with his empire built, it seems he wanted to be seen as the father of his people, a kind of Chinese Asoka, but one who never renounced war.

Despite his adventurous (and licentious) life, Kublai survived to a ripe old age. He died in 1294, just short of his eightieth birthday. At his death China was once more a united country, something it had not been for 300 years. If its population had not yet made good its loss of numbers, its culture had regained its former brilliance. But within fifty years, disaster struck yet again.

In 1331, an outbreak of plague occurred in Hupeh province, in central China, which is said to have caused the death of 90 per cent of the population. The source was almost certainly a long-established reservoir of infection in the rodent population in the mountains of Yunnan and Burma, 500 miles to the south-west. During the next twenty years the pestilence worked its way across the whole country. Reliable statistics are hard to come by, but given the figures in later censuses, it is difficult to see how the total number of deaths could have been less than 20 million, possibly more. The damage was not confined to China. The great camel caravans, up to 10,000 strong, that bore the flourishing trade along the Silk Road offered a cosy ride to plague-carrying fleas. By 1338, these agents of death had reached the rich oases of Central Asia. By 1346, they were feasting on the blood of that Mongol army outside Caffa in the Crimea, whose dead comrades made Europe the present of the Black Death.

The dynasty that Kublai founded did not last long. Intensifying climate change caused a succession of poor harvests. As famine struck and millions died, festering resentment against what was perceived as foreign domination led to a series of peasant uprisings. Beginning in 1325, and continuing through the plague years, they reached a climax in 1353, when they found a gifted leader in a former monk and orphaned peasant named Zhu Yuan-Zhang, who was the leader of a secret society called the Red Turban. Zhu obtained the support of members of the educated elite, who introduced him to the Confucian classics and persuaded him to present himself as a national liberator. After a fifteen-year campaign, he proclaimed himself emperor in 1368, in the name of Hung-Wu ('most warlike'). In doing so, he inaugurated a dynasty – the Ming – which would rule China for the next three centuries, during which the nomad warriors of the steppes were never again able to inflict serious harm on the settled peoples of the empire.

The extreme swings between expansion and contraction that occurred in Europe and China between 1100 to 1450 did not form part of the experience of the peoples of India. Climate change had nothing like the same effect in these more southerly regions, and the armies of Genghis Khan, which massacred whole populations in Persia and Afghanistan, did not reach the north Indian plains. This different experience is reflected in the population statistics for the period. In 1200 the population of India amounted to a mere 70 million compared with China's 120 million. By 1300 it had shot up to 100 million, while China's had crashed to 80 million: an increase of around 40 per cent, compared with China's fall of more than 30 per cent.

The basis of this century of prosperity was one of the most important events in Indian history, the creation in 1206 of the Muslim dynasty that goes under the name of the Delhi Sultanate. Its founder was a redoubtable warrior named

Muhammad Ghuri, a cultured, Persian-speaking member of an aristocratic family. In a series of brilliant campaigns between 1175 and 1192, the forces under his command overcame two powerful Hindu kingdoms, and took control of the whole of north India, including the great river valleys of the Indus and the Ganges. These conquests were further evidence of the power of the highly mobile tactics they shared with the Mongols. It was also a tribute to the speed and stamina of the grass-fed horses of Central Asia and the skill of the men who rode them. Despite the wealth and manpower of the kingdoms of the plain, their war elephants, provided on an ad hoc basis by local aristocrats, were no match for tough, professional cavalry who spent their lives in the saddle.

Unlike the Mongols, these Muslim warriors and their descendants were conquerors, not tribute-taking terrorists. Where they conquered, they stayed to rule. In 1193, Muhammad Ghuri established a permanent garrison in the small town of Delhi. When he died in 1206, the Afghan segment of his domain split from the rest, and Delhi thereafter became the capital of the sultanate that took its name. His descendants worked hard to make it a centre of culture and learning, while they continued to add new territories to those they already controlled.

The Delhi Sultanate reached a peak of power and prosperity during the reign of Ala ud-din Khalji, from 1296 to 1316. He was a ruthless dictator, who usurped the throne after murdering the rightful occupant. But he was a brilliant soldier, conquering one rich south Indian kingdom after another in a seven-year campaign that brought him territory and treasure on an enormous scale. He also crushed a Mongol army that had invaded the Punjab, thereby ensuring that India would be free from such incursions for the best part of a century. Like his near contemporary, Kublai Khan, Ala ud-din displayed a strange mix of megalomania and fatherly concern for the peoples whose lands he conquered. Under him, India, or at least its land-owners and its merchants, prospered.

As the fourteenth century progressed, the peoples of India were caught up in an ever-widening web of commerce and culture made up of two separate networks. One consisted of contacts with the Muslim worlds of Central and South-west Asia, opened up by the conversion of the Mongol peoples to Islam. The other comprised the shipping routes across the Indian Ocean, which generated ever-growing flows of trade with Africa, South-east Asia and China. As people moved along these networks, India itself became more and more cos-mopolitan. The scale of these networks, and the ease with which people could move around them, is demonstrated by the career of the greatest of all Muslim travellers, Ibn Battutah, who spent several years in India in the mid-fourteenth century.

Ibn Battutah grew up in Tangier, Morocco, in a family that had produced a number of distinguished judges. It was this background, and his academic distinction, that opened doors wherever he travelled. After studying in Egypt, Syria and Hejaz, he developed a wanderlust that consumed him for nearly thirty years, during which he is estimated to have trav-elled about 75,000 miles: equivalent to travelling three times around the equator. After completing the pilgrimage to Mecca, he travelled through Arabia, Iraq and southern Iran, before returning to Mecca and Medina, in which cities he passed the next several years. His wanderlust then took him along the coast of East Africa as far as present-day Tanzania. Having heard of the wonders of the Delhi Sultanate, he decided to see it for himself. He was forced to take a roundabout route via Anatolia, so he stopped off to call on the khan of the Golden Horde, who ruled the lands around the River Volga, and to visit Samarkand, in Central Asia. After several years in Delhi, where he held high office and enjoyed the consolations of a harem of wives and concubines, he was appointed the sultan's ambassador to China. On the way, he spent two years in the Maldive Islands, where he married into the ruling family, before completing his journey to China. While there, he explored the inland waterways as far as Beijing.

Having survived shipwreck and having witnessed – and avoided – the plague, he arrived back in Morocco in 1348. Settling down at last, he dictated an account of his travels, casually dropping in the names of over 2000 eminent people he had met, most of which have been verified from independent sources. His book, known as *Rihlah*, is still the most vivid evocation available of this golden age of travel and commerce.

Half a century later, the Indian Ocean was the scene of another feat of exploration, the scale of which still amazes. This was a complete contrast: not the wide-eyed wanderings of a curious traveller, but a 'show-the flag' expedition by the greatest fleet the world had ever seen. The year was 1405, and the person responsible was a Chinese admiral named Zheng He.

When he was ten years old, Zheng, who was of Mongol parentage, had been taken prisoner by the soldiers of a Chinese army engaged in the 'pacification' of the south-western province of Yunnan. At the age of thirteen, he had been subjected to the customary castration administered to young male captives, which involved the severing of both penis and testicles with a single stroke of a sword. Having – as many did not – survived the ordeal, he was taken into the service of a prince of the royal house, Zhu Di, with whom he began a life-time of friendship and mutual regard. When Zhu Di became emperor, Zheng was made an admiral. In 1404, he set sail on the first of a series of trading and 'show-the-flag' missions, with a fleet of 317 ships of assorted sizes, carrying 28,000 men. Among these ships was a group of gigantic nine-masted vessels fitted with palatial cabins, and laden with silk, porcelain and other choice items to be exchanged for luxuries the Chinese hoped to obtain on their travels.

This was the first of seven such expeditions under Zheng's command over a period of nearly thirty years. There were plans for expeditions as far ahead as 1470, and there is no knowing how far they might have travelled and what discoveries they might have made. But the death of the emperor, and his suc-cession by his seven-year-old son, opened up a long-simmering power struggle within the imperial court, in which the oppo-nents of foreign involvement won the upper hand. In 1500, it became a capital offence to build a boat with more than two masts. In 1525, just three years after the first round-the-world voyage by a European ship, an imperial edict ordered the destruction of all ocean-going ships, and the arrest of the traders who sailed in them.

The greatest fleet the world had ever seen had been destroyed. The mercantile classes had been put firmly in their place. And the 'middle kingdom' had returned to its traditional disdain for the lesser breeds beyond the seas.

An alien visitor conducting an audit of the human race in the year that Gutenberg published his Great Bible would have concluded that the species was more than holding its own. Most of the population losses suffered across Eurasia through war and plague had been made good. And thanks to increases in numbers elsewhere, world population was now back at the 400 million level it had first reached around the year 1200. China, admittedly, had still not fully recovered from the double blow of the Black Death and the Mongol conquest, but this was balanced by the increase achieved in two regions – sub-Saharan Africa and the Americas – that the plague had not reached.

In terms of sheer numbers, Africa south of the Sahara had been the greatest success story of the previous three centuries. Starting from around 30 million in 1100, its total population had more than doubled, and was now, at nearly 70 million, greater than Europe's, and within striking distance of China's. This impressive increase was attributable to three factors: more and better food; improved technology; and the benefits of trade.

In the central rainforests, a multitude of gatherer-hunter societies pursued their traditional ways of life. In the highland regions to the east, tribes of pastoral nomads still travelled with their cattle from pasture to pasture. In the area around the River Limpopo, on the borders of present-day Zimbabwe and Mozambique, the wealth generated by such herds supported a state whose capital city, Great Zimbabwe, was home to a permanent population of something like 20,000. Through its ports on the east coast, it exported gold and ivory across the Indian Ocean, and imported glass beads and cotton textiles from India, and porcelain from China. In the Bantu-speaking regions of the southern half of the continent, kings whose wealth lay in vast herds of cattle ruled over a multitude of highly developed farming cultures that between them supported populations measured in millions.

In northern and western Africa, the most important trade was the trade in slaves. It was also one of the oldest, dating back to Roman times. In some parts of North Africa, nearly half the population consisted of slaves, and in addition there was a substantial export trade in slaves to Muslim countries around the Mediterranean, to Arabia and into South-west Asia. Some of these were captives taken in war, but many were the product of raids mounted for the specific purpose of acquiring them. In the mid-fifteenth century, villages in the western part of the continent were still plagued by raiders who appeared out of the blue to carry off the able-bodied young. Within a hundred years, these slave-traders would find a huge new market in the Americas. But in 1455, the existence of the Americas was still unknown to the rest of the world.

In the Americas, isolated from Eurasia's germs, and sustained by highly efficient farming cultures, the population had been increasing for centuries, and now numbered about 50 million, speaking around 2000 mutually unintelligible languages. A sizeable portion of this total was accounted for by two recently established civilizations: one in Mexico, and the other on the Andean Plateau, from Bolivia, through Peru, to northern Chile.

The civilization that occupied the Central Valley of Mexico was the creation of a people known as the Aztecs, who had entered the region from the north around 1200. For a hundred years or so, they had moved about, hiring out their services as mercenaries to their neighbours. In 1325 they had established a city-state of their own, called Tenochtitlán, on a series of islands in Lake Texcoco, the great stretch of water that then filled the area where Mexico City now stands. By 1456, they had conquered the whole of the Central Valley. Tenochtitlán, already as big as any city in Europe – indeed, any outside China – was in the middle of a building programme that would within another 50 years turn it into one of the world's greatest cities.

Although Tenochtitlán was laid out on a virgin site, the architects who created it were not starting from scratch. They were heirs to a tradition that stretched back over a thousand years to the metropolis of Teotihuacán, whose ruins were not far away. The wealth that made their work possible, and supported the luxurious lifestyle of the rulers who employed them, came from the tribute exacted from subject peoples in adjoining regions. These peoples were, in effect, farmed; not just for their tribute, but for their contribution to the maintenance of the Aztec religion. The Aztecs believed that their god, Huitzilopochtli, required a continuous supply of human hearts, which had to come from the living bodies of warriors taken in battle. Without this, the sun would cease to rise, and the world would come to an end. This put the Aztecs in the position of having to find excuses for recurring wars against peoples already under their domination. The hatred and resentment that this created would prove a decisive factor in the later downfall of this seemingly invincible empire.

Three thousand miles away, in the Andes of South America, the Inca empire was just emerging. In the twelfth century, the empire of Tiahuanacu, which had dominated the mountain valleys on the borders of Bolivia and Peru for close on 1000 years, had finally collapsed. In its wake, a host of small kingdoms had arisen, most of which were confined to single valleys. Then, between the thirteenth and fifteenth centuries, a successor empire had arisen – the Chimu – that eventually controlled a 700-mile stretch of country along the coast of Peru. Around 1200 the Inca had established a city at Cuzco, north of Tiahuanacu, which over the course of the next two centuries became the capital of a growing empire. Then, in a series of campaigns beginning in 1438, and continuing over the next thirty years, the Inca succeeded in conquering all the rival states in the region, including the Chimu, and establishing themselves as undisputed masters of western South America, from Ecuador to central Chile.

The Inca were the inheritors of a farming tradition more than 4000 years old and had developed one of the world's most sophisticated systems of agriculture, featuring massive irrigation works and backed up by a magnificent network of roads. To administer their far-flung dominions, they employed a large corps of administrators, whose training and skills might have impressed even the self-satisfied mandarins of imperial China.

The people of the Pacific coast of South America and the people of Mexico knew of one another's existence, and limited cultural exchanges had occurred over many centuries, via intermediaries along the coast of the two continents. But 3000 miles was a long way in the fifteenth century, and for all practical purposes these civilizations might as well have been on different planets. The state of mind that such isolation created was reflected in the name – Cuzco – the Inca gave to their capital city. It meant 'navel'. For them, as for the Chinese, their homeland was the centre of the world. Had they, or the Aztecs, known that there were other centres elsewhere, and that 6000 miles away other sailors were tentatively exploring the waters off the coast of Africa, they would have been astounded, though they would not have been concerned. But within seventy years, a storm was destined to sweep across those miles of ocean that would rip their civilizations to shreds.

In North America at this time, around 50 per cent of the area now occupied by the United States was home to farming cultures that supported a multitude of prosperous villages and small towns. The Mississippian culture that had flourished so strongly in the eleventh century was still vibrantly alive. An earthquake, and a run of devastating droughts, had forced the abandonment of Cahokia, the city that had dominated the region for three centuries. But elsewhere, in present-day Alabama, Georgia and eastern Oklahoma, substantial towns, ruled over by proud chiefs and defended by disciplined warriors, looked out across extensive fields of maize.

Maize was also the staple crop along much of the eastern seaboard. Here, a typical farming landscape would consist of three or four villages surrounded by up to 5 or 6 square miles of cornfields. Beyond the fields, there was often a belt of sweet chestnut or hickory trees, deliberately planted in cleared ground, to provide a supplement to a corn-based diet. In the more arid south-west, a different kind of agriculture was practised on terraced hillsides watered by artificial irrigation. But whatever style of agriculture was practised, in a forest landscape rich in small game, there was usually a source of meat close at hand.

Away from the lands of the settled farmers native peoples of many tribes pursued a traditional gatherer-hunter lifestyle. But these were not lands teeming with prey. When humans had arrived in the Americas thousands of years before, they had made short work of the large mammals, whose numbers had never recovered. In the mid-fifteenth century, there were no herds of bison thundering across the prairie. That picture belongs to a later time, when humans once again became thin upon the ground, and it was the turn of the big herbivores to fill the empty spaces.

On the other side of the Pacific, the people of Japan still lived much as their ancestors had done three centuries earlier. Thanks to the failure of Kublai Khan's attempted invasions, they had escaped the turmoil that their Chinese neighbours had been subjected to. Their numbers had continued to increase, and in 1455 stood at 10 million, twice what it had been 300 years earlier. Their emperor was still a member of the Yamato family, but he now merely reigned: he did not rule. Since 1192, real power had been in the hands of a succession of shoguns, military rulers who controlled the life of everyone outside the immediate circle of the imperial court. Under the shogun, the people were governed by, and existed to serve, a military aristocracy. These were the samurai, the highest caste in a rigidly stratified society, in which the lowest class, as in India, was untouchable. But by 1455, increased prosperity had encouraged a series of uprisings by a rebellious peasantry, whose determination to obtain some degree of control over their own lives led to weakening of the power of the shogunate, and of the samurai aristocracy in general.

In China, the overthrow of the Mongol dynasty in 1368 and its replacement by the Ming dynasty, which had roots in northern China, had led to a reversal of the long-running trend of population and prosperity from north to south. The creation of a new capital, Peking (modern Beijing), and the completion of the Grand Canal to supply it, had provided the motive power for a revival, not just of the north, but of the country as a whole. In 1456, China's population of around 75 million was still well short of what it had been before the Black Death and the Mongol invasion. But in an atmosphere of internal peace and increasing prosperity, it was on a rising curve that would carry it to record levels during the next two centuries.

'Ming' means 'brilliance', and artistically this was one of the most brilliant periods in Chinese history. By the mid-fifteenth century, the country's craft workers were turning out great quantities of fine carpets and carvings, and exquisite embroidery. Particularly notable was the beautiful blue and white porcelain, some of which was of eggshell thinness.

China at this time was more inward-looking than perhaps it had ever been. The explorations that might have taken the nation's navies across the Pacific, and into the Atlantic, had been abandoned. The ancient links with Central Asia had been broken, and instead, enormous efforts had gone into strengthening defences against possible nomad invasions. Advanced technology provided the underpinning for artistic achievement, and for the luxurious lifestyle of the upper classes. But something had happened to the country's genius for innovation. Potentially, it was as powerful as ever: the genetic makeup of the Chinese people had not changed. But inventive genius is like a plant. If it is to flourish, it needs favourable soil, and room to grow. In the restrictive, inward- and backward-looking atmosphere of the Ming dynasty, scientific enquiry was discouraged, and commercial enterprise was tightly controlled.

This was no immediate obstacle to material progress. A country with advanced technology, efficient administration and a literate culture can prosper on the basis of its accumulated wisdom for a long time. But in a fundamental sense, this society was marking time. Half a world away, in Europe, other societies were changing fast, and a series of revolutions – scientific, technological and commercial – was imminent, that would eventually leave China, and all the nations of Asia, trailing hopelessly in their wake.

The only Chinese ships now met with on the high seas were pirate ships. For them, the pickings were good. The Indian Ocean and the seas of South-east Asia were crowded with sails, riding the monsoon winds. From Timor in the East Indies to Zanzibar on the east coast of Africa, merchants plied back and forth. The centres of this Indian Ocean trade were the trading cities of south India, where Arabs, Jews and Christians alike gathered to transact business. From their quays, ships bound for the Mediterranean left carrying pepper, sandalwood, teak, sugar and spices, and returned laden with copper and gold. On the west, or Malabar coast the free port of Calicut (modern Kozhikode) attracted so many Arab merchants that a Chinese visitor, Ma Huan, reported that the entire population was Muslim.

We have no firm evidence that any of this sea-borne trade extended as far as Australia, or that any of its practitioners knew of Australia's existence. But there are tantalizing remains that suggest that the north coast at least may have had visitors from Asia. Whether this was the case, it is clear that in the fifteenth century most native Australians continued in their traditional way of life: small family groups that occasionally met up with other groups for celebration and exchange of information. Their culture was not stagnating, but compared with what was happening elsewhere, its rate of change was glacially slow.

The prosperity of the southern part of the Indian subcontinent was not shared by the peoples further north. Northern India in 1455 was still licking its wounds after a nomad invasion sixty years earlier. In the last great wave of conquest these horsemen of the steppes would ever mount, they had exploded out of Central Asia in 1383, under a ruthless leader of Turkish extraction named Tamerlane (Tamberlane, or 'Timur the Lame'), whose capacity for slaughter would have impressed even Genghis Khan. Over a fifteen-year period, his armies had rampaged across southern Russia, Persia and Afghanistan, leaving ruined cities and mountains of skulls in their wake. A Sunni Muslim, he had dressed up his murderous conquests in the garb of jihad. Like other Central Asian thugs before and after him, he had a soft spot for both religion and learning. During his reign, and his successors', the beautiful cities of Herat, Samarkand and Bukhara, created by captive artisans from the far corners of his empire, rose out of the desert sands to join the ranks of the greatest centres of learning in the world. In 1398, his forces had descended on Delhi itself, capturing and then killing 100,000 prisoners en route. In a three-day orgy of destruction, the city had been looted and razed to the ground, and its inhabitants massacred. The Delhi Sultanate had survived as a political entity, but had been permanently weakened, and it would take more than a century for its capital city to recover.

Like Genghis Khan's before him, Tamerlane's westerly advance scorched Poland and Hungary, but got no further. Saved from nomad incursions, the other countries of Europe had had to make do with fighting among themselves. This they had done with a will. But in spite of their efforts to reduce one another's numbers, the population of the continent had continued to creep back towards the level it had reached before the Black Death. In 1455, at around 65 million, it was only slightly below its 1300 total.

In the furnace of Europe's wars, a new kind of entity was being forged: the nation-state. The year 1453 had brought the end of the long period of conflict between England and France that goes by the name of the Hundred Years War. England lost its French domains, apart from the town of Calais, which it would retain for another hundred years. It was from this date that England and France can be said to have become nation-states, in the sense in which we use the term today. Spain, too, was well on its way to nationhood. The kingdoms of Aragon and Castile had reconquered substantial territories from the Moors – the Islamic rulers who had governed much of the peninsula for the previous 600 years. Within fifty years, the two kingdoms would be united by a dynastic marriage, and another nation would be born. Italy and Germany were still a long way from the unified entities we know today, but the kingdoms and principalities into which those lands were divided already displayed most of the characteristics that define a nation-state.

The papacy had lost the struggle for earthly power over the continent's rulers, but its spiritual authority still gave enormous leverage in European politics. And over much of the continent they possessed absolute power of life and death over those who dared to challenge them in matters of faith, conscience and learning. But there was a spirit of intellectual and religious restlessness at large that threatened that authority. The printing revolution inaugurated by the publication of Gutenberg's Great Bible in 1455 gave that spirit a voice, and it would in due course deal that authority a blow from which it would never recover.

2 0

THE BRIDGING OF THE ATLANTIC

The capture of Constantinople by the Turks in 1453 had badly affected the once lucrative trade in spices from the East, and traders throughout western Europe were consumed by the dream of finding a route by which they might bypass the Turkish domains. None dreamt of it more ardently than a young Genoese merchant and sailor named Cristoforo Colombo. Colombo, known in English-speaking countries as Christopher Columbus, had married the daughter of the governor of the Portuguese colony of Madeira. By doing so, he gained Portuguese nationality and an entrée to the highest ranks of Portuguese society.

Portugal, with a population of only about a million, had little in the way of natural resources. But it had a strong mercantile tradition, and its sailors had led the way in a wave of exploration along the coasts of Africa, under a succession of rulers sympathetic to trade.

In 1480, after only a year of marriage, Columbus's wife died, leaving him a 28-year-old widower with a small son. By this time his dream of finding a new route to the East had given rise to a conviction that such a route could be found by sailing west. It was not a revolutionary idea. Educated Europeans in the fifteenth century were well aware that the earth was round, just as educated Greeks had known it more than 1500 years before them. The Greek-Egyptian mathematician Eratosthenes had written as long ago as the third century BC 'If the immensity of the Atlantic Sea did not prevent it, we could sail from Iberia [Spain and Portugal] to India along the same parallel.'

The unanswered questions were, not what shape the earth was, but how big it was, and just where on the earth's surface did East Asia lie? Eratosthenes had estimated the circumference of the earth to be about 25,000 miles, only 1000 miles short of what we now know to be the correct figure. But Columbus preferred the calculations of the Genoese mathematician Toscanelli, who believed that the earth was only 20,000 miles round at the Equator. He had also read the works of the thirteenth-century traveller Marco Polo, who believed that Japan lay 1500 miles to the east of China. Given that the earth's circumference was so much smaller at the latitude of Spain than it was at the Equator, Columbus reckoned that he would only have to sail about 3000 miles to reach Japan. Armed with this comforting assumption, he approached the Portuguese king, who was sympathetic, but was persuaded by the opposition of his geographers, unconvinced by Columbus's sums.

In 1488, another Portuguese navigator, Bartolomé Dias, rounded the Cape of Good Hope, proving that it was possible to reach the Indian Ocean by a round-Africa route. Columbus realized that he would now have to look elsewhere for patronage. He therefore approached the king and queen of the newly united kingdom of Spain. This time he was successful. On 3 August 1492, he left the Spanish port of Palos in command of three small ships: the 120-foot-long *Santa María* and two others, the *Pinta* and the *Niña*, which were less than half this size. He made first for the Canaries, and then, on 6 September, sailed due west, trusting to the sun and the stars to tell him whether he was keeping to a straight line. (His compass helped him set a westerly course, but he needed the sun and stars to tell him whether he was keeping to it.) On 11 October, after five weeks sailing in superb conditions, and having sailed almost exactly as far as he had expected, he sighted land. The next day he dropped anchor, chatted to the natives and planted a flag, claiming the territory, which was somewhere in the Bahamas, in the name of the Spanish monarchy. When he set sail for home, he took with him, as proof of his success, gold, cotton and two painted native Americans, whom he called 'Indians' on the assumption that he had reached the Indies. Till the day he died, he remained convinced he had reached Asia.

Columbus's discoveries, following on those made around the coast of Africa, gave rise to concern in Spain and Portugal about future rivalries between the two countries. In 1494, in one of the most stupefying acts of high-handedness in the history of the human race, the two nations signed the Treaty of Tordesillas. This stated that their respective territorial rights were henceforth to be defined by a north–south line (drawn by the pope), passing a thousand miles west of the mid-Atlantic Cape Verde Islands, and continuing round the entire globe. Spain was entitled to all lands 'other than Christian lands' to the west of the line, and Portugal all those to the east.

Once Columbus had proved the possibility of finding land by sailing west, others followed. In 1519, another Portuguese explorer with dreams of reaching the 'Spice Islands' (the Moluccas) by sailing west was turned down by his king, and he, too, successfully approached the king of Spain. His name was Ferdinand Magellan, and in 1519, he set sail with a fleet of five ships. After exploring the eastern coastline of South America, he found a way through to the Pacific, via the straits that now bear his name. After a three-and-a-half-month non-stop voyage across the Pacific, during which the crews were reduced to eating leather, rats and sawdust, they dropped anchor in the Philippines, where Magellan met his death as a result of a misunderstanding with the local inhabitants. On 22 September 1522, one remaining ship – the first to sail around the world – dropped anchor in Seville, carrying fewer than twenty survivors of the 250 who had set out three years before.

In the century and a half after this first round-the-world voyage, countless groups of would-be colonizers made their way from Europe to the Americas. Their objectives differed, but their motivations may be summarized under three main headings: gold, religion and land.

From the first discovery of the Americas, the prospect of finding gold was one of the main incentives for those who braved the hardships of the crossing. Columbus had been presented with objects made of gold by the first native Americans he met. He did not himself reach the mainland of Central America, but he returned with stories of a land where gold could be had in plenty. These stories were an undoubted factor contributing to the willingness of the Spanish crown to sponsor transatlantic explorations. The principal source of gold at this time was the 'Gold Coast' of West Africa, where the Portuguese had an effective monopoly of the trade. The belief in the existence of a Land of Gold ('El Dorado') was the motivation behind two of the most horrific episodes that disfigured the subsequent colonization of the Americas: the conquest of the Aztecs of Mexico, and the destruction of the Inca civilization of Peru. Both were remarkable for the speed with which the native civilizations collapsed, and for the apparently insuperable odds that confronted the Europeans who conquered them.

The first of these civilizations to fall to a European assault was that of the Aztecs, whose Emperor Montezuma ruled over at least 10 million people, and probably more. His capital city, Tenochtitlán, had a population of around 200,000, greater than that of any European city of the time. The year was 1519, and the man who brought this empire low was Hernan Cortés, the 33-year-old Spanish-born mayor of the city of Santiago, on the island of Cuba. Talk of a mysterious civilization far away in the Central Valley of Mexico had excited his ambition, and he had raised a force of 500 soldiers, 100 sailors and 16 horses, with which he set sail for the mainland of Yucatan. On arrival, he ordered his men to burn their boats, committing them, and himself, to either glory or certain death.

Cortés had the advantage of guns and gunpowder against a Stone Age civilization, and also the shock effect of cavalry on people who had never seen a horse. But these advantages would have counted for little, had he not been blessed with three strokes of luck. The first of these was that the Aztec empire was riven with internal disputes, which meant that there were forces in the country ready to welcome anyone who presented a threat to the ruling power. Secondly, his troops, without knowing it, were armed with a deadly weapon – the smallpox virus – to which the native population had never been exposed, and to which they were therefore extraordinarily vulnerable. Thirdly, he had the assistance of a captured native princess named la Malinche, who spoke the Aztec language, Nahuatl. He taught her Spanish, and she became both his mistress and his negotiator. Thanks to her, he succeeded in putting together an alliance that was ultimately able to field a force more than 100,000 strong.

20.1 The Re-peopling of the Americas 1500–1800

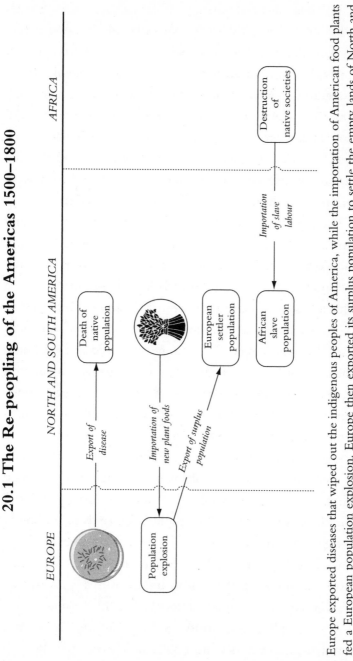

Europe exported diseases that wiped out the indigenous peoples of America, while the importation of American food plants fed a European population explosion. Europe then exported its surplus population to settle the empty lands of North and South America, and these settlers imported slave labour from Africa to work for them.

Before he obtained the support of these native allies, Cortés and his small force had some extraordinarily narrow escapes from total disaster. And even with their aid, his conquest of Tenochtitlán was not achieved without a long, bloody street-by-street battle, in which up to 100,000 people were massacred. But by 1521, Cortés was master of the entire empire. A less loyal servant of his emperor, so far from home, might have been tempted to make himself a king. But Cortés ensured that the wealth of this extraordinary civilization – for gold there was, in abundance – went to swell the treasury of his royal master.

The next adventurer to achieve the destruction and enslavement of an American civilization was another Spaniard, Francisco Pizarro. He had travelled to the Americas in search of a fortune, and had accumulated the makings of one while serving as mayor of Panama between 1519 and 1523. In the latter year, when he was about forty-eight years of age, no doubt inspired by the example of Cortés, he organized an exploration of the coast of Ecuador. Returning to Panama with no discoveries to boast of, he managed to scrape together enough money to finance a second attempt. On this voyage, one of his companions encountered a raft laden with fine embroidery and precious metals, which convinced Pizarro of the existence of a rich civilization in the mountains of the interior. Faced with opposition from the governor of Panama, he travelled to Spain to plead for royal authority to explore the lands to the south. The reigning queen, Isabella, also fired by the example of Cortés, who happened to be in Seville at the time, appointed Pizarro governor of the still-to-be-discovered province of 'New Castile' stretching 600 miles south from Panama.

Armed with this authority, and accompanied by a small force of men and horses, he landed on the coast of Peru in

April 1531. Six years after his first expedition, and fifty-five years old, he was more determined than ever to make his dream a reality. Like Cortés, he was lucky in his timing. Had he found his sought-after empire at his first attempt in 1525, its forces would have disposed of his expedition as easily as he himself would have swatted away a fly. At that time the Inca empire had been at the height of its power and prosperity. Extending over more than 2000 miles, from Quito in the north to the Maule River in the south, it had a population of at least 6 million, and possibly nearer 10 million. It also had a superb system of communications based on 20,000 miles of roads, and a large and disciplined army. But by 1528 it had been devastated by an epidemic of European origin – almost certainly smallpox – to which its people had no resistance. Among the millions who died was the empire's brilliant ruler, Huayna Capac. The resulting dislocation had been intensified by a civil war over the succession.

When Pizarro landed in Peru for the second time, he found a country ravaged by war and pestilence, and subject peoples in a state of near mutiny. It must have seemed an opportunity made in heaven. All that was needed was a little treachery. Pizarro had studied Cortés's successful strategy in Mexico, and had learned the necessary lessons. Having invited the new emperor, Atahualpa, to meet him, Pizarro succeeded in taking him prisoner during a mêlée in which the emperor's escort was terrorized by a surprise attack featuring firearms and charging horses, neither of which they had experienced before. Atahualpa offered, as his ransom, to fill the hall in which he was held prisoner with gold, silver and precious objects. When the room was filled to the ceiling, and the wealth of the empire proved beyond doubt, Pizarro had Atahualpa strangled.

The death of their ruler, whom they revered as a god, destroyed most of what fighting spirit the Inca had left. After a series of mopping-up operations, the vast Inca domain became part of the Spanish empire, and those fit enough were put to work mining gold and silver, and melting down treasure, to fill the coffers of the Spanish queen.

21

The Remaking of North America

No treasure awaited the adventurers who explored the coasts of America north of Mexico. They found no gold and no urban civilizations. But if the process of occupation there was more protracted, the result was the same. Throughout the Americas most of the native population was wiped out by European diseases. In North America, the wave of pestilence travelled ahead of the settlers who brought it, so that new arrivals sometimes found themselves passing through villages peopled only by the corpses of those they had unwittingly infected. Statistics of deaths are hard to come by, and estimates vary considerably. But that tens of millions of native Americans died from Old World diseases is beyond question: the only legitimate question is just how many tens of millions succumbed to diseases from which their forebears had been isolated for more than 10,000 years. These included not just smallpox, but infections like influenza and measles, often little more than an inconvenience to Europeans, but lethal to people with no inherited resistance.

Some have called the destruction of the native peoples of the Americas genocide, but that is an abuse of the word. 'Genocide' implies intention, and for that we have no evidence. 'Massacres' is the right word, and the deaths in those massacres are to be counted in millions. There were undoubtedly those who harboured genocidal desires, such as the notorious Lord Jeffrey Amherst, who was involved in an early example of germ warfare during the French and Indian War of 1754–63, when native Americans were deliberately issued with blankets used by smallpox victims. But the tidal wave of death that swept across the two continents was caused by microbes that needed no assistance from any human agency. It was one of the greatest tragedies in the history of the human race, destroying two advanced civilizations and countless highly developed cultures. In the process it robbed the world of a store of knowledge, and ways of thought, that had taken thousands of years to build up and are now gone for ever.

From the moment the first settlements were established, tragedy was inevitable. To the stupendous massacre of the native peoples by the new Americans' germs, we must add the lesser, but still substantial massacre by their guns. The exact extent of the combined effect is a matter of dispute, but we can say with confidence that between 1550 and 1750, it reduced the native population of the Americas by at least 50 per cent. The true figure may lie closer to 90 per cent.

During the course of the sixteenth and seventeenth centuries, four European countries – Spain, Portugal, France and England – acquired substantial territories in the Americas. The Portuguese, who seemed at first to have been excluded from the New World by the line drawn by the pope down the middle of the Atlantic, discovered that there was a part of South America that lay to the east of it. Technically, this should only have given them just a small part of the land we now know as Brazil. But seeing what their Spanish neighbours had gained from the division, they refused to be deprived of this new colony's potential by a technicality, and they proceeded to drive deep into the interior, planting the flag as they went.

England and France were latecomers to American colonization. In the sixteenth century they were more concerned with establishing their positions in the cockpit of European politics. England in particular lacked the resources to match the efforts of the Spanish and Portuguese. But as the seventeenth century dawned, England and France woke up to the potential of these newly discovered continents. The English crown, unfazed by Spanish and Portuguese pretensions, began to exercise a greater interest in the lands on the eastern seaboard of the northern continent, where English settlers had attempted, so far unsuccessfully, to establish a permanent foothold. On 14 May 1607 the first successful English settlement was founded on a peninsula in the James River, in a territory that was named Virginia. This was Jamestown, a community that would later notch up a notable list of 'firsts': the first colony to grow tobacco; the first to import African slaves; and, in 1619, the first to introduce representative government.

Further north, the French also had had a presence on the continent since the beginning of the century. Their most important settlement was Quebec, which was settled in 1608, just one year after Jamestown. In 1634, the French began a serious effort at colonization with the establishment of the Company of New France, which was set up to develop the fur trade. When the English created the Hudson's Bay Company in 1670, to exploit the resources of the region around the great bay of that name, a rivalry ensued that would not be resolved until nearly a century later.

There was one other maritime nation that aspired to colonize the eastern seaboard: the Dutch. In 1626, Peter Minuit, Director General of the New Netherland Province, purchased an island in the Hudson River from a tribe called the

Manhattan, and established a colony that later acquired the proud name of New Amsterdam. In 1664, it was taken by an English force, and renamed New York.

Not every European who landed in the Americas was looking for glory or treasure. Many, courageous and hard-working, were simply looking for land, and the chance of a new life, free of the religious persecution they had suffered in the lands of their birth. One such settlement is the most famous of them all: the one founded in Plymouth, Massachusetts, by the group known today as the Pilgrim Fathers and Mothers. They had sailed from the English port of Plymouth in the *Mayflower* in 1620. About half of the 102 people who survived the winter crossing died from sickness during the first year, and the rest would have starved, had it not been for the help extended them by some of the native population. When their first harvest was taken in, these neighbours joined in the first Thanksgiving. The settlers later signed a number of treaties of friendship with these neighbouring tribes, but it was a friendship that could not last.

The very fact that some settlers survived encouraged others, and the drive to master this new environment placed a premium on the breeding of a new generation to help till the soil. As their numbers increased, settlers everywhere sought out more land. In their eyes, ownership resided in a piece of paper, and the lands around them were ownerless, since the native population had no such pieces of paper. Their view, that land was a common good to be enjoyed, like the air, and that if it could be said to be owned at all, it could only be owned by an entire people, was something outside the newcomers' experience. As for the native Americans, it gradually became clear to them that an alien civilization was intent on dispossessing them of their ancestral lands. The choice that confronted them was either to risk death in the defence of their inheritance, or to let it go, and reconcile themselves to the extinction of their peoples.

As the years went by, the trickle of transatlantic settlement swelled. The mixture of motives persisted. Some settlements were created by government decree, others by companies, or rich sponsors, in pursuit of profit. Yet others were created by groups of friends, in pursuit of religious freedom, or in the hope of escaping from the hardship of life in their overcrowded homelands.

As the new arrivals attempted to exploit the lands on which they had planted their flags, a challenge presented itself. In Europe, their biggest problem was finding enough land to feed a growing population. Here, the challenge was the opposite one: not shortage of land, but of people to work it. This was not a pressing problem in New England, where family labour supplied family subsistence. But further south, and in Brazil and the Caribbean in particular, plantation owners producing crops for export found their pursuit of profit frustrated by a shortage of hands to work the land available to them.

One crop in particular – sugar – held out the prospect of gratifying returns, if labour shortages could be overcome. Refined sugar had first been produced in India around 700 BC, and had reached Europe by the twelfth century. There it had remained a luxury product, used primarily as a medicine. Sweetness was still provided by honey, as it had been since the days of the ancient Egyptians.

Around 1530, the Portuguese, who already cultivated sugar on their Atlantic Islands, introduced it to Brazil. In these sun-drenched lands, sugar cane could be grown very cheaply, provided there was the labour to plant and harvest it. Unfortunately, having killed off the settled farmers whom they might have been able to enlist in their workforces, the plantation owners were forced to look further afield.

A solution soon presented itself. On the other side of the Atlantic, in Africa, there were people who were used to working outdoors in a hot climate. There were also established slave markets, where such people could be bought, as one might buy any other piece of equipment – a spade or a cart – to till the soil or harvest crops. Behind these markets were slave-traders, who could supply unlimited quantities of people captured in war or kidnapped in raids. The trade was an old one. For centuries, young men and women in their thousands had been marched in chains from West Africa across the Sahara, to spend what remained of their lives in the service of the 'civilized' races who lived around the Mediterranean and in South-west Asia. Why should the 'civilized' landowners of the Americas not have a share of this wonderful resource?

Insistent demand will always find a supply. As the plantation owners' money was brought to bear on the problem, slave markets sprang up on the coast of West Africa. New patterns of raiding developed to service them, and Christian merchants from Europe appeared with the ships needed to transport the slaves. The conditions were horrific. Chained together in dark, confined spaces below deck, terrified out of their wits, lying in their own filth, and breathing in the germs of those around them, it was only to be expected that many would die before they reached their journey's end. But it was not always necessary to die of one's afflictions. Sick slaves were worthless in America, so some ships' masters simply threw them overboard, and claimed on their insurance. On average, only about 80 per cent of the slaves who were embarked survived the journey.

The plantation owners of Brazil and the Caribbean struggled to meet the insatiable demand for cheap food from the burgeoning populations of Europe. For most of the seventeenth century, about 10,000 slaves a year were transported across the Atlantic. By 1700, this figure had risen to 40,000. In 1760, when the numbers peaked, the annual figure was close to 70,000. By then, a total of some 6 million Africans had been torn from their homes, shipped like cattle and sold to landowners to whom they were essentially two-legged beasts.

Most of these early arrivals ended up on the sugar plantations of the Caribbean and Brazil. As the eighteenth century progressed, an increasing number found their way to plantations in Virginia and the states of the Mississippi basin, where two other crops, tobacco and cotton, were becoming important. On these plantations, they were treated like other farm animals: vilely or humanely, according to the nature of the people who owned them.

Important though sugar, cotton and tobacco were, the greatest gifts of American agriculture to the peoples of Europe, and to the peoples of temperate climes throughout the world, were two plants that were transplanted, not exported: maize and the potato. When Columbus sailed from Palos in 1492, no one outside the Americas had even heard of them, let alone seen them.

The home of the potato was in the Andes of South America. It was a staple food of the Inca, and it was Pizarro's conquest that led to its introduction to Europe, and from Europe to the rest of the world. But the Inca did not invent it. The people of the Andean civilization of Tiahuanaco had been harvesting 10,000 tons of potatoes a year 1000 years before Pizarro was born. And the people to whom we truly owe this most magical of foods had lived 3000 years before them.

Maize, too, was the fruit of conquest. First developed from its wild precursor, teosinte, by the peoples of Central America around 3000 BC, it was a staple food of the Aztecs. As a consequence of Cortés's victory, it, too spread around the world. Today, more than 400 years after the last shipment of Aztec gold left American shores, maize is a major crop, from the southern states of the USA to south-west China, and it provides the breakfast cereal of millions.

Another American food plant that travelled the world was the sweet potato. This found its way to China, which finished up growing more of this American vegetable than the rest of the world, and where it would become one of the country's chief mainstays against famine.

By 1750, 90 per cent of the population of the Americas were the subjects of one or other of four European empires. The Portuguese already controlled much of Brazil. The Spanish crown exercised sovereignty over most of the remainder of South America, over Mexico and over a sizeable portion of the lands east of the Mississippi. Britain and France between them controlled large parts of the eastern half of North America, and disputed who had legal claim to the rest.

Between 1756 and 1763, these two countries engaged in the worldwide struggle for territory and influence that we know as the Seven Years War. It ended with the signing of the Treaty of Paris, under which Britain gained the whole of Canada and East and West Florida, and the French abandoned their claims to territories east of the Mississippi. The British representatives at its signing possibly felt they were witnessing the greatest triumph in the nation's history. If so, they were mistaken. The long war had been a costly enterprise, and the British government now had to face up to the question of how their enlarged empire was to be defended, and how that defence was to be paid for. Most important of all, the eviction of the French from North America had removed a threat that had been hanging over these fast-growing colonies. If there was no longer a French enemy on their frontier, did they need a mother country at all?

Between Columbus's first expedition in 1492 and the Treaty of Paris in 1763, the population of the world outside America more or less doubled. But the devastation wrought by the Europeans' arrival had been so great that even after more than two centuries of immigration and slave transportation the population of the Americas in 1763 was still only a third of what it had been in 1492.

America's loss was many countries' gain. American food plants found their way into the markets, and on to the farms, of the Old World. Two in particular – maize and the potato – provided stunning new sources of nourishment from land that would have been incapable of generating anything like the same food value from any other crop. As the calories available increased, Old World populations raced ahead. Europe, in particular, benefited from this bonanza of food. But Europeans received another benefit from their transatlantic adventure undreamt of by Columbus.

The modern city of Potosí, in Southern Bolivia, stands on a cold, bare plateau 13,000 feet above sea-level, in the shadow of the mountain from which it takes its name. In 1532, when Pizarro made his second visit to Peru, no city stood there. But thirteen years later a Spanish expedition discovered that the mountain contained substantial amounts of silver. Before long it became clear that the mountain was effectively made of silver. In the century or so that followed, stupendous quantities of the metal were mined and shipped back to Spain. By 1650, the population of Potosí had reached 160,000.

Potosí was far and away the most spectacular confirmation of the hopes of the conquistadores who defeated and enslaved the peoples of Latin America. But it was just one of many sources of precious metals that were uncovered in the years that followed. In the decade 1551–60, 43 tons of gold entered the Spanish port of Seville. In the whole period from 1500 to 1650, recorded imports of American gold through Spanish ports amounted to 181 tons. How much was smuggled in, or pirated, will never be known. But these totals were dwarfed by the recorded imports of silver during the same period, which amounted to nearly 17,000 tons.

These astounding transactions initiated a transformation of the economy of an entire continent. Silver ingots were soon being made into coins with which to buy goods and services. American silver and gold oiled the wheels of trade, and made it possible for Europeans to enjoy the fruits of the labour of other peoples around the world.

Prior to the discovery of America, Europeans still largely operated a barter economy. The trouble with barter is that if two traders don't each have what the other wants, no trade is possible. For its economy to function smoothly, and for its commerce to thrive, Europe desperately needed more cash: precious metals in the form of currency. This was even more necessary if the continent was to be able to acquire the goods it could not produce for itself: pepper, spices, silk, cotton goods, tropical hardwood and all the other products that had become available. The value of Europe's exports to countries further east had habitually run short of the amount needed to pay for their imports from them. This shortfall was made good with exports of gold and silver. The great emporium of the Indian Ocean was both an inexhaustible source of luxury goods and an insatiable outlet for precious metals. No matter how much silver the merchants of Arabia, India, South-east Asia and China succeeded in laying their hands on, they were always ready for more. In 1570, when the Chinese government simplified its tax system by imposing a single tax, payable in silver, demand for the metal went through the roof. For most of the seventeenth century, something like two-thirds of the world's output of silver finished up in China. Thanks to China, the silver deposits that Europeans discovered in the Americas became the key that opened up the markets of the world.

It would be difficult to exaggerate the importance of these two European discoveries – the discovery of the Americas and the discovery of their mineral wealth. They set in train a series of events that led directly to the world we inhabit.

The modern world was born when the first consignment of American silver sailed into the port of Seville. Its significance lay in its timing. By the mid-sixteenth century, the peoples of western Europe had recovered from the disaster of the Black Death, and had found their confidence again. In addition, the turmoil of those terrible times had, over much of the region, dissolved away the world of feudal obligations, and substituted money payment of rent and wages. Only a shortage of money prevented cash payment becoming the norm across the whole economy. When that constraint was removed, barter quickly disappeared.

As the Spanish and the Portuguese spent their new wealth – on buildings, on luxuries and on wars – their spending sent a wave of prosperity washing through the countries around them.

22.1 Europe's Asian Transfusion

Europe used cheap American labour to mine American silver, and used this to pay for luxury goods produced by Asian labour.

22.2 The Growth of World Population since AD 1000

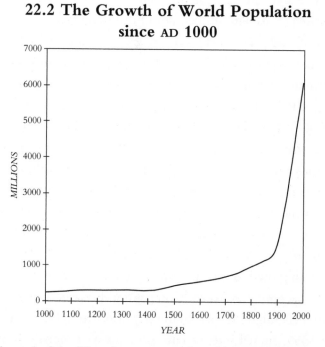

By the end of the fifteenth century, total world population had more than made good the falls resulting from famine and plague during the fourteenth century, and had embarked on the uninterrupted rise that has continued ever since.

They were assisted in this endeavour by the piratical activities of countries such as England, whose sailors (and monarchs) did not see why the Spanish should have all the fun, and helpfully relieved their ships of precious metals, for distribution elsewhere.

The volume of trade along the coasts of north-west Europe, and even more so around the Mediterranean, had been growing steadily for a century before the Americas were discovered. On the back of this, a sophisticated private banking system had come into existence. When American silver arrived, both the volume of trade and the proportion that was paid for in cash increased considerably. With so much more cash in the system, the size and influence of the banks increased. And with the increased availability of methods of deferred payment, the volume of trade also increased. In great trading cities such as Florence, Venice, London and Antwerp, the wealth generated by banking became a source of enormous power and patronage. One of the most important services that these banks rendered was by making available bills of exchange. These were documents that traders could use to obtain funds in a foreign city to pay for goods or services, on the understanding that they would honour the bills (that is, repay the credit extended) at a future date, which was termed the 'maturity date'. These bills were effectively post-dated cheques, for which the trader had to find the money by the agreed settlement date.

This growth of private banking did not just result in more credit becoming available. Competition between banks led to credit becoming cheaper. In the city of Antwerp between 1500 and 1550, annual interest rates on borrowed money dropped from 25 per cent to 9 per cent. This gave a huge advantage to local traders, and was an important factor in establishing the city as the leading port in the region.

The massive expansion of the banking system that occurred in Europe in the two centuries after 1456 was a pre-condition for the take-off into rapid economic growth of the eighteenth and nineteenth centuries. There were a lot of accidents on the way. It was said in Venice in 1585, that of the 103 private banks that had opened in the city up to that date, 96 had gone bankrupt. But it was pain that Europe had to go through. Without the development of banking, modern economies could never have come into existence. Bank lending is the lubricant that keeps the wheels of business turning. Without it, commercial life would come to a juddering halt. Unfortunately, like some other lubricants, bank lending can be highly inflammable.

There is a difference between lending for productive investment (buildings, machinery, etc.) and lending for speculation. All investment decisions contain an element of speculation, because all investment involves the commitment of present wealth in the hope of future gain, and the future is unknowable. But some investments are so speculative as to amount to sheer gambling. When too much borrowed money is used to fund investment of this kind, it can do serious damage. There cannot be a borrower without a lender, and just as there is unwise borrowing, so there is ill-considered lending, or as it is sometimes called, excessive credit. One example of this stands out.

In 1554, in Constantinople, the Austrian ambassador to Turkey was shown a flower he had not seen before. It was a tulip. He described it in a letter home, and accompanied his letter with some bulbs, which were later planted in the imperial garden in Vienna. In 1502, when the garden's curator was appointed to a similar post at the University of Leiden in The Netherlands, he took some bulbs with him. He could not have foreseen the consequences of his action. Within twenty years of the flower's introduction to The Netherlands, it formed the basis of a flourishing trade, both at home and for export. Within thirty years, a bulb of the most sought-after variety, the 'Semper Augustus', had changed hands for 1000 guilders – enough to buy a smart carriage and a horse to go with it.

This was the beginning of the tulip mania, the most famous of all financial manias. In 1634, many Dutch people went tulip mad. Tulips, and their values, became a topic of everyday conversation, and otherwise rational citizens were consumed with dreams of the wealth that could be theirs by merely buying, and then reselling, tulip bulbs. In 1637, the bubble burst, quite literally overnight. On 3 February that year, a rumour started to the effect that there were no more buyers of bulbs in the market. Within twenty-four hours, bulbs were unsaleable at any price. People who had contracted to buy bulbs at high prices after the harvest found excuses to renege on their commitments, and would-be sellers who had laid out large sums in the hope of profit suffered substantial losses. It was many years before the more desirable varieties recovered even their pre-mania value. The prices of the more ordinary varieties, which had formed the principal vehicle of speculation for most of those involved, never recovered.

The tulip mania is the perfect model of a speculative bubble. It seems so outlandish that there is a temptation to think of it as a 'one-off', without parallel at any other time. Nothing could be further from the truth. There has not been a single generation in the last 400 years when some prosperous country has not been seized with a comparable frenzy. Examples include the Mississippi scheme in eighteenth-century France; the South Sea Bubble in eighteenth-century England; the canal and railway manias in nineteenth-century England; the Wall Street boom and the Florida land boom in 1920s America; the stock market and property booms in 1980s Japan; and Wall Street's love affair with the internet in the 1990s.

At the height of the tulip mania, people were essentially paying for their tulips with IOUs. This made it easy to pay crazy prices for tulip bulbs, just as the availability of mortgages nowadays makes it easy for people to pay high prices for houses. In sixteenth-century Holland people were used to trading on credit, so IOUs made out by respectable citizens seemed a perfectly proper basis for the conduct of business.

If that seems strange, it is worth going over both this explanation and the story of the tulip mania again. What might seem like nothing more than an example of the madness and delusion of crowds is in fact an example of the same principle that brought about the Industrial Revolution of the eighteenth and nineteenth centuries. The people who made it were able to find the money to build their factories and buy their machines because banks and their customers between them can effectively create money out of thin air any time they like, provided only that they feel confident in doing so.

In the event, the tulip mania did not have as disastrous an effect as it might have done. Many of the wealthier and more worldly-wise members of Amsterdam's trading community had refused to get drawn in. So although it brought ruin to a lot of ordinary folk, it didn't bring down the economy. And the tulip has been a good friend to the Dutch ever since.

No matter how sophisticated the continent's commercial and financial systems had become, Europe would never have caught up with China, either in power or in wealth, had it not made equivalent progress in technology. Fortunately, by 1500,

Europe's industrial and agricultural technology was easily the equal of China's. More to the point, it was advancing at a faster rate. This achievement was to a considerable extent the result of having benefited from discoveries made in China centuries earlier. But Europe had proved a good learner, and the teacher was now in the process of being left behind. The Chinese did not know this, of course. Ensconced behind the psychological Great Wall of their own self-absorption, it would take another three centuries before the shock of realization would hit them, and by that time the former pupil would have grown into a hulking brute without respect, unaware of how much it had been taught, and by whom.

There was an important technology possessed by the Chinese that the Europeans were still unacquainted with. This was the plough with an iron-faced, concave mouldboard. The secret of how to make cast iron had reached Europe in the thirteenth century, but even after the introduction of the iron ploughshare, European ploughs required large teams of draught animals to turn over heavy soils. It would not be until the American Thomas Jefferson worked out the mathematics of the concave mouldboard in the eighteenth century, and an iron-faced mouldboard was combined with an iron frame, that Europe's farmers would be able to match China's in the efficiency of their ploughing.

Ploughing apart, sixteenth-century European farming practices showed considerable progress. With improved techniques, a greater understanding of the processes of plant growth and animal breeding, and operating within the framework of a cash economy, the continent's farmers were able to deliver the food needed to support a growing population. And this increased efficiency of food production, and of food marketing, made possible the even more rapid rate of growth of the towns and cities that were now bursting into vibrant life. Throughout the seventeenth and into the eighteenth century, the rate of agricultural innovation would increase, providing the underpinning for the massive increase in population that accompanied, and drove, the transformation known as the Industrial Revolution.

EUROPE'S DISCOVERY OF ART AND SCIENCE

The discovery of new lands created a ferment of excitement in Europe. Every young man of spirit and good family yearned to take part in the adventure of exploration. Every old man of wealth and position wanted to have a stake in it. But there was a psychological impact as well. The discoveries had demonstrated that sitting around and thinking was not the only way of acquiring knowledge of the world. Some knowledge could only be obtained by experimenting: by going out and looking for it. It also showed that not all knowledge was contained in a secret store accessible only to a select few. Once this was understood, the excitement of discovery spilled over into other areas of enquiry. Men (it was men, because only they had the time and the opportunity) began to question accepted ideas, and to wonder what other kinds of discoveries there were to be made.

This new enthusiasm for enquiry was encouraged by two fifteenth-century developments that provided powerful new means for the exchange and spread of ideas. The first was the expansion of universities across the continent during the fifteenth century. Between 1400 and 1500, the number of universities in Europe increased from twenty to seventy. These not only created a forum in which scholars could discuss theories, new and old; they also welcomed students from universities elsewhere, ensuring a constant flow of fresh ideas. Reinforcing this effect was the printing revolution of the

1450s, which quickened the flow of ideas between the universities, and brought readers outside them into the web of knowledge exchange.

The buzz created by the flood of printed books was intensified by a side-effect of the fall of Constantinople in 1453. One of the last groups to escape from the city had been a party of scholars who brought with them manuscripts containing some of the most important texts of Greek science. These yielded a treasure trove of scientific knowledge. They also stimulated a search for similar texts elsewhere, many of which were discovered in Arabic translations whose contents had until then remained unknown to Christian scholars.

These three influences – the new universities, the printing presses and the rediscovery of ancient knowledge – together created an explosion of scientific enquiry that transformed people's understanding of the natural world. It was the beginning of the process known as the Scientific Revolution.

The first triumph of this new enterprise came in 1543, when a Polish priest named Mikolaj Kopernik – Nicholas Copernicus – published (in Latin, of course) a book entitled *On the Revolutions of the Heavenly Spheres*. Copernicus's work was a perfect illustration of the intellectual explorations that paralleled the physical explorations of the navigators. He began his university studies in 1491, just as Columbus was making the final preparations for his voyage. While Columbus was criss-crossing the Atlantic on his successive journeys, Copernicus was criss-crossing Europe, sharing ideas with scholars in Poland, Italy and Germany.

At this time the accepted view of the solar system was that of the first-century Greek astronomer Ptolemy, who postulated a universe in which the Sun and the planets revolved around a stationary Earth. Copernicus, inspired by recently translated works by Greek astronomers who lived before Ptolemy, suggested a new model, in which the earth and the planets revolved around the Sun. Thanks to the printing presses that now existed in every European city, his ideas quickly became known across the continent.

Sixty years later, in 1609, another university-trained scientist, the Italian mathematician Galileo Galilei, turned the newly invented telescope on the heavens, saw spots on the Sun, and used them to calculate the speed at which it turned on its axis. He also observed the satellites of Jupiter revolving around their parent planet, just as Copernicus had imagined the Earth revolving around the Sun. This convinced him of the truth of the Copernican theory, which he promoted in a book entitled *Dialogue on the Two Chief World Systems*, published in 1632.

Galileo's promotion of Copernican theory was too much for the pope, who held that it was contrary to the Church's teaching. Galileo was arraigned before the Holy Inquisition, the body charged with preserving the faith and rooting out heresy. Faced with the threat of being burned alive, he was compelled to retract, and he spent his last eight years under house arrest. With four years left to live, his sun-damaged sight failed him and his stargazing ended.

The trial of Galileo was the last great set-piece in the struggle of the Church of Rome to direct the thoughts of the faithful in matters of science. Although the Church had won this particular battle, it quickly became clear that it had lost the war.

One reason why the Church had felt compelled to act against Galileo was that he had written in Italian, the language of the common people, rather than in Latin. Unfortunately for the Church, he was a master of the language, and the power of the book's arguments outweighed his formal retraction. The cat, as the saying goes, was out of the bag. There would be other occasions in the years to come when popes would plaintively warn their flocks not to read books that were placed on the *Index Librorum Prohibitorum* (the list of books that Catholics were forbidden to read). But they might as well have saved their breath. Even if their warnings curbed the curiosity of their own flocks, there were now too many scientists outside the Church's reach. The Reformation initiated by Martin Luther in 1517 had freed scientists in Protestant lands from any obligation to follow the Church's guidance.

In 1609, while Galileo was putting the finishing touches to his telescope, the German mathematician Johannes Kepler published *The New Astronomy*. This introduced his three laws of planetary motion that explained the mathematical relationships governing the movements of the earth, the moon, the sun and the planets. In 1687, less than eighty years after this book was published, a professor of mathematics in the University of Cambridge in England, Isaac Newton, published *Principia*, the most famous book in the history of science. In it, he used Kepler's laws and Galileo's studies of the mechanics of moving bodies to arrive at his Law of Universal Gravitation. This established the existence of the force of gravity, and gave us the formulae we use to weigh the stars and calculate the flight paths of rockets bound for the moon.

Although this chain of discoveries linking Copernicus to Newton, through Kepler and Galileo, is the most famous illustration of the Scientific Revolution in action, equally striking examples could be quoted from other sciences. What they all show is the extent to which scientific advance is dependent on the simultaneous presence of a range of beneficial influences.

These include:

1 a society rich enough to be able to support a sizeable class of people who spend their time reading and talking, and carrying out possibly fruitless experiments

2 opportunities for networking (such as universities and learned societies)

3 access to the accumulated knowledge of the both the past and the present (in the form of, for example, libraries and printed books)

4 appropriate technology (microscopes, telescopes, accurate time measurement)

5 freedom from obstructive censorship

6 a culture in which enquiry is a habit, and challenging accepted ideas is the norm.

This list does not include 'scientific genius', because genius is present in every age. The items in the list are those that are not present in every age. Scientific progress occurs in some places, and some ages, but not in others, because the factors that enable scientific genius to manifest itself and to achieve particular kinds of results are present. Archimedes, the great mathematician and engineer of second-century BC Sicily, and Zhang Heng, the second-century Chinese astronomer, painter and poet, were both unquestionably geniuses. But they and their contemporaries could not have created a scientific revolution, because they were living in the wrong places, at the wrong time. The people who created the Scientific Revolution of the sixteenth and seventeenth centuries had the good fortune to be living in the right places, at the right time.

Just to drive the point home, let us consider the context in which Newton formulated his theory of universal gravitation. He belonged to one of the most privileged groups in Europe. He was a professor in a well-endowed college in a prestigious university, where he had had the opportunity to mix with some of the best minds of his generation. He had little teaching to do, plenty of time to think and access to the accumulated wisdom contained in a fine library of printed books. He had the good fortune to be living in an age that was heir to the recent work of Copernicus, Galileo and Kepler. He lived in a rich Protestant country, in which – thanks to the religious revolution wrought by people like Martin Luther in the previous century – he was free of the censorship of an overbearing Church. He was a member of the Royal Society, a gentlemen's club in which he could pick the brains of some of the finest scientists in Europe, both face to face and by correspondence. That Society was protected by a king, Charles II, whose father had lost his head as a result of civil strife, and who was determined to maintain a climate of toleration in which he would keep his own head. One certainly can't say that Newton lived at a bad time for making scientific discoveries.

There was another group of people who similarly had the good luck to be living in the right places at the right time. These were the artistic and literary geniuses whose work adorned the period of European history we know as the Renaissance (meaning 'rebirth'). The Renaissance was an explosion of magnificence in all the arts, but especially in literature, painting, architecture and sculpture. It partly predated, and partly overlapped, the Scientific Revolution. It had its immediate origins in two developments: the rediscovery of Greek and Roman art and literature and the maturation of a group of new languages (notably Italian, Spanish, French and English). But the fuel that powered it was the same that drove the revolution in science: the wealth generated by trade, the possibilities opened up by new technology and the excitement arising from the discovery of new lands and previously unknown works of the past. It is no coincidence that the power-house of this stupendous outpouring of artistic achievement was Florence, the richest city in Europe, and one presided over by cultured rulers who valued the work of artists both for its own sake and for the prestige derived from its display.

Looking back on the Renaissance, many later artists must have echoed the words of the English poet William Wordsworth, who said, in a different context:

> Bliss was it in that dawn to be alive,
> But to be young, was very Heaven!

For the artists living at this time, and for their patrons, this really must have felt like the dawn of a new age. So much was being attempted for the first time, or for the first time in many centuries.

As in the case of the scientists, this outpouring was the product of the special circumstances of the time, which gave genius a unique opportunity. The sort of masterpieces that were being created at this time included:

The Netherlands
1434: van Eyck's painting *The Arnolfini Marriage*

Italy
c. 1320: Dante's epic poem *The Divine Comedy*
1504: Michelangelo's sculpture *David*

England
1601: Shakespeare's comedy *Twelfth Night*

Spain
1605: Cervantes's romance *Don Quixote*

What characterizes so many of these and other great works of art produced at this time is that they are trail-blazing explorations of new forms, new materials or recently evolved languages, and yet they are at the same time mature masterpieces. Van Eyck's exquisite painting is exploiting a brand-new medium – oil paint – to serve a new kind of secular domestic market. Dante is reaching back to biblical themes, but handling them in a new language that he himself is helping to create. Shakespeare, too, is luxuriating in a new language that he is helping to create. His play is written for the entertainment of a royal patron, but it is performed by actors whose skills have been honed in the first public theatres since Roman times. Michelangelo is, like Dante, supposedly telling a biblical story, but he is really inviting comparison with the greatest of Greek sculptors. Cervantes is inventing a new form – the novel – to fill the leisure hours of readers made rich by American silver.

Just as certain factors were the precondition for the Scientific Revolution, so these creative geniuses benefited from:

1 the urban context in which their art was developed

2 the food surpluses that made that urban context possible

3 the new opportunities and technologies they were exploiting

4 the accumulated wealth with which their patrons supported them.

Which is to say, that no man (or woman) is an island, and that great works of art, like great works of science, owe at least as much to their social context as they do to their creators.

2 4

EMPIRES OF EAST
AND SOUTH ASIA

The period between 1455 and 1763, which witnessed the end of the isolation of Europe from the Americas, also saw the end of the isolation of Europe from the life of South and East Asia.

Before the fifteenth century, contact between Europe and the more distant parts of Asia was almost entirely through intermediaries, along either the vast distances of the Silk Road or the sea lanes of the Persian Gulf and the Red Sea. From the late sixteenth century, the establishment of new sea routes across the Indian Ocean initiated an era of trade and conquest that had as profound an impact as the opening up of the routes across the Atlantic.

It was again Portuguese ships that led the way. Portuguese sailors had been exploring the waters off the west coast of Africa from the beginning of the fifteenth century. Finding those coasts bare, and knowing nothing of the rich kingdoms of the interior, they had supposed that that they were skirting the fringes of a barren and empty continent. In late 1497, one of their number, Vasco da Gama, a sea captain from a minor aristocratic family, rounded the Cape of Good Hope. In 1498 he explored the coast as far as the port of Malindi (in modern Kenya), where the local sultan made available the services of a pilot, who took him to Calicut (modern Kozhikode) in southern India. It was the beginning of a century of Portuguese monopoly of the sea-borne trade between Europe and South and South-east Asia.

During this period the Islamic Mughal empire established its dominance over a large part of the Indian subcontinent. The empire was initiated by the conquests of a Muslim Turk named Babur, a grandson of Tamerlane on his father's side and a descendant of the great Genghis Khan himself on his mother's. His childhood was spent in the rich and cultured city of Samarkand, in Central Asia. He became king of Fhargana (in present-day Turkmenistan) at the age of eleven, but lost his kingdom and suffered twenty years of wandering and hardship, during which he acquired skills of generalship in a long series of battles. His ancestry made him ambitious to repeat his fore-bears' exploits, but, unable to fulfil this ambition in Central Asia, he turned his attention to India. In 1526, from a base in Afghanistan, he conquered first the Punjab and then the Delhi Sultanate. By 1529 he was the master of an empire that extended from Afghanistan all the way to the frontier of Bengal.

Babur was followed by a glittering succession of rulers who expanded the empire further. Outstanding among these was Akbar the Great, who ruled from 1556 to 1605. During his reign, and the reigns of those who came after him, the empire was enlarged to include Bengal, Kashmir, Gujarat and the Deccan.

Although the Mughal empire was officially a Muslim state, its rulers did not administer their realm on strict Islamic lines. This was particularly the case with Akbar, who established the principle of equal recognition of all religions – and showed his sincerity by marrying a Hindu princess. His enlightened rule initiated a period of tolerance and prosperity, and created a new sense of unity. This toleration contained a hard core of realism in an empire where 70 per cent of the people were Hindus, another 10 per cent were Buddhists or subscribers to other faiths and only 20 per cent were followers of Islam.

In 1608, an English ambassador named William Hawkins journeyed to the capital Agra to present his credentials at the glittering court of Akbar's son, Jahangir. His purpose was to solicit trading rights for the recently formed 'Company of Merchants of London Trading into the East Indies', the body known to history as the English East India Company. The company had been created with the objective of exploiting the spice trade with the East Indies (present-day Indonesia). Financed by the subscriptions of a group of wealthy London merchants, it had been incorporated by Royal Charter in 1600, with the enthusiastic support of Elizabeth I, who had in mind the mouth-watering possibilities of customs duties levied on the company's imports. European trade with India at this time was largely monopolized by the Portuguese, and although Jahangir took a fancy to Hawkins, and even found him a wife, nothing commercial came of the visit. However, after an English naval victory over Portugal in 1612, another ambassador, the courteous, diplomatic and patient (it took him three years) Sir Thomas Roe, was able to obtain rights for the company to trade out of a number of south Indian ports. This apparently modest achievement would, in the long term, turn out to be one of the most momentous developments in both British and Indian history.

The Mughal emperors depended for the biggest portion of their revenues on the taxes paid by India's farmers, who eventually numbered 150 million. They did not overburden them unduly, and for nearly a century and a half their dominions continued to prosper. Peace and prosperity permitted the flowering of one of the world's great periods of artistic achievement, whose riches include the exquisite miniature paintings that have become the hallmark of the Mughal period. Its greatest treasure is the beautiful monument known as the Taj Mahal. This was raised by Shah Jehan to the memory of his wife, Mumtaz Mahal, who died in childbirth in 1631, after nineteen years of marriage during which they had been inseparable companions. Beautiful and moving as it is, it is also a memorial to a man whose outlook on life, and attitude to his subjects, resembled that of an Egyptian pharaoh. The Peacock Throne from which he ruled his empire sparkled with 10 million rupees' worth of jewels.

The nature of the Mughal empire gradually changed during the seventeenth century and its hold over its subject peoples began to weaken. Under Emperor Aurangzeb (1658–1707) it reached its greatest extent, stretching 1500 miles from Afghanistan in the north to Mysore in the south, and 1500 miles from the Indus in the west to beyond the Ganges. But the religious toleration of Akbar's reign was now a distant memory. Aurangzeb embarked upon a persecution of Hindus. Since they were by far the greatest segment of his subjects, it is hardly surprising that he was rewarded with rebellion. He also weakened his realm further by a series of expensive military campaigns.

As the empire began to fracture, a group of wily operators stood ready to pick up the pieces. Decade after decade, the English East India Company had been skilfully accumulating concessions and alliances. It had also been accumulating arms. While still in theory a purely commercial undertaking, it had gradually acquired the character of a state within a state. After a Persian emperor attacked Delhi in 1739 and carried off the Peacock Throne to his own palace, there was no effective central power left. And in its absence, there was nothing to prevent the 'Company of Merchants in London' – and its private army – from gradually acquiring control over an entire subcontinent, one containing twice as many people, and twice as much wealth, as the whole of Europe.

The other great sixteenth-century empire of Asia – the Ming dynasty of China – had begun to decline even earlier than the Mughal empire. This decline was hastened by external attacks that greatly disturbed the peace of what had been a secure and prosperous empire. The first took the form of a series of invasions by forces led by a descendant of Genghis Khan named Altan. His people pastured their flocks and herds in a part of Inner Mongolia, to the north of Shansi province, and several times during the first half of the sixteenth century they descended into Shansi and Hopei to pillage those provinces in the time-honoured Mongol fashion. On one occasion they got as far as the gates of Beijing, where the citizens had the dubious pleasure of having their streets illuminated by their campfires. While the authorities were still worrying about how to defend themselves from these incursions, a new enemy appeared off the country's coasts: the Japanese.

Japan in the mid-sixteenth century was just emerging from a hundred-year period of civil war. As these internal disturbances came to an end, the warlike energy they had generated was turned against the outside world. At first it took the form of locally organized acts of piracy against the Chinese mainland, and armed brigands began to infest the coasts of Chekiang, Fukien and Canton. But then one of the most famous Japanese soldiers and statesmen, Hideyoshi, conceived the idea of conquering China. This may now appear foolhardy, but often a foreign invader has succeeded in gaining control of that vast country when a declining dynasty seemed to be losing the Mandate of Heaven, so perhaps it was not a hopeless quest. Whatever the inspiration, the plan was to attack China from the territory of Japan's traditional enemy, Korea. A 200,000-strong Japanese army was assembled, and on 12 June 1592 its advance troops entered the Korean capital, Seoul. What happened next sounds eerily like a later invasion, in the 1950s. Having reached Pyongyang, the Japanese forces were poised to cross the Yalu River. But the fierce defence put up by the Koreans had given the Chinese time to organize their forces, and the invaders were driven back. The Japanese had another go four years later, with even less success. It would be 300 years before they would again attempt the conquest of their giant neighbour.

The defeat of this upstart neighbour from the south bought the Ming only a short breathing space. Within thirty years, another enemy appeared in the north, and within fifty, that threat proved fatal. The invaders on this occasion were the Manchus, a race of forest dwellers who lived on China's northern frontier, in Northern Manchuria. In 1622, under a forceful leader, Nurhaci, they succeeded in capturing the whole of Southern Manchuria, but were stopped at the Great Wall.

Five years later, Nurhaci died, and was succeeded by his son Abahai. He was one of those leaders of genius in the Kublai Khan mould, who appeared from time to time on China's borders, combining the passion and endurance of the tough-living barbarian with an appreciation of the achievements of civilization. He had dedicated himself to the task of becoming emperor of China. In 1630 his forces reached the gates of Beijing, but were not equipped for a prolonged siege. Returning to his capital, Mukden, where he had many Chinese advisers, Abahai had himself proclaimed emperor.

Events now conspired to make it unnecessary for the Manchus to lift a finger to achieve their objective. In time-honoured Chinese fashion, the waning of a dynasty brought forth uprisings. In April 1644, while the imperial army was guarding the frontier against the Manchus, a rebel force attacked Beijing, where sympathizers opened the gates to them. To escape their clutches, the emperor hanged himself with his sash. When the commander of the imperial army heard what had happened, he marched on the city. Finding himself out-numbered, he solicited the help of the leader of the Manchu army. The Manchus obliged, but when the rebellion had been put down, they declared Abahai's seven-year-old son emperor. (His father had died a few months earlier.) Since they were installed in the imperial capital with an army 100,000 strong, there was not much anyone could do about it. They slotted Manchu officials into senior positions alongside existing offi-cials, and, after a few years of mopping-up operations in distant provinces, the empire continued in its usual manner. With an infusion of new blood at the top, and a successful conquest, it could reasonably be claimed that the Mandate of Heaven had been renewed. Thus began the Manchu, or Ch'ing, dynasty that would rule China for the next two and a half centuries.

While first the Japanese, and then the Manchu, had been testing the Ming empire to destruction, a new power had been quietly establishing a presence on China's western and northern frontiers. Early in the sixteenth century, Russian fur traders had begun to explore the lands to the east of the Ural Mountains. In 1582, a powerful industrial family in north-eastern Russia, the Stroganovs, had sent a 1600-strong party of Cossack horsemen into these eastern territories to subdue the troublesome local tribes. Despite their small numbers, they had achieved impressive victories over both the native population and their Mongol overlords. These successes encouraged the Tsar, Ivan IV (Ivan the Terrible), to adopt their adventure as his own, and Siberia was formally annexed to Russia. Making use of the great rivers, the Ob, the Yenisei and the Lena, fur traders had travelled further and further to the east, until by 1638 they had reached the shores of the Pacific. Fur was to Russians what gold had been to the Spanish, and these traders behaved with the same rapaciousness and ruthlessness as the sixteenth-century conquistadores. As gold and silver had flooded into Seville, so furs began to pour into Moscow.

Defeated in their attempt to conquer China, the attention of the Japanese was now concentrated on their own islands. These were mountainous, to an exceptional degree. Unlike, for example, the Inca, the Japanese did not develop a system of agriculture that responded to the mountainous character of their environment. Instead they concentrated on the potential of their extensive coastline, and the limited amount of flat land the country contained. During the seventeenth and early eighteenth centuries they developed a fishing industry of enormous productivity and an agricultural system based on a new variety of rice that delivered exceptional yields. With the aid of these new food sources, the population entered a period of explosive growth. The Japanese preference for living on flat land near the coast ensured that most of this increase was funnelled into the fast-growing towns. Japan had embarked upon the path that would turn it into a nation of city dwellers – one of the world's first.

As the population increased, Japan's rulers moved to isolate the country from foreign influence. Portuguese traders had reached Japan as early as 1542, and they had been followed seven years later by Jesuit missionaries. Within fifty years they had made 150,000 Christian converts. Dismayed by this perceived threat to the Japanese way of life, the authorities had banned Christianity in 1587, and put many Christians to death. In 1603 the shogun Tokugawa Ieyasu introduced rules forbidding native Japanese to leave the country. Foreign merchants were also banned, saving only the Chinese – and the Dutch, who were regarded as trustworthy because they did not attempt to make converts. But even the Dutch were not allowed onshore; their business had to be transacted on an island in Nagasaki Bay to which they were confined. For the Japanese, it was the beginning of a period of national isolation that would last for over 200 years.

25

THE WORLD IN 1763

The three centuries following the printing of Gutenberg's Great Bible had been a period of increased prosperity in many parts of the world. The total human population had doubled, from around 400 million to nearly 800 million, in spite of the huge reduction in numbers in the Americas. Half of this 800 million lived in India and China and they accounted for more than half of the world's wealth and income. India's population, having experienced a rapid expansion, had settled down at around 180 million. Of these, 35 million lived in the province of Bengal, whose stupendous wealth was now at Britain's command, following Robert Clive's victory over a Mughal army at Plassey in 1756. It is a stunning reflection that the population of Britain itself at this time was only about 8 million. Britain's Indian empire had originated less than a hundred years earlier, when King Charles II, desperate for money, had leased Bombay to the East India Company, after acquiring it as part of his wife's dowry. The company had built a fort there, and had succeeded by a combination of trade, chicanery and force in obtaining control of a large part of the subcontinent.

China's population, after suffering serious setbacks from the combined effects of famine and Mongol invasion, had once again overtaken India's. It now exceeded 200 million, and was rising fast. Some of this was attributable to the conquest of new territories, including Tibet and Chinese Turkestan. With these additions, the Chinese empire had reached its greatest ever extent. But for once this increase in population had not been accompanied by a fall in living standards. Peasants in China, like peasants everywhere in the eighteenth century, had a miserable standard of living. But it seems pretty certain that in 1763, average living standards were higher in China than they were in Europe, and a great deal higher than those in most of the rest of the world.

The wealth of China at this date came largely from its role as the hub of a vast network of trade from the Philippines to the coast of Africa. China itself continued to export huge quantities of its traditional specialities, porcelain and silk, and remained the world's most important customer for the spices that the countries of South-east Asia exported. Slaves and gold were exported from the busy ports of East Africa, and India exported huge quantities of cotton textiles. Spanish ships crossed the Pacific, bringing the Peruvian silver that Chinese merchants needed to pay their taxes, while ships of other European nations provided most of the transport in the Indian Ocean. The centre of gravity of world trade would eventually shift to the Atlantic, but in 1763, it was the seas leading to and from China that saw most of the action.

A century and a half earlier, much of this trade would have been in Japanese hands, but after Japanese merchants were forbidden to trade overseas in 1603, that country had ceased to have any significant trading relations with the outside world. Despite this, the Japanese economy had prospered mightily, and the country's population was now around 25 million. This prosperity flowed from the country's merchant classes, who were less subject to government interference than their counterparts in China. It was reflected in the growth of towns, which now held something like 15 per cent of the population – a percentage matched by hardly any other country in the world.

Unaffected by, and totally ignorant of, this hubbub of trade on the oceans to the north and west of them, the peoples of Australia continued in their traditional ways of life. Their number probably amounted to something like 500,000, although estimates vary widely on either side of this figure. In the more densely populated spots around the coasts, there were on average about five people to the square mile, but in the interior there were large areas where the average density was more like five people for every 100 square miles. Separated by long distances into a multitude of tribal groups, they had developed a wide variety of languages. Depending on how one defines a language, the total was somewhere between 1000 and 2000. Their ancestors had had this land to themselves for the best part of 60,000 years. A few who lived near the northern and western coasts had tales to tell of strangers who had arrived in boats, lingered for a while and sailed away again, leaving them undisturbed. But they would not stay undisturbed for much longer. In just fifteen years' time, a party of strangers would arrive and not go away – and those quiet lives would be turned upside-down.

The doubling of the world's population between 1456 and 1763 reflected a resumption of the pre-1250 rate of growth in Eurasia that had been interrupted by a cooling climate, by plague and by nomad assault. With a better climate, less plague and an end to the Mongol threat, the settled peoples of Europe and Asia had been able to exploit their improved technology to increase food production, and to extend the scale and the range of their trade with one another.

Although the web of trade had grown, it still moved at much the same speed as it had 2000 years earlier. The fastest transport on land was still horse-drawn; the fastest transport on water was still powered by the wind. Nowhere were there any roads better than the Romans had made, and in many places the roads were worse than they had been in Roman times. The year 1456 had been close to the low point of inland communication, and the high point of coastal cities and populations. Improvement had since been made, but in 1763 access to navigable water was still an overwhelming factor in the location of towns and industry. European sailors routinely traversed the oceans of the world. But if the Governors of the English or Dutch East India Company sent an urgent message to their agents in Calcutta or Batavia, they did so in the knowledge that it would be twelve months before they could receive a reply.

At the heart of the Eurasian super-continent, a new Great Power – Russia – had appeared upon the scene. This hitherto land-locked collection of peoples that had barely qualified as a nation in 1456 was now a force to be reckoned with. Under the leadership of two strong and ambitious rulers – Peter the Great and his daughter Elizabeth – the country had been opened up to European ideas and European technology. Peter had found himself in 1682 the ruler of a country that had at last recovered from the effects of the Mongol invasions of the fifteenth century, but was in many respects 200 years behind its European rivals. For the next forty-three years, he devoted himself to the strengthening and modernization of his backward domains. Having travelled extensively in western Europe to see what other nations were capable of, he had moved his capital from Moscow to St Petersburg, compelling a substantial portion of the nobility and the merchant class to move with him. He had introduced western technology, and completely overhauled the Russian government and military system. At the same time he had greatly increased his country's security by successful campaigns against Sweden, Persia and the Ottoman Turks, gaining access to the Baltic and control over the western shores of the Caspian Sea. In 1724, the year before he died, he had inaugurated the Imperial Academy of Sciences in St Petersburg.

Towards the end of Peter's reign, in 1721, Russia was declared an empire. This was done with the conscious intention of invoking the image of the Roman empire, at a time when Europe was enjoying a love affair with all things Roman. But the empire that Peter ruled over was a rag-bag collection of subject peoples that bore little resemblance to the integrated and efficiently run empire of the Caesars. For one thing, it was essentially rural. Even as late as the 1760s, town dwellers made up only 3 per cent of the population. Unlike western European nations, it had only a thin layer of middle-class enterprise and energy, sandwiched between its preening nobility and the poverty-stricken peasantry that made up 90 per cent of its population. It had nothing resembling the trained administrators of Rome, let alone contemporary China. In 1763, St Petersburg was in the middle of a massive building programme, in the course of which the breathtaking vistas that now make it one of Europe's most glittering cities were created. But away from the capital, Russia remained a poor and backward country. To hold this ramshackle empire together, its rulers employed the vicious and all-pervading apparatus of a police state. Russia had come a long way, but was still weak, and there was no knowing how much resilience it would be able to display, if it should be tested by a determined outside force.

Divided into a multitude of nation-states, the peoples of Europe had got into the habit of fighting wars. These were typically fought between groups of nations in temporary alliance, with the aid of mercenary soldiers recruited from third parties. As the balance of power changed, so did the alliances. The names of the wars – the Thirty Years War, the Seven Years War – tell their own story. Armies moved back and forth across the continent, doing increasing damage with their constantly improving weapons, destroying harvests and leaving devastation in their wake. But in spite of the deaths that these wars caused, such was the efficiency of Europe's improved agriculture, and so rich the harvest of trade from its expanding overseas empires, that the population continued to grow. The total population of the continent, excluding Russia, had doubled since 1456. It was now around 110 million, and rising fast.

The cities of western Europe were not only large and numerous, they were expanding. The two biggest were Paris and London, which had recently caught up with Paris. At around 700,000, London's population was fractionally the larger, but it was growing fast, and during the coming decades it would leave its French rival far behind.

The growth of London's population was the consequence, not of an increase in births, but of a reduction in the number of deaths. A turning-point had been reached in 1751, with the imposition of sharply increased taxes on liquor, and restrictions on its sale. Before that date, London's notorious gin cellars, with their boast of 'Drunk for a penny. Dead drunk for two pence', had played a leading part in shortening the lives of its poorer citizens, for whom drink was a temporary escape from an often unbearable existence. After strong liquor was priced out of their reach, and beer, then tea, became the everyday drink, the death-rate came tumbling down. But the condition of many of the survivors remained pitiable, in a society characterized by extremes of poverty and wealth.

The most populous, and the wealthiest, country in western Europe was still France. It was also the leading military power, despite having lost a worldwide seven-year war with Britain, which had a population of less than 10 million, compared with France's 20 million. Britain had a superior navy and could control the seas, and was also able to organize, and subsidize, alliances on the mainland of Europe. The decisive battles in North America and India, although fought on land, were really won on the sea, thanks to the control that the British navy was able to exercise over France's supply lines.

In North America, the British colonial settlements were still essentially confined to the eastern seaboard: none of them extended more than 300 miles inland. Across those 300 miles, a pattern had become established. As wealthier settlers had taken over nearest the coast, the poorer, and the more recently arrived, had been forced inland. As the years passed, two different lifestyles had come to characterize the two regions. In the eastern cities, fashion-conscious ladies and gentlemen practised metropolitan manners in European-style houses. In the frontier regions, plain living, plain speaking folk lived in log cabins built with their own hands; fought with nature to gain a living from the soil; and, from time to time, fought with the remaining native Americans to assert their right to stay there. It was the beginning of a division between frontiersmen and women on the one hand and city slickers on the other that would become more marked as the frontier moved further west.

To the south, in British, French and Portuguese colonies, plantation owners were growing rich, using armies of imported,

25.1 The Eighteenth-Century 'Triangular Atlantic Trade'

Manufactured goods were shipped to West Africa, especially from Liverpool and Bristol. Slaves were shipped to the plantations of the West Indies and the southern states of North America. Charlestown was by far the most important port of transhipment. The triangle was completed by the shipment of sugar, cotton and tobacco to England.

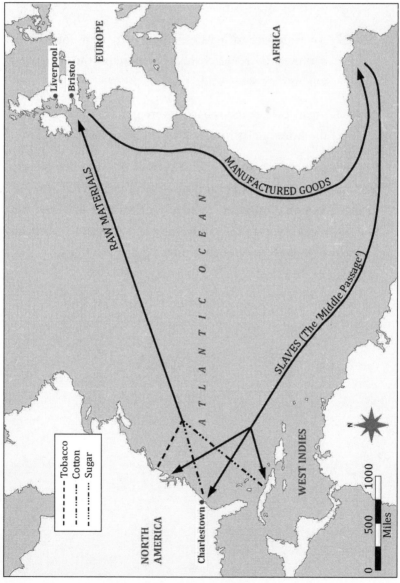

short-lived slaves to grow crops of tobacco, sugar and cotton
for export to Europe. Their economies were tied in to what
became known as the 'triangular trade':

Side 1: ships sailed from ports such as Liverpool and Bristol,
carrying manufactured goods to be sold in the slave
ports of West Africa.

Side 2: slaves purchased in West Africa were transported – in
darkness, filth and chains – to ports in the Americas,
where they were sold.

Side 3: sugar, cotton and tobacco were purchased for resale in
the home ports from which the ships had set out.

Its neatness was one of the marvels of the age. The hell on
earth it created did not perturb those who managed it. And its
reality was something from which the fragrant ladies, and the
not-so-fragrant gentlemen, in Europe and America who lived
on its proceeds were carefully protected.

2 6
THE AGE OF REVOLUTION

One of the key events in the struggle between Britain and France for control of Canada had been the capture by the British of the city of Quebec in 1759. In this engagement, a thirty-year-old British naval officer named James Cook marked himself out as a commander and surveyor of exceptional promise. When the question later arose as to who should lead a scientific expedition to the Pacific, Cook's record recommended him, despite his junior rank.

The official task of the expedition was to conduct observations of a transit of the planet Venus across the face of the Sun. This was expected in June 1769, and would not occur again until 1874. The observation would enable a precise calculation to be made of the distance of the Earth from the Sun, and the location was the recently discovered island of Tahiti, with its exceptionally clear skies. To enable him to carry out this assignment, Cook was given a four-year-old coal boat, appropriately renamed *Endeavour*. In the event, the day of the transit was cloudy, and the observations turned out to be largely useless. But the expedition achieved other, unexpected results that more than compensated for this disappointment.

Having completed his measurements, Cook opened his sealed instructions, to discover that he was charged with the task of making a search for the 'great southern continent' it was thought must lie in regions close to the South Pole. Instead of taking the easy way eastward across the southern Pacific, riding on prevailing westerly winds, he headed west, and on 9 October 1769 he and his companions landed on what we know as the north island of New Zealand. After spending six months charting the coastline of both islands, they continued west, and on 19 April 1770 bumped into the east coast of Australia. They were not the first Europeans to set foot on the continent. Others had landed, or been shipwrecked on, various stretches of the south, west and north coasts, without realizing that these were not simply isolated islands. What Cook discovered was a lengthy, continuous coastline that offered superb harbours and attractive locations for future settlement. After charting 2000 miles of it, he sailed home via the Indies and the Cape of Good Hope.

Cook was rewarded with the command of two subsequent expeditions, during the first of which he circumnavigated the entire Antarctic continent, meeting ice all the way, but without actually finding land. On his third voyage, he sailed north, as far as the entrance to the Bering Strait, before sailing once more to Tahiti, which he reached in 1779. There, as a result of an unfortunate and quite untypical misunderstanding with the natives, he met his death.

Cook's explorations, the most extensive made by any mariner in history, would later yield the British crown a huge addition to its overseas empire. But while he was still just a highly regarded ship's master engaged in surveying Canadian waters, a chain of circumstances had been set in motion that would lose Britain the largest tract of territory it possessed.

The British colonies in North America were 3000 miles from London. To send a message from one side of the ocean to the other, and receive a reply, took at least four months.

This alone led to problems of communication between Britain and its North American colonies. But the feelings of alienation were intensified by the fact that the day-to-day administration of the colonies was in most cases in the hands of officials who were American-born, whereas the orders they were expected to carry out were formulated in Europe. There was also a real difference in the character of the two societies that became more marked as the years went by. There were rich and poor in America, as there were in Britain. But in America there was no hereditary aristocracy, and no bishops to support its pretensions. Even the poor had the hope that by hard work they could improve their situation. It was essentially a more middle-class society. Between 1764 and 1775, the insensitivity of the government in London and the touchiness of its independent-minded subjects in America combined to create an explosion of resentment that finally blew the relationship apart.

The immediate causes of the falling-out were two in number: the home government's attempt to impose new taxes, and a fresh prohibition on settlement further west. This latter caused particular outrage, as the belief grew that the government was planning to sell some of the newly acquired territories to pay off debts incurred in the war against France.

In this heated atmosphere, the words 'America' and 'American' began to acquire new meanings. At an emergency congress of nine colonies called in 1765 to protest against the new Stamp Act, the representative of South Carolina, Christopher Gadsden, said that 'there ought to be no New England man; no New Yorker, known on the Continent: but all of us Americans.' Over the next ten years, the word 'American', which had till then been little more than a geographical label, acquired two new shades of meaning: a mark of distinction, separating it from 'British', and a badge of membership, bringing the thirteen colonies together in a shared identity.

To politicians in London it seemed reasonable that, as the war had been partly fought to protect the colonies, the colonies should bear some of the cost. To this the colonists replied with one of the most effective slogans ever devised: 'no taxation without representation'. That is to say, since the colonies could not elect members to the British Parliament, they should not have to suffer taxes they had had no say in devising. Protests against the new taxes led to demonstrations. When these were met with brutality, resistance intensified. Even so, at this stage there was no widespread desire for a complete break. But continued British insensitivity led to a rapid growth of separatist propaganda.

In 1773, the British Parliament passed a Tea Act, prohibiting anyone but the British East India Company from importing tea into the colonies. On the night of 16 December, a group of patriots, disguised as Mohawk Indians, threw 342 chests of tea belonging to the Company into the harbour in Boston, Massachusetts. When the governor reacted with violence, the other colonies rallied to the province's cause. A new Continental Congress authorized the formation of an army to resist British oppression, under the command of a 43-year-old Virginia plantation owner named George Washington. He was well qualified for the task, having fought under the British colours against the French.

In August 1775, Britain declared the American colonies to be in a state of rebellion. On 4 July 1776, the colonies replied with a declaration of their own. By twelve votes to none, with New York abstaining, they approved what has come to be seen as one of the most momentous resolutions ever agreed upon by any assembly anywhere: the Declaration of Independence.

The colonists had the support of the French, who were hoping to make a comeback in North America, and of the Spanish and the Dutch, who were able to prevent the British from establishing control of the seas. But even so, the war lasted for eight years, and the rebel forces at one point came close to total defeat. But they – and the French – triumphed in the end, and in 1783, in another treaty signed in Paris, Britain finally recognized the independence of its thirteen former colonies. Four years later, in 1787, their representatives convened in Philadelphia to approve a constitution, under the chairmanship of their victorious commander. In the summer of 1788, after the assemblies of nine states had ratified it, it came into force, and the United States of America formally came into existence. As it happened, the votes in the tenth and eleventh states to ratify, Virginia and New York, were desperately close. Had those votes gone the other way, the Union would still have come into existence, but it would have done so in a very weakened form. In April 1789, the now 57-year-old Washington took the oath of office, and became the new republic's first president.

Ironically, the loss of this major portion of its North American possessions was the direct cause of Britain's acquiring a substantial colony on the other side of the world. The revolution in agriculture had led to increased population, and at the same time to reduced demand for workers on the land, creating an army of desperate unemployed people. Conditions in the towns, and the death rates there, were appalling, but the influx of people was such that numbers continued to rise. A rootless underclass generated an increase in crime, especially theft, which the English judicial system was ill equipped to deal with. Imprisonment was scarcely available as a punishment: there were very few lock-ups and almost no prisons as we understand the term. By the mid-eighteenth century a long list of offences had become punishable by hanging, including what we would now regard as very minor crimes, such as stealing a handkerchief. Juries were understandably reluctant to find defendants guilty. In an attempt to restore an element of deterrence to the system – and, it should be said, out of compassion on the part of many reformers – a new punishment of 'transportation to places beyond the seas' had been introduced as an alternative to hanging. For many years, the 'place beyond the seas' had been the American colonies. With their loss, Britain also lost a destination for future transportees. As the judges continued to sentence people to transportation, a log-jam built up, which was dealt with by accommodating the condemned on 'hulks': old warships, anchored in the Thames estuary and in harbours elsewhere. But as the hulks filled up, a desperate search began to find another solution.

The first location considered was the West Coast of Africa, but considerations of health, and unfriendly natives, made this impracticable. Then a bright civil servant remembered Cook's glowing description of the superb harbours and beautiful landscape around the area in south-east Australia he had christened Botany Bay. This not only sounded like a suitable place for convict settlement, it also held out the possibility of establishing a support base for naval operations in South and South-east Asia.

A list of transportees was drawn up, and in 1787 a flotilla was assembled: eleven ships that would for ever be known to Australians as the First Fleet. On board were 262 convicts: 140 men and youths, and 122 women and girls; mostly aged between 16 and 35. They left England on 13 May 1787. Eight months later, on 19 January 1788, they reached Botany Bay. But they did not stay there. The commander, Captain Arthur Phillip, decided that the area was too arid, and established his settlement further along the coast at a spot called Port Jackson. It looked out on to one of the most magnificent natural harbours on earth, the one we know as Sydney harbour.

The place where the new settlement was established already had a resident population, albeit not a settled one. Its first discoverers had found it 20,000 years earlier, and their descendants had been living there ever since. When Phillip later reconnoitred the surrounding area he estimated the local population at around 1500, but they were split into small tribal groups, and in any case they did not have guns. Provided that the next fleet was not too long in arriving, the future of his little township looked reasonably secure.

In the Europe these pioneers had left behind, events were moving towards one of the most dramatic upheavals in the continent's history. The seven-year war with England had left Louis XVI of France with debts he could not service, and without the means to continue the way of life to which he and his court had grown accustomed. In desperation, the king summoned the Estates-General, the nearest thing that France had to a parliament, representing the aristocracy, the clergy and well-to-do commoners. No Estates-General had been convened for 175 years, a fact that summed up the arrogance with which France had traditionally been governed. Governed, that is to say, from the king's 1000-room palace at Versailles, 20 miles from Paris, where Louis, his queen Marie Antoinette and his courtiers lived in luxurious idleness, with the help of 4000 servants.

Louis assumed that the Estates-General would agree upon new taxes, which could then be levied with its authority. In earlier times such a proceeding would have been considered beneath the king's dignity. It was an indication of the seriousness of the situation that it was now considered essential, with the country in a state of near-revolution, after a series of crop failures, and under the burden of crippling taxes from which nobles and clergymen were exempt.

The traditional arrangement in the Estates-General was that the sectional votes of the three groups – nobility, clergy and Third Estate (lawyers, doctors, lesser landlords, etc.) – were treated equally. But on this occasion the members of the Third Estate refused to be counted as a mere third, and instead formed themselves into a National Assembly, inviting the nobles and the clergy to join them. When Louis forbade them to meet in their usual place, they adjourned to an outdoor tennis court, and took their famous Tennis Court Oath, that they would not disband until they had given the country a constitution. After the failure of the harvest in the autumn of 1788, the price of bread shot to impossible heights, and a near-starving populace cracked. On the 14 July 1789, a crowd stormed and set fire to Paris's notorious prison, the Bastille. This was followed by uprisings across the country. The response of the National Assembly was to abolish the tax exemptions of the nobles and the clergy, and to publish a Declaration of the Rights of Man, written in the same defiant tone as the American Declaration of Independence.

Events now began to unfold at whirlwind speed. In October 1789, hundreds of women marched the 20 miles to Versailles demanding bread, and almost succeeded in lynching the queen. The royal couple fled, but were caught, and ignominiously brought back to Paris. The National Assembly confiscated Church lands, abolished slavery in France's American colonies and introduced the promised constitution, giving all better-off taxpayers the vote. Eighteen months later, it tried and condemned the king, who was publicly decapitated by the newly invented guillotine.

The leaders of the new republic, confronted by opposition within France, and by the enmity of surrounding countries, whose rulers feared for their own necks, were driven to violent reaction. Between 1793 and 1794, a Committee of Public Safety instituted a reign of terror, during which 20,000 people followed the king to the guillotine. The appalling damage that this orgy of killing, and the atmosphere of terror that accompanied it, did to France's intellectual life and the country's incipient industrial revolution comes across clearly in the story of one man's fate.

One of the greatest names in the history of science is that of Antoine-Laurent Lavoisier, universally acknowledged as the father of modern chemistry. Lavoisier was the son of a lawyer, and was himself intended for the law. But after hearing a lecture by the astronomer Lacaille, he resolved to devote his life to science. In 1776, when he was only twenty-three, he was awarded the Gold Medal of the Academy of Sciences for an essay on the best way of lighting a small town. To provide himself with an income while he and his gifted wife were working at their researches, he invested his capital in the *Ferme Générale*, the system whereby individuals were awarded the right to collect taxes on behalf of the state, and to retain a significant portion as their remuneration. This was very profitable, and enabled him to build what was probably the best-equipped laboratory in the world. It became a meeting-place for France's leading scientists, as well as notable visitors such as Benjamin Franklin and Thomas Jefferson. To be living off tax revenues was bad enough, in the eyes of the Revolutionary Tribunal. But Lavoisier compounded his crime by making an enemy of an inferior, but later very influential would-be scientist named Jean-Paul Marat, who settled scores by denouncing him. On the morning of 8 May 1794, the 53-year-old Lavoisier was tried and condemned to death. When he asked for a couple of weeks' stay of execution to enable him to complete some experiments, the presiding judge replied, 'The revolution has no need of scientists.' One of his contemporaries, the astronomer Joseph-Louis Lagrange, commented, 'It took them only an instant to cut off that head, but France may not produce another like it in a century.'

In June 1794, revulsion in the National Assembly led to the return of some kind of sanity, and the terror ended. But the battle against the forces of reaction within, and enemies without, continued unabated.

Fired by a belief in the justice of their cause, French armies won victory after victory. But somewhere along the line, wars of self-defence became wars of liberation, which in turn became nothing more than old-fashioned wars of territorial expansion. These were directed by a young general named Napoleon Bonaparte. In 1799 he staged a *coup d'état*, effectively making him dictator of France. He then set about creating a European empire. Paradoxically, one of his first acts was to dispose of an overseas possession that enabled the fledgling United States of America to more than double the extent of its own territory. This was the Louisiana Purchase of 1803 (see Chapter 31).

In 1804 he abandoned all pretence of republican rule by declaring himself emperor, deliberately invoking memories of the not-yet-forgotten Holy Roman Empire. As a leader of armies he seemed invincible. There was only one enemy he could not touch. Safe on their island fortress, the British continued to orchestrate continental opposition to his ambitions, while their navy conducted a blockade of his ports. But on land, his forces swept all before them. He defeated Austria and Prussia, and conquered most of Italy and Spain. Had he remained content with what he already had, he could have consolidated an empire that embraced most of Europe, and one that might have lasted for some time. But in an eye-watering error of judgement, which would be repeated by Adolf Hitler 130 years later, he decided to invade Russia.

This backward empire must have seemed easy meat, but Napoleon underestimated the Russian bear's capacity for punishment. In the century preceding this trial of strength, the rulers of Russia had been engaged upon two huge tasks: the conquest and settlement of the regions beyond their borders and the modernization of the Russian economy. This twofold challenge had been taken up by Peter the Great, and it had been continued by another outstanding ruler, Catherine II (Catherine the Great), empress from 1762 to 1796.

Catherine, a German princess, had been married at sixteen to the then heir to the throne, Peter's grandson. Having secured the throne for herself when she was thirty-three, she had worked tirelessly throughout her 34-year reign to complete the programme that Peter had begun. A woman of great energy, intelligence and strength of purpose, she had the support in this task of a brilliant administrator, Prince Grigory Potemkin, who was for many years her lover, and who remained her ally long after they had both found consolation elsewhere. By the end of her reign, they had extended Russia's southern and western territories by a massive 200,000 square miles, adding 40 million to its population, and providing it with a defensive cordon without which the blow that now fell could not possibly have been withstood.

It was the new Russia created by these two extraordinary rulers, Peter and Catherine, that was tested in the fire of Napoleon's assault. At first his armies were unstoppable, and his campaign took him quickly to the gates of Moscow. But Moscow held. And while the siege of the city continued, the Russian winter took command. Unable to make further progress, and with his lines of supply dangerously over-extended, Napoleon led his frost-bitten and half-starved troops on a desperate retreat, harried by a vengeful Russian army, and suffering enormous losses on the way. It was the end of his dream of European domination.

The tearing apart of his 600,000-strong army opened the door to rebellious forces within the empire. It also changed the attitude of the few allies he possessed. First Germany rose against him, then Sweden. In 1814 he abdicated, and was exiled to the island of Elba. He escaped in 1815 and raised one last army, which was defeated by the combined forces of Britain and Prussia outside a village called Waterloo (in present-day Belgium) on 18 June 1815. This time, his enemies were taking no chances. He was transported to the island of St Helena, in the middle of the Atlantic, where he lived out his remaining years in well-attended, disappointed exile.

Although Napoleon's empire was short-lived, the changes he wrought in the legal, political and social structure of France would never be undone. He may have been tainted with megalomania, but his spirit was that of a democrat, albeit a despotic one. He swept away the antique, oppressive and arbi-trary structure of the French state, and replaced it with a legal code based on the principle of equality before the law. This code – the *Code Napoléon* – still provides the framework of civil life in France, and the many countries around the globe that have been touched by French civilization. He concluded an agreement with the pope that guaranteed the permanence of the separation between Church and State that has kept France a rigorously secular country ever since. The Church never recovered the lands that had been confiscated during the Revolution, nor the wealth that land represented. His redrawing of the map of France, based on the regional units known as *départements*, still forms the basis of the country's administration. And the reformed system of weights and measures he introduced – the metric system – is today the most widespread in the world.

After Napoleon's defeat, his enemies met in Vienna to redraw the map of Europe, and to recreate, as far as possible, the regimes that had governed the continent before the revolutionary wars had removed them. Among other restorations, another Louis – the eighteenth – was placed on the throne of France. But although the thrones had been refilled, the revolutionary spirit kindled in 1789 had not been quenched, and during the coming decades it would flare up repeatedly. Before the end of the century, representative government would be the norm over most of the continent, and France would take its place alongside the United States as the home, and joint originator, of republican government.

Although revolution had been defeated in France itself, the fire that France had lit now spread far and wide. Among the regimes it consumed were the European empires that had governed Latin America for the past 300 years. In a mere fifteen years, between 1810 and 1825, they were swept away.

The first colony to assert its independence was the jewel in the Portuguese crown, Brazil. The liberation of this, the largest of all the European colonies, was peaceful. Portugal and Britain had been allies for centuries, and Napoleon had invaded Portugal in 1807, specifically in order to injure British trade. When this happened, the Portuguese regent (later King John VI), transferred his court across the Atlantic to Rio de Janeiro. Once there, he introduced legislation that effectively made Brazil the constitutional equal of Portugal, and opened the country to the trade of all nations, to the benefit of the local economy. When he returned to Portugal in 1821, the Portuguese assembly, the *Cortes*, proceeded to enact legislation aimed at reversing many of the reforms he had instituted. This so incensed the Brazilians that they persuaded his son, Dom Pedro, who was acting as regent in his father's absence, to convoke a legislative assembly. On 7 September 1822 it proclaimed the country's independence. And that was it, without a shot having been fired.

The first Spanish colony to declare its independence – the nucleus of what is now Argentina – also did so without an uprising. In 1808, Napoleon forced the abdication of the king of Spain, and placed his own brother, Joseph, on the throne. The Creole element of the Buenos Aires Municipal Council – the merchant and landlord classes of the region known as the Viceroyalty of La Plata – responded by taking advantage of an old law to declare interim independence, pending the restoration of the deposed king. But when he was restored, it quickly became evident that he was one of the worst kings that Spain had ever had. So on 9 July 1816, an assembly representing most of the territory declared permanent independence, under the name of the United Provinces of La Plata.

The liberation movement that freed the remainder of Spain's South American colonies was a more violent affair. Its hero was a man whose gifts and achievement bear comparison with any freedom-fighter in any country in any age: a man who has gone down in history as *El Libertador* – the Liberator. His name was Simón Bolívar, and he was born in Caracas, in Venezuela, into a family of wealthy aristocrats. Educated in Europe, he came into contact with a number of radical thinkers, and in 1805, at the age of twenty-one, while standing on the Monte Sacro in Rome, he made a vow to liberate his country. In 1813, while living in New Granada (the future Bolivia) he published the *Cartagena Manifesto*, the first of several great political theses in which he called upon the people of Venezuela to cast off Spanish rule. As commander of an expeditionary force, he succeeded in occupying Caracas, but was defeated and forced to flee to Jamaica. It was there that he published his most famous political statement, *Letter from Jamaica*, in which he advocated a series of Latin American republics, with constitutions modelled on that of Britain. In 1819, in one of the most astounding feats in military history, he led a small army out of the Orinoco Basin, over supposedly impassable mountain terrain, to a memorable victory at the Battle of Boyacá on 7 August 1819. In May 1821, he repeated this triumph at the Battle of Carabobo, which freed his native city, and prepared the way for the independent future of three new republics: Colombia, Ecuador and Venezuela.

In 1824, Bolívar met another hero of Latin American liberation: José de San Martín. A former Spanish general, San Martín had also led an army across the Andes to liberate Chile. He had then entered Peru, and taken possession of Lima, but he did not have the resources to defeat the Spanish army in the north. Bolívar and San Martín did not hit it off. San Martin was an autocratic and stand-offish figure, who believed that every country needed a king and had already proclaimed himself emperor of Peru. Bolívar, by contrast, was a firm believer in republican and democratic principles, and this stand had won him the support of many Peruvians who resented San Martín's aristocratic airs. More importantly, it was clear that Bolívar wanted the glory of the final defeat of the Spanish empire for himself, and had no intention of sharing it with anyone. In the face of this difference in aims, and conscious of the dissatisfaction around him, San Martín withdrew from the scene, and ended his days in exile. On 9 December 1824, Bolívar won a last great battle at Ayacucho in Peru, which liberated that country and ended Spanish rule in South America. In 1825, Upper Peru took the name of Bolivia in honour of its liberator, and completed the roll-call of the new American republics.

The independent republic of Mexico had come into existence just two years earlier. The struggle there had been the most long-drawn-out of all. It had begun with a popular uprising in 1810, under the leadership of a poor but charismatic priest named Manuel Hidalgo y Costilla. His army had reached the gates of Mexico City, but the untrained force was easily defeated by government troops. An uprising in 1814 was similarly crushed. Resistance expressed itself in guerrilla warfare, without any decisive outcome until May 1821, when the representative of the Spanish government was forced to accede to the Treaty of Cordoba, under which New Spain, as the country was still called, was to become independent under its own locally chosen emperor. The country did not formally become a republic until two years later, but 24 May 1821 would always be celebrated as the republic's founding date.

The citizens of Paris, whose uprising had initiated this turmoil, had lost their own republic, and would not see another for a generation. But they had the consolation of knowing that, as a direct consequence of their actions, two once-great empires had disappeared from the map, and the people of a dozen new republics had won the right to manage their own affairs.

The governments of the restored monarchies in Europe would have liked to reimpose their rule over Latin America, and they started discussions as to how they might bring this about. Faced with opposition from Britain and the United States, they were forced to abandon the idea. Britain, the world's foremost naval power and trading nation, had no intention of letting these strategically important countries, with their mouth-watering commercial potential, fall back under Spanish and Portuguese control. The United States, which was now flexing its international muscles, felt the same way, and had no intention of letting them come under Spanish, Portuguese or British domination.

In December 1823 the president of the United States, James Monroe, enunciated what has come to be called the Monroe Doctrine: a move against any American nation would be regarded as a hostile act against the United States. That effectively settled the matter. What may have appeared to be a statement of principle in defence of republican liberties was really an announcement that there was a new player in the game of international power politics, and that there was going to be only one empire in the Americas in future: an American one.

2 8
A New Way of Working

1776, the year in which the American colonies issued their Declaration of Independence, also saw the publication of the book that would become the founding document of the science of economics, Adam Smith's *The Wealth of Nations*.

At the time of its publication, Smith was a 53-year-old professor in the University of Glasgow, in Scotland. His book was a cool, dispassionate look at changes then occurring in the commercial life of Britain, and the implications of the emerging factory system. He emphasized the enormous increase in output that could be obtained by the division of labour: the splitting-up of the process of production into highly specialized operations, each allocated to an individual worker. But the most important idea in the book was that of the 'unseen hand'. This was what Smith called the process by which competition between businesses seeking profits drove them to seek out the most efficient means of achieving customer satisfaction, which resulted in the maximization of the value and quality delivered to those customers.

Smith was not a businessman, nor was he starry-eyed about business behaviour. He was quite clear about what he saw as the unquenchable greed of the commercial classes, and adamant that it needed to be kept within bounds by government action. But he was equally convinced that, beyond ensuring fair competition, government intervention in trade was an unmitigated evil. The book in which these ideas were worked through remains one of the most influential ever written. Apologists for business never tire of quoting its advocacy of the benefits of competition, and the dangers of government intervention. For some reason, they always seem to overlook its equally powerful warnings about the dangers of uncontrolled business greed.

Smith could see that he and his contemporaries were standing on the threshold of a new world, and his book was written to help people understand that world. It was inspired by the new factories and the markets that were opening up for their products. A consideration of one of the industries he had in mind will help us understand the changes that were taking place in Britain, and the fever of excitement they were generating.

About 150 miles to the north-west of London lies the district known as the Potteries. It gets its name from the local specialization in the manufacture of earthenware and china, which goes back several centuries, and started there because of local deposits of suitable clay. Pot making requires substantial amounts of fuel to heat the kilns in which the pots are fired. This had been done by wood fires, but when wood became scarce the Potteries, being blessed with local supplies of good quality coal, began to use coal instead.

At the beginning of the eighteenth century, pottery manufacture was carried on in small workshops by master potters and their apprentices. By the time *The Wealth of Nations* was published, the industry had undergone a transformation. In a factory in the village of Burslem, a manufacturer named Josiah Wedgwood employed one of the largest workforces in Europe. His factory was one of the best examples of the division of labour that so excited Smith. It was not highly mechanized.

Even in the late eighteenth century, pottery manufacture was still a craft industry. But the volume of business passing through it enabled him to organize his production according to the successive stages in the manufacturing process, and to employ teams of people, with each team being concerned with just one stage.

Wedgwood had himself once been a small-time master potter, having served an apprenticeship with an older brother after leaving school at the age of nine. But he was a man of great gifts and wide reading, and a keen scientific curiosity. And he had had the support of a dearly loved and capable wife, who had brought him a dowry sufficient to get his business off to a good start. Thanks to her, and to his own gifts, he had become rich and famous: potter to the Queen, supplier to the nobility and a pioneer of modern methods of manufacturing. In 1774 he supplied an exquisite, hand-decorated dinner service of 952 pieces to Catherine the Great of Russia. It was an order he was able to fulfil because a recently constructed canal, of which he had been a principal sponsor, enabled him to deliver his products safely to their port of embarkation, without having to trust them to a still execrable road system. The canal, with its access to the sea, also enabled him to obtain the Cornish china clay he needed. In 1782, on the suggestion of his bosom friend, the scientist and poet Erasmus Darwin, he became the first factory owner in the world to use steam to power a line of machines. Erasmus had been able to offer this suggestion because he was a friend of a Birmingham factory owner, Matthew Boulton, the partner of a Scottish engineer named James Watt, who had invented the kind of steam engine in question.

The invention of the steam-driven pump at the beginning of the seventeenth century had made it possible to get the water out of coal mines, which in turn made it possible to extract the coal that England needed to make good its lack of timber. Had the steam pump not been invented just then, the expansion of the English coal industry would have been stopped in its tracks. As early as 1702, one pit in Warwickshire had been using 500 horses simply to work the pumps that kept its water level under control.

The early steam engines that took over from the horses were not exactly marvels of efficiency. They delivered only one unit of power for every 100 units of heat equivalent consumed: an efficiency of just 1 per cent. Watt's experiments transformed the prospects for steam power in two ways. First, by inventing the apparatus known as the condenser, he increased the efficiency of the engines ten times. Second, by devising a means of converting reciprocal (in and out) motion into rotary motion, he produced engines that could be adapted to a wide range of applications; most importantly, in the powering of belt drives for machinery.

Once the usefulness of steam for driving machinery had been demonstrated, Boulton and Watt engines began to be installed in factories throughout Britain. They also began to be exported. But in the first quarter of a century after the patent was first registered, the number installed overseas was a tiny fraction of the total. It has been calculated that in 1800, at least 40 per cent, and possibly 50 per cent, of all the non-human power used in the world was used in Britain, and that the per capita consumption of power in Britain was something like fifteen times as great as that in France. It is a statistic that goes some way to explaining how Britain, with less than half the population of France, was able to wage such an effective war against it.

This new power source opened up the possibility of large-scale manufacture, utilizing novel production methods. Closeness to the sea and access to a canal system made it possible to transport the coal and other raw materials cheaply to a large number of inland locations. Already some of the factors that caused that unique phenomenon, the eighteenth-century Industrial Revolution, to occur just when and where it did are becoming clear.

So much for the supply side: the making and marketing of goods. But trade is a matter of supply and demand. Without demand there can be no supply. And it is a circular process: increases in demand generate increases in output. Higher levels of output make possible increased specialization, bigger batches and lower production costs. Lower production costs make it possible to quote keener prices, which further increases demand, opening up the possibility of further economies of scale, and so on. And those canals, linked to coastwise traffic around the small island country, didn't just make it easy to get fuel and raw materials to factories. They also made it easy to get goods to customers in distant cities. That gave manufacturers access to bigger markets, which made it possible for them to produce even bigger batches at even lower cost. Wedgwood's great factory, with its mass production employing the latest technology, was viable because he could pack his fragile products on the spot, and convey them safely by water to any destination – St Petersburg included. Access to far-distant markets, and the resulting large scale of operation, also encouraged the employment of specialized workers and the development of specialized machines.

But what causes such increases in demand in the first place? Well, suppose the efficiency of agriculture increases, or a new high-yielding, nutritious vegetable is introduced (potatoes, anyone?). This means that the same amount of farmland can support a bigger population, leading to increased demand. This more efficient farming requires fewer farm workers, which creates cheap surplus labour for the factories to absorb. The fewer people needed on farms, the more there are available to work in factories, producing cheap goods that no one could afford before.

If this argument should seem a bit breathless, that is deliberate. It is impossible to understand the whirlwind of change that constituted the Industrial Revolution of the eighteenth century without appreciating that it really was a whirlwind. There was no ordered sequence in which A led to B, which led to C, which caused D, and so on. It was a great churning of interacting forces, against a background of lucky chances. Everything necessary just happened to come together in a particular place, England, at a particular time, the mid- to late-eighteenth century. Eighteenth-century Englishmen (supported by their wives, and their wives' dowries) were no cleverer than fourth-century BC Greeks or sixteenth-century Inca. They just happened to be in the right place, at the right time, with the right attitude.

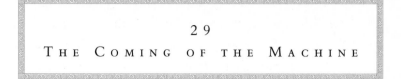

The pottery industry serves well to illustrate the influences that created the Industrial Revolution in eighteenth-century England, but it was in another industry – iron manufacture – that the most important developments occurred. It was already highly developed in China in the first century BC, and China was producing huge quantities of cast iron a thousand years ago. But that iron was used essentially for structural purposes. China had never got around to using iron for mechanical purposes. In truth, China had never got around to the systematic use of machinery at all; it just was not a machine-minded civilization. The contrast in this respect between England in the eighteenth century and China at any earlier time is striking. Many Englishmen in the eighteenth century were infatuated with machinery.

This fascination was not confined to mechanics. As in the case of Josiah Wedgwood and his friends, there was continuous networking between industrialists, scientists and practical engineers. And although England certainly had its sharp-edged class distinctions, there was no rigid segmentation of society into mandarins, intellectuals, craftsmen, scientists, farmers, landed aristocrats, and so on. Unlike the mandarins of classical China, who cultivated long fingernails as a sign of their freedom from manual labour, and unlike the philosophers of ancient Greece, who regarded manual labour as the business of slaves, the gentlemen who sponsored the Industrial Revolution in England loved the nitty-gritty of mechanical invention. The most influential force in the development of the country's early canal system was the partnership of an aristocrat – the Duke of Bridgewater – and a millwright of humble origins turned engineer, James Brindley. It originated when the duke, wounded by a broken engagement, retired to his estate and commissioned Brindley to build a canal to transport coal mined on the estate to nearby Manchester, where both the population and the demand for heating fuel were growing fast. It was a very English kind of partnership, and it was matched by many others, not just in transport, but in mining, manufacturing and agriculture. There was a revolution in agriculture that paralleled, and indeed made possible, the revolution in industry. Aristocrats by the dozen teamed up with gardeners and animal breeders in a competitive drive to improve their herds and their estates. This was a time when English landowners took as much pride in the size of their bulls, and the yields of their crops, as they did in the speed of their racehorses or the sagacity of their foxhounds.

But why were such people caught up in the excitement of agricultural improvement and mechanical invention? Quite simply, because there were fortunes to be made. A rapidly increasing population, falling transport costs and a culture of continuous invention were throwing up opportunities of profit on an almost daily basis. And most important of all, English entrepreneurs were free to pursue those profits. There was no government monopoly reserving to itself the right to conduct inland trade and exploit invention. Nor was there any direct taxation of business profits. The necessary infrastructure was in place, too. English patent law, while far from infallible, provided a reasonable guarantee that the person who invented a new process would share in the profits of its exploitation. It was an assurance that an inventor in France, for example, did not have. Bills of exchange were also backed by the force of law. They made it possible for raw materials to be paid for after the finished goods had been sold, or for goods to be sold safely in a distant location, to a customer who was not personally known to the factory owner who made them. Finally, the invention of the joint-stock company made it possible for groups of people who were not actively engaged in business to contribute some of the capital required, and to receive a proportionate share of the profits earned.

Business in England at this time had many of the characteristics of a gold rush. Stories abounded of lucky strikes and fortunes made. It also had something of a Wild West character. Frauds abounded, and risks were great. Banks were small, and bank failures frequent. The principle of limited liability, whereby shareholders in a failed company are not responsible for its debts, had not yet been enshrined in law, and so in the late eighteenth century, the liability of shareholders was unlimited.

The reason why it was in the iron industry that the most important developments occurred is that without mass-produced iron – and its later derivative, steel – there would never have been a machine-based civilization. One of the key developments in modern iron making occurred very early in the eighteenth century. The place was the village of Coalbrookdale in Shropshire, in the English Midlands. It was there that an iron founder named Abraham Darby, the first of three generations of iron founders with the same name, heated iron with coke, instead of coal. Coke was free of the impurities that made coal an unsuitable fuel for this purpose. It also had strength that charcoal did not possess.

Prior to 1709, iron making was dependent upon supplies of charcoal. This was why most early English ironworks were located in forested areas. It was also why Sweden, with its abundant supplies of both timber and iron ore, was a pioneer of iron manufacture, and – in the seventeenth century – Europe's leading producer. England's increasing shortage of timber had raised the cost of charcoal to a level that threatened the very survival of its iron industry, which had to compete with imports of iron from richly forested countries such as Sweden and Russia, and even from North America. But the use of coke, which had the strength to support the weight of large quantities of iron ore, made it possible to build bigger blast furnaces. These added economies of scale to the cheapness of the fuel. The cheaper iron was competitive in new uses, with a consequent increased demand for both iron and coking coal, the coal that yielded good coke.

Coal was one thing that England had plenty of, and because of the shortage of timber, mining was already a major industry. Already in 1662, when Charles II granted the Royal Society its charter, Britain's mines were producing five times as much coal as the rest of the world. But the kind of coal that industry needed was deep underground, and Britain was a wet country. The deeper the shafts went, the greater was the problem of flooding. It was this that created the urgent need for mechanical pumps. And it was the need for mechanical pumps that was the incentive for the development of an efficient steam engine, which, once invented, was found to have a multitude of other uses.

It is not unreasonable to say that when the first Abraham Darby introduced coke-fired smelting of iron in 1709, he fired the starting pistol for the Industrial Revolution. It was not a flying start. It needed other advances in iron manufacture before the metal could meet the demands that population growth and inventions elsewhere were generating. It was not until 1748 that the second Abraham Darby succeeded, by careful selection of ores, in making a cast iron that was suitable for the manufacture of large forgings. But by 1779, the villages of Shropshire were producing a quarter of all the iron being made in Britain, and more than was being made in any other country in the world. It was in that year that the third Abraham Darby constructed the Industrial Revolution's most famous monument: the cast-iron bridge over the River Severn. And it was in his works that the iron boiler was made that powered the world's first steam-driven locomotive. It made its debut in south Wales in 1804, when it pulled a 10-ton load at 5 miles an hour along a 10-mile stretch of line between the Penydarran Ironworks and the Glamorganshire Canal.

Although it was coal and iron that made the Industrial Revolution, the most spectacular developments occurred in the cotton industry. This was concentrated in the county of Lancashire, between the fast-growing towns of Liverpool and Manchester that were the industry's twin headquarters. Liverpool was the port through which raw cotton was imported and cotton goods exported. Manchester and its satellite towns were the centres of manufacture.

'Fast-growing' hardly does justice to the phenomenal expansion of these two towns. Liverpool was a prosperous place before the cotton trade began. A mere fishing village in the fourteenth century, it had blossomed into one of the busiest centres of commerce in the land. In 1600, its population had been little more than 1000 – less than before the Black Death. By 1700, thanks to the sugar and tobacco trades, it had grown into an elegant and spacious town, with a population of 5000. But it was slaves and cotton that made its fortune. By 1800 its population had exploded to 70,000, and was increasing at the rate of 2000 a year. Manchester's growth had followed an almost identical path, with almost identical numbers. Its early prosperity had been based on other textiles, linen and, especially, wool. But from the opening of its first cotton mill in 1780, cotton manufacture became its *raison d'être*.

Long before anyone in a Lancashire factory had spun a cotton thread, the workshops of Isfahan and Tabriz in Persia (present-day Iran) provided employment for thousands of weavers of both cotton and silk. As late as 1700, India was the world's only significant exporter, not only of cotton goods, but of woven textiles generally. But with the coming of mechanization and cheap energy, standardization and mass production, and the development of the port of Liverpool, Lancashire acquired a brute strength, and a cost advantage, that wiped its overseas competitors off the map. This was not how the mill owners of Lancashire would have put it, of course. Within two generations, they would be telling themselves – and the world – that their near-monopoly was attributable to Lancashire's unique spirit, Lancashire's exceptional talents and the altogether special nature of the Lancashire climate. Within a hundred years, it would be Manchester's boast that there were more spindles within 20 miles of the city centre than there were in the rest of the world.

The combination of entrepreneurial drive and inventive craftsmanship that was powering the Industrial Revolution in other parts of England was working overtime in cotton. In a twenty-year burst, between 1770 and 1790, the technical basis of the industry was transformed. Developments in spinning forced changes in weaving – and vice versa – in a breathless merry-go-round of invention. As factories multiplied, and grew larger; as first water-powered and then steam-powered machinery replaced hand spinning and hand weaving; and as shift working became the norm, output increased prodigiously. In 1765, England's total output of cotton, which was then spun by hand, weighed in at 500,000 pounds. Just nineteen years later, in 1784, it weighed 16 million pounds. By 1840, textile manufacturers would be employing 75 per cent of the country's industrial workforce, half of them in cotton.

In 1820, Lancashire, which didn't, and couldn't, grow cotton, had a stranglehold on the world's cotton goods markets that would last for a hundred years. And this was in spite of the fact that it had no natural advantages for carrying on the trade whatsoever. It was a perfect example of the maxim that 'nothing succeeds like success'. It got in first, and established a scale of operation that brought costs down to a level that made it impossible for manufacturers elsewhere to survive, let alone modernize. Even the Americans, who, after 1800, were the principal suppliers of the cotton that Lancashire used, were unable to compete in Britain's markets. They settled instead for growing the raw material. They had the climate, and they had cheap slave labour. After the American engineer Eli Whitney invented the cotton gin – a machine that made it possible to use a variety that could be grown inland – the area of land available for cotton cultivation was vastly increased.

The excitement of this brave new world did not trickle down to the bottom of the industrial heap. It was not shared by the agricultural workers who were forced out of their villages into crowded, unhealthy towns, where the average life expectancy was a mere twenty years, to work as machine minders under brutal overseers. It was not shared by the malnourished five- and six-year-olds, who worked ten or twelve hours a day, fell asleep at their work, and ended up in the clattering machines. It was not shared by the worn-out women who crawled like moles underground, hauling wagons of coal attached to ropes around their waists. And it was certainly not shared by the little boys (they had to be little) who climbed with their brushes, in the dark, up the tall chimneys of the elegant houses that this new wealth had built. In the streets outside these houses, and in the miserable hovels in which the majority of the population lived, grown-ups and children alike went about in rags, and children went barefoot.

Not all those who lived in fine houses were blind to the realities of the world that provided them with such a delightful existence. Josiah Wedgwood and Erasmus Darwin, for example, were energetic supporters of the movement for the abolition of the slave trade. They did not live to see it, but on 25 March 1807, their friend and fellow campaigner, William Wilberforce, after a nineteen-year parliamentary struggle, persuaded his fellow Members of Parliament to pass a bill outlawing the slave trade. The abolition of slavery itself throughout the British empire, which was the end he really sought, came about in 1833, just one month after he died.

3 0
IRON HORSES AND IRON SHIPS

By 1820, the first stage of the Industrial Revolution was complete. Factories with large labour forces, equipped with steam-driven machinery, and with a high degree of job specialization, were widespread in northern Europe and the United States. In many industries, the processes of production had been transformed. Most of this activity was still located in Britain, whose early start had gained it an advantage that it would retain for another thirty or forty years. But it was no longer the world's only industrial nation. Other countries were catching up fast.

What had not changed were the processes by which raw materials found their way to the factories, and finished goods found their way to the customer. In 1820, goods and people still moved at the same speed, and by the same means, as they had in the Roman empire. Horses on land, and sails on water, were still the fastest and the most efficient means of transport. If industry was to prosper, this was a problem that had to be solved.

The solution was the replacing of horse and sail by the device that had already replaced horse power and human power in manufacturing: the steam engine. It was solved in Britain and America almost simultaneously. Both countries had had short-distance railroads, on which horses pulled loads along iron rails, for many years. All that was needed was an engine to replace the horse. The possibility of using steam power to haul loads had been demonstrated in south Wales in 1804, but it was not until the development of sufficiently strong rails, and a locomotive with smooth wheels that could adhere to them, that rail transport became viable. It is not surprising that when the first public railway offering transport of both goods and passengers was opened in 1830, it should have been one connecting those twin hubs of the cotton industry, Liverpool and Manchester.

The world that witnessed the opening of the Liverpool and Manchester Railway was very different from that of Abraham Darby's coke-fired blast furnace. Britain was still the world's industrial champion, in output and in machine power available. But when it came to the application of science, or the rate of industrial innovation, half a dozen countries – most notably France, Germany and the United States – were snapping at Britain's heels. In some respects they were already out in front. The first stage of America's Baltimore and Ohio Railroad actually opened several months before the Liverpool and Manchester, and only the technicality of being a 'public' railroad allowed the latter to insist on its claim to priority. Having been formed to exploit British technology, the Baltimore and Ohio's engineers quickly developed an expertise of their own, with techniques more appropriate to American conditions, earning the company the byname 'university of railroad engineering'.

Once the practicality of steam locomotion had been demonstrated, its application in every country connected to the industrial web quickly followed. On Christmas Day 1830, the South Carolina Canal and Railroad Company became the first American railroad to offer scheduled passenger services using steam locomotives. In France the St Etienne to Lyon line was opened in 1832, and in Germany the line from Nuremberg to Fürth opened in 1835. The world's first international line, between Strasbourg and Basel, followed in 1841.

30.1 Installed Steam Engine Capacity in Europe, 1840–80

| | Steam Engines (1000 Horse power) | | |
	1840	1860	1880
Gt Britain	620	2450	7600
Germany	40	850	5120
France	90	1120	3070
Austria	20	330	1560
Belgium	40	160	610
Russia	20	200	1740
Italy	10	50	500
Spain	10	100	470
The Netherlands	–	30	250
Sweden	–	20	220

Source: C.M. Cipolla (ed), *Fontana Economic History of Europe*, Vol. 3, (Collins, 1973) p.165

Britain, still the most industrialized country, developed its railroad system more rapidly and extensively than any other. This was accompanied by a railway mania that echoed the Dutch tulip mania of two centuries earlier. The opening of the Liverpool and Manchester Railway had coincided with a cyclical upturn in the economy as a whole. When the cycle turned down a few years later, the enthusiasm faded. But in that brief period, 2000 miles of track had been laid.

When the economy recovered in the 1840s, Britain went railway mad. Within a decade, the country's track mileage went from 2000 to 8000 miles. In a single year, 1846, Parliament passed 270 Railway Acts, authorizing the construction of 5000 miles of new lines. In England, investors in their thousands committed all they had, and much borrowed money as well, in railway stocks. Scotland became, in the words of the poet William Wordsworth 'an asylum for railway lunatics'. It had to end in tears, and it did. Thousands were bankrupted, and the crash that followed led to an economy-wide recession. But the nation had a railway system, and a mastery of the skills of railroad and locomotive construction that would later take British-made railroads around the globe.

Railroads transformed the map of human settlement and the entire economy of nations. For centuries, access to navigable water had been the key to prosperity. Railroads made it possible for cities to arise wherever there was a good reason for them, navigable water or no navigable water. And they brought not only accessibility, but speed, and in addition, reliability. Only the harshest weather stopped them.

If ever there was a nation made by the railroad, the United States of America is that nation. It, too, had its railroad mania, and, in 1837, its railroad panic. As in Britain, much damage was done, but the country emerged with 2800 miles of track laid. With the aid of public subsidies, track laying then began in earnest. The effort put into railroad construction during the 1850s was phenomenal: by 1860 there was 30,000 miles of it.

The most striking feature of the American system as it emerged in the 1860s was not so much its extent as its pattern. Unlike Britain, where unrestricted competition resulted in many lines serving the same routes, this northern network was notable for the great east–west routes that were established either as single- or joint-company lines. These connected the Atlantic ports with leading commercial centres in the west, such as Chicago, Pittsburgh and St Louis. They transformed the patterns of movement within the continent, hitherto heavily influenced by the north–south orientation of the great waterways, especially the Mississippi and the St Lawrence.

Another invention that made distances shrink was the electric telegraph. Early versions were demonstrated in Britain, France and Spain in the eighteenth century, but it was not until the development of suitable batteries that it became a practical technology. The first commercial installation was in 1838, on a line out of London, belonging to the Great Western Railway Company. This installation had a sensational success in 1845, when a suspected murderer was seen boarding a London-bound train at Slough. A message sent to the terminus at London's Paddington station led to his arrest, and subsequent conviction and execution. This triumph was not sufficient to ensure the invention's commercial future. It depended on receivers that individually recorded specific letters of the alphabet, and was later rejected in favour of a system based on the Morse code.

The Morse code was the brainchild of a multi-talented American portrait painter, Samuel F.B. Morse. He had been interested in electricity since his youth, and had been attracted to the problem of the electric telegraph as a result of a conversation overheard during a transatlantic crossing. Having obtained Congressional support for a line between Baltimore and Washington, he gave a successful demonstration of his device in 1844. Further lines soon followed. As the railroad network crept – or rather, raced – across the continent, the telegraph spread with it. By the 1850s, the telegraph had become an indispensable tool of both commerce and government. Within four years of Morse's first demonstration, his system had been installed in every state but Florida. In Europe, too, the telegraph quickly transformed communications. By 1852, Britain had 4000 miles of telegraph lines, and an undersea link with France.

The 1840s also witnessed the development of modern postal systems. The earliest known mention of what might be called a postal system comes from Egypt, around 2000 BC. The Chinese appear to have been the first to possess a system based on post houses and relays of messengers, in around 1000 BC. The highly developed Roman system was one of the keys to the control of that vast empire. After it fell, Europe was without anything comparable for more than a thousand years. With the coming of the mail coach in the late eighteenth century, reasonably speedy communication over long distances was once more possible. But it was not until the introduction of nationally administered systems that letters became a medium of mass communication. High-speed carriage of letters began in Britain in 1838, with the introduction of a railway post office with on-train sorting. When a flat-rate charging system, using prepaid stamps, was introduced in 1840, the volume of postal traffic exploded. During the next twenty years, similar operations were established around the world.

Important developments were also occurring in the technology of movement on water. There had been experiments in the application of steam power to ship propulsion in several countries in the late eighteenth and early nineteenth centuries. Early steam engines were bulky and heavy, so pioneer French engineers first tried to harness them to water, rather than land transport. An 8-inch cylinder engine was tried out on the Seine in 1775, but turned out to be insufficiently powerful. In 1783, the marquis Jouffroy d'Abbans successfully ascended the River Saône in a 180-ton paddlewheel streamer, the *Pyroscaphe*. There is no reason to doubt that the French would have continued to lead the field, had the horror of the revolution not brought such aristocratic experiments to an abrupt end.

In 1801, an engineer named William Symington demonstrated a 22-inch cylinder engine on a paddlewheel steamer called the *Charlotte Dundas* on the Forth and Clyde Canal in Scotland. Six years later, the American engineer Robert Fulton, who had witnessed the *Charlotte Dundas* trials, achieved the first commercial success with steam propulsion by using a Boulton and Watt beam engine to drive the paddle steamer *Clermont* on a service between New York and Albany. It was the crossing of the Atlantic by the American steamship *Savannah* in 1819 that gave the world notice of the birth of a new age of international travel. The *Savannah* was actually propelled by its sails for nearly 90 per cent of the journey, but the point had been made. The future, on water, as on land, belonged to steam.

A decisive change in steamship design occurred in 1838, when the first screw-driven steamer, the 240-ton British-built *Archimedes*, was launched. The screw drive, which would form the basis of all later developments in ship propulsion, was the simultaneous invention of an Englishman, Francis Pettit Smith, and a Swede, John Ericsson. Ericsson left England for America and sold his patent to the United States Navy. In 1842, the US Navy launched the world's first screw-driven warship, the USS *Princeton*. In 1843, the British-built, iron-framed merchantman *Great Britain* became the first screw-driven ship to cross the Atlantic. Steam had truly come of age.

The short period of thirty years between the Battle of Waterloo in 1815 and the apprehension of that suspected murderer on Paddington station in 1845 saw the transition from what one might call, without much distortion, the *Age of Then* to what is recognizably the *Age of Now*. The world of the express train and the electric telegraph is one we can imagine ourselves in; that of the cavalry horse and the mail coach seems altogether more distant. Yet it was a transition that many people not only lived through, but lived to look back on. As a way of illustrating that transition, let us examine a slice of the life of someone who did live through it, and whose work expresses the break between the *Age of Then* and the *Age of Now*.

The creation of the South American republics out of the Spanish and Portuguese empires created mouth-watering opportunities for the trading nations that had hitherto watched from the sidelines. Chief among these was Britain, whose population needed food and raw materials, and whose expanding factories needed customers. President Monroe had pronounced his doctrine, but had said nothing about buying and selling, so everything was up for grabs. But to trade safely on the other side of the ocean one needed maps and charts.

Cometh the hour, cometh the man. In Francis Beaufort, hydrographer to the Navy, Britain found a leader of vision, who was determined to provide his country with the maps it needed. In 1825 he had sent a three-masted sailing ship, the *Beagle*, to survey the coast of South America. Its captain had succumbed to the loneliness of command in the waters around Tierra del Fuego, and had shot himself; but his task had been taken over by a brilliant young officer named Robert Fitzroy, who was passionately interested in science. He had completed the survey with distinction, and when the question of a follow-up arose, he was the natural choice to conduct it. Remembering what loneliness had done to his predecessor, he took as his shipboard companion an even younger man (twenty-two years of age to his twenty-eight) who was as mad about science as he was. His name was Charles Darwin, and he was the grandson (through his mother) of the potter Josiah Wedgwood, and (through his father) of Wedgwood's friend, the scientist Erasmus Darwin.

After visiting the ship at its mooring in Plymouth, Darwin travelled back to London by mail coach, and wrote an excited letter to Fitzroy, to which he added the words 'P.S. 250 miles in 24 hours!!!'.

The *Beagle* left England in December 1831, and returned in October 1836, having completed a five-year circumnavigation of the globe. For Darwin, the sights he had seen, and the thinking he had done, laid the foundation for a piece of work – *On the Origin of Species* – that would eventually cause him to be ranked alongside Newton. On the homeward stage of its journey, in January 1836, the ship anchored off Sydney, the city that now stood where the First Fleet had unloaded its cargo of convicts less than fifty years earlier. Darwin, the respectable son of a rich father, stared in wonder at the well-dressed descendants of the transportees who had been dumped there during the previous half century. Writing home to his sisters, he said:

> Ancient Rome, in her Imperial grandeur, would not have been ashamed of such an offspring. . . . There are men now living, who came out as convicts . . . who are said to possess, without doubt, an income of from 12 to 15,000 pounds per annum.

He was right to be impressed. That's a million pounds in today's money.

In March 1838, just a year and a half after his return, he went to the zoo to see Jenny the orang-utan. She was the first great ape he had seen, and one of the first ever seen in London. When he got home, he wrote in his secret notebook:

> Let man visit the ouran-outang in domestication. . . . see its intelligence. Man in his arrogance thinks he is a great work . . . More humble I believe and true to consider him created from animals.

It was the most potent sentence he would ever write. Thirty years later, it provided the inspiration for another book – *The Descent of Man* – in which he would overturn the beliefs of his age concerning human origins.

In January 1839, he travelled to London by train – the first train journey of his life. He had missed the railway mania, having been exploring the Andes at the time. The 22-year-old who had been so excited at covering 250 miles in twenty-four hours was now a twenty-nine-year-old who didn't consider a journey to London in a horseless carriage at 50 miles an hour anything to write home about. It was a measure of the way the world had changed in little more than six years.

In 1844, as the noise of riveting filled the yard in Bristol where the *Great Britain* was being prepared for its voyage across the Atlantic, Darwin sat quietly writing in his study in the Kent countryside. He was putting the finishing touches to a 230-page outline of a theory – evolution by natural selection – that would leave the cosy world of his rich, respectable friends in turmoil, and inspire a century and a half of scientific research and discovery. The world was not, he thought, yet ready for it, so he wrapped it up and hid it under the stairs, where it would lie unopened for the next fifteen years.

In 1851, like almost everyone of his class and age, Darwin went to London to visit the Great Exhibition. A shop window for British manufactures and a glorification of the British empire, its British visitors bathed in a glow of pride, and went home with understandable feelings of superiority. Foreign visitors took notes, and went home to carry on with their plans to beat the Brits at their own game. In fact, the Brits were already being overtaken – but they would be the last to find out.

3 1

THE CHANGING BALANCE
OF POWER

In a single generation after 1830, the railway and the steamship dramatically reduced travelling times. During the course of the next generation – from the 1850s to the 1880s – they also made possible migration on a massive scale. In combination with new technologies of war, such as heavy artillery and machine guns, they gave industrialized nations an overwhelming advantage. By the 1880s, a new set of power relationships had emerged that would dictate the course of world history for nearly a century. These changes occurred in four major regions of the world: North America, South Asia, East Asia and Europe.

When the nineteenth century began, the population of the United States was only 6 million, some five or six times that of London. Its territory consisted of the original thirteen states of the Atlantic seaboard, plus the lands as far west as the Mississippi and as far north as the Great Lakes that had been acquired from Britain as a consequence of the War of Independence. By 1870, the USA was a nation of nearly 40 million, occupying a territory that extended from the Atlantic to the Pacific, from the Rio Grande to the St Lawrence, and including the whole of Alaska. It remains one of the most astonishing exercises in nation building; an achievement that involved the expenditure of a certain amount of money, and a considerable quantity of blood.

The biggest slice of money was spent in 1803, in a spectacular real estate transaction known as the Louisiana Purchase.

31.1 The Growth of the United States

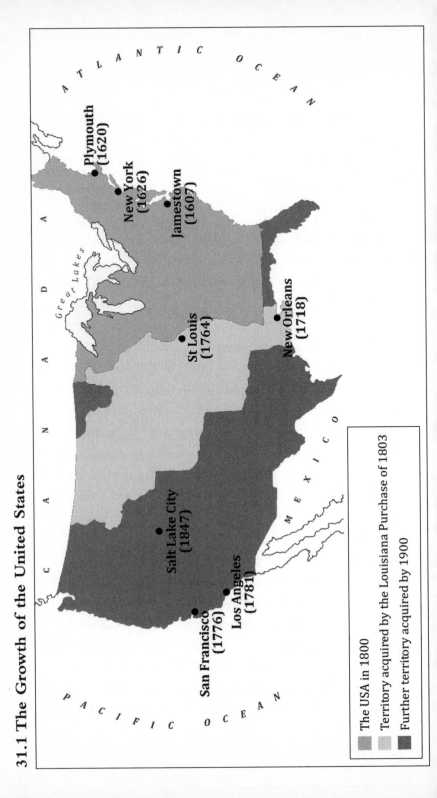

ATLANTIC OCEAN

Plymouth (1620)

New York (1626)

Jamestown (1607)

C A N A D A

Great Lakes

New Orleans (1718)

St Louis (1764)

M E X I C O

Salt Lake City (1847)

Los Angeles (1781)

San Francisco (1776)

PACIFIC OCEAN

The USA in 1800

Territory acquired by the Louisiana Purchase of 1803

Further territory acquired by 1900

For a mere $11.25 million, the 27-year-old nation acquired from France territories covering a greater area than its own, including what is now Louisiana, Iowa, Arkansas, Nebraska, North and South Dakota, together with much of Oklahoma, Minnesota, Kansas, Wyoming, Montana and Colorado.

Another huge tract was added when Texas became the twenty-eighth state in 1845. It had originally formed part of the Spanish colony of New Spain, and then, from 1821, part of the Republic of Mexico. But in 1836, its citizens (many of whom were American settlers) had declared themselves independent of Mexico, and had for almost ten years administered their own Republic of Texas. The admission of Texas to the United States led to war with Mexico, after which that country was compelled to cede further huge tracts of territory to the USA, including present-day California, Utah and Nevada, and most of Arizona.

Well before Texas joined the Union, the phrase 'manifest destiny' had entered the American political lexicon. It meant that it was somehow preordained that the 'American nation' – meaning that part of the population with European forebears – should become the owners and developers of whatever portion of the continent they were able to wrest from the previous occupants. This 'destiny' was not so manifest to the native Americans who were already in occupation, and it required a considerable amount of force to persuade them move to their 'reservations'. It required an even greater effort to exterminate those who could not be persuaded to move, and who insisted on displaying an inordinate amount of courage in defence of their ancestral lands. But within a century of the Declaration of Independence, with its assertion of the right of all men to 'life, liberty and the pursuit of happiness', the task of subjugation and extermination had been largely completed.

As new lands were cleared of their native American populations, they began to fill up with immigrant replacements: mainly African Americans (slaves) in the areas of the Louisiana Purchase, and mostly European Americans (free men and women) elsewhere. This differential pattern of immigration sowed the seeds of a dispute that would require the blood of hundreds of thousands of European Americans to be added to that of the millions of native Americans already killed, before the process of nation building could be completed.

The dispute that arose in 1860 was between the slave-owning states of the South – Kentucky, Alabama, and so on – and the largely slave-free states in the North. One of the consequences of the enormous expansion of the cotton industry in England had been a corresponding increase in the number of slaves employed in growing cotton in America. The simultaneous growth of population in England's industrial cities had also led to a greatly increased demand for cheap food energy in the form of sugar. This, too, had required a matching increase in the slave labour force in the Americas. Between 1800 and 1860, the number of slaves in the southern USA increased fivefold, and similar increases were seen in the Caribbean and Brazil. In the eighteenth century the increase in slave numbers had been largely through importation. But now, with the gradual enforcement of the ban on slave trading, the increase had to come from the growth of the existing black population, whose offspring were in essence being bred for the purpose.

Chile and Mexico had abolished slavery when they achieved independence in 1820. In 1833, an enlargement of the franchise in Britain increased the representation of the middle classes in Parliament, making possible the passage of an Emancipation Act that freed 750,000 slaves in the British empire. In 1848, the installation of a revolutionary government in France was followed by the freeing of 300,000 slaves in the French empire. These acts of emancipation encouraged those – mostly in the North – who wished to see similar action in the USA. But slavery was now the foundation of the economy of the southern states. The 700,000-strong slave labour force of 1776 had grown to 4 million. For many southern whites, slavery was not just the basis of their economy, it was a defining feature of their civilization. There were other factors, too. Slaves were property, and the idea of emancipation conflicted with the right to enjoy private property embodied in the constitution. Finally, there was the unsettled question of where power ultimately resided: was it in the Federal Congress, or in the state legislatures?

When a Republican candidate, Abraham Lincoln, who was committed to the prohibition of slavery in any future states admitted to the Union, was elected to the presidency, it was the parting of the ways for many southern citizens. South Carolina seceded from the Union, to be followed by fourteen other states, forming the fifteen-state Confederacy. The war that followed was essentially about whether the Union should continue or whether the Confederate states should be permitted to go their own way.

It took four years of civil war to decide the outcome. It was in many ways the first 'modern' war. By the time it ended in 1865, it had claimed 600,000 lives. The immediate consequences were the abolition of slavery throughout the USA, and desperate injury to the economy of the southern states. The war's longer-term significance can hardly be exaggerated. It ensured that there would henceforth be one single nation, rather than two or three, or more, over the entire territory between Canada and Mexico. Much of the subsequent history of the world was decided on the battlefields of what the defeated Confederacy termed 'the war between the states'.

While the future boundaries and character of the United States were being determined, another great nation was being forged in the heart of Europe. At the end of the Napoleonic Wars, the region we now know as Germany was still divided into a number of independent sovereign states, some of which were very small. Foremost among them was Prussia, which occupied a substantial stretch of country on the southern shores of the Baltic Sea, with its capital in Berlin. It was Prussia that formed the nucleus of modern Germany, and it was the genius of Prussia's prime minister, Prince Otto von Bismarck, that engineered its creation.

Bismarck, one of the greatest nation-builders in European history, displayed what, to modern eyes, was a strange mixture of reactionary attitudes and reformist zeal. He was a great patriot, but he was no democrat. Rigidly traditional in his view of rank and social obligation, he yet had a revolutionary vision of the importance of science and technical education. He was a supreme master of the game of power politics, but still found time to design and install the world's first state old age pension. In the course of a single generation, his contradictory genius not only brought the modern German state into existence, but made it into one of the most formidable players on the inter-national stage.

When, in 1862, his task began, Prussia was still a small country, with a population and military capacity dwarfed by that of France. By the time he had completed it, in 1871, Germany was the most powerful military force on the continent, and in many ways the most advanced industrial country in the world.

Bismarck's programme of nation building began in 1864, with a war against Denmark that gained Prussia the duchies of Schleswig and Holstein. Almost immediately afterwards he engineered another brief war, this time against Austria. Victory on this occasion enabled Prussia to annex the territories of several smaller states that had made the mistake of allying themselves with Austria, and ensured the exclusion of that country from any further involvement in German affairs. This cleared the way for the decisive clash of arms that was initiated when Napoleon III of France allowed himself to be provoked into declaring war on Prussia in September 1870. When Prussia emerged victorious from this conflict – the Franco-Prussian War – it extracted as part of the spoils of war two rich French provinces, Alsace and Lorraine. The prestige of this defeat of what had hitherto been the continent's leading military power made it easy for Prussia to assume the leadership of all the German states, which it did in 1871 with the creation of the German empire. Nominally a confederation of sovereign states, this was in reality a Prussian empire, into which the former French provinces of Alsace and Lorraine were incorporated. It was the beginning of modern Germany. The former division of the homeland of the German-speaking peoples into a multitude of individual sovereign states, many of them very small, had left them disadvantaged by comparison with Britain and France. Now, with its unified home market, its extended borders and its modern industry, Germany was ready to take its place as one of the Great Powers.

Although it was these two newly forged nations, the USA and Germany, that would dominate the next hundred years, the world's leading power at mid-century was still the British empire. In the 1850s and 60s, it advanced in wealth and strength, as did the assurance of the British that the country's power in the world derived from the innate virtues of its people.

The forces that drove Britain's colonial enterprise were the search for cheap sources of raw materials and the desire to eliminate competition. But these objectives were transformed in British minds into a belief that Britons were engaged in a mission to bring the benefits of civilization to less fortunate peoples. It was a belief every bit as self-serving as America's 'manifest destiny', and was held with equal sincerity.

The principal field of operation for this 'mission' continued to be the vast Indian subcontinent. Thanks to their guns, their gunboats and their enormous financial resources, the rulers of a little island off the coast of north-west Europe were able to rule 200 million people living in a country 6000 miles away, and to administer their affairs so as to provide the maximum benefit to the inhabitants of the sweetly-named 'mother country'. One consequence was that India was prevented from developing its indigenous industries. This perception that Britain was deliberately holding India back fed the resentments that boiled over into the uprising in 1857 that the British labelled the Indian Mutiny. This uprising achieved considerable early success, and had there been a greater degree of unity among the various rebel forces, it is quite possible that it might have marked the end of British India.

After this so-called mutiny had been successfully – and brutally – put down, the British Parliament passed the 1858

Government of India Act, which took control of Indian affairs out of the hands of the East India Company. Henceforth India was the direct responsibility of a British minister in London – the Secretary of State for India – advised by a fifteen-member council. The day-to-day administration of the country was overseen by a viceroy, who was advised by a council of his own.

Britain's response to the 1857 rebellion, which combined outrage with the disappointment of a parent at the behaviour of an ungrateful child, opened up an unfortunate gap between the Indian people and their British rulers. It created a feeling of distrust on both sides, and an attitude of opposition to reform that made desirable political changes more difficult to achieve. Subsequent conservatism in Indian affairs was further ensured by the guarantee of support that the British government extended to the rulers of the princely states, who were thereby enlisted as reciprocal guarantors of the continuance of British influence. It was a brilliant arrangement that enabled a few thousand British administrators to continue to control the lives of 200 million people.

The control of the imports and exports, and the internal trading arrangements, not only of this vast subcontinent but of the continent of Australia and of the whole of Canada as well might have been thought sufficient to assuage the commercial appetite of an island of shopkeepers in the North Atlantic, but 'enough' was a word that did not feature in the British commercial lexicon. The next prize to set British mouths watering was the immensely rich and, from their point of view, unexploited Chinese market. Here was a country with a population of nearly 400 million, with one of the highest per capita incomes in the world. It was surely desperate for the goods that British enterprise had to offer. British merchants were certainly desperate for Chinese silk and porcelain. What they needed was something to offer in exchange.

The British could, however, obtain copious supplies of one product very cheaply. This product was Indian-grown opium. China originally consumed little of it, but the British set about creating a demand. Their success in doing so was such that, for a time, the opium trade became the greatest single trade in the world. The Chinese authorities took exception to the smuggling of this illegal and dangerous drug, and in 1839 their officials descended upon the British warehouses in Canton (Gwangzhou) and seized 20,000 cases of the stuff. The response of the British was to send warships to besiege the port. Thus began the first of several Opium Wars. When it ended in 1842, the Chinese were forced to sign the Treaty of Nanking, under which a number of ports were opened up to foreign trade, and the island of Hong Kong was ceded to Britain. Between 1856 and 1860, the two countries fought a second Opium War, at the end of which the British forced the opening of more ports. Britain's example was followed by several other countries, which insisted on the Chinese signing further 'unequal treaties', as the Chinese understandably called them. It was an end to the isolation from outside influences that Chinese governments had sought so strenuously to preserve.

These assaults from outside would at any time have represented a severe threat to China's ability to maintain control of its affairs. But they were made more serious by the fact that they came when the internal politics of the country were in a state of total disarray. In the late 1840s, a spate of crop failures had led to widespread famines. These contributed to a series of uprisings by peasants demanding a reorganization of the country's system of land tenure. Into this volatile situation stepped two charismatic leaders. One of these was Hung Hsiu-ch'üan, a disappointed civil service examination candidate who thought he was the younger brother of Jesus of Nazareth. The other was his friend Feng Yün-shan, who organized a peasant grouping, based on Hung's teaching, called Pai Shang-ti Hui (the God Worshippers' Society). They joined forces, and in January 1861, Hung proclaimed a new dynasty – the Taiping Tien Kuo – and himself as T'ien-wang (Heavenly King).

This movement, which advocated the redistribution of land holdings, attracted a large number of followers among both peasants and miners, and very soon Hung and Feng were the commanders of a highly disciplined fighting force of more than a million. Between 1851 and 1853 these armies swept across the Yangtze Valley and into the Central Plain, where they captured the great city of Nanking. This was the high water mark of what is called the Taiping Rebellion. If Chinese history at this point had proceeded according to precedent, the mandarin class would have deserted the ruling dynasty as it lost the Mandate of Heaven, and the Taiping dynasty would have inherited its mantle. But two factors prevented the time-honoured precedent from being followed. One was the mandarins' fear of a socialistic revolution that threatened the basis of their own aristocratic power. The other was the involvement of foreign commanders, who were able to provide a stiffening of the authorities' resistance. Countries such as Britain and America had no desire to see a new dynasty in command of China's affairs, especially such a fiercely anti-capitalist one. They preferred to deal with a weak and pliant government with a proper respect for the rights of private property. Whether this wasin the best interests of the Chinese people was not their concern.

With assistance from these foreign commanders, who

included an American adventurer named Frederick Townsend Ward and a British army officer named Charles George Gordon (later famous as Gordon of Khartoum), the rebellion was eventually crushed. In 1864, after a two-year siege, the Chinese General Tseng Kuo-fan captured the rebel stronghold of Nanking. To the victors' astonishment, 100,000 of the city's defenders chose death, rather than surrender. Sporadic fighting continued for four more years, but it was by then a lost cause. Something like 20 million people had been killed, and the already weakened country had been reduced to a condition that ensured that it would remain impoverished and undeveloped for another half century.

The dreamers who had led the rebellion had achieved nothing for themselves, but they had sown a seed that would bear fruit in the twentieth century. The Nationalist Revolution of 1911, and the Communist Revolution of 1949, would both draw powerful inspiration from the memories that the Taiping Rebellion left behind.

With the industrializing nations on the rampage, no country could hope to remain undisturbed for long. In 1853, it was the turn of the Japanese to be humiliated by foreign steamships and foreign guns. The bearer of bad tidings on this occasion was an American naval officer, Commodore Matthew Perry, who appeared in Tokyo Bay with four warships and a demand that Japanese ports be opened for trade and refuelling to ships travelling between San Francisco and Shanghai. The granting of these rights led to similar demands by Britain, France, Russia and The Netherlands. These raised such discontent among the country's clan leaders that in 1868 they engineered a coup in which the ruling shogun was removed and the emperor's power restored. This event, which became known as the Meiji

Restoration, was a turning-point in Japanese history. The Japanese reaction to the exercise of technology-based blackmail was quite different from that of the rulers of India and China. Recognizing that if they wished to beat their humiliators, they would first have to join them, the country's ruling class embarked on a crash programme of modernization, involving massive investment in education and in industry, and later in military and naval technology. For the time being, the power of the Americans and the Europeans was irresistible, in East Asia as everywhere else. But they had poked a stick into a sleeping tiger's den. They were to discover that this tiger had teeth and claws.

3 2

A MESSAGE OF HOPE

By the 1840s, northern Europe's Industrial Revolution was in full swing, generating enormous fortunes for factory owners and their financial backers. Very little of this new wealth found its way into the pockets of the factory workers, who lived and worked in appalling conditions. Nowhere was this juxtaposition of riotous wealth creation and grinding poverty more conspicuous than in Manchester, which was now Britain's second city, and the heart of the world cotton industry.

In 1842, a 22-year-old newly discharged Prussian cavalry officer named Friedrich Engels arrived in Manchester to begin a period of service with the textile firm of Ermen and Engels, in which his father was a partner. Engels had leapt at the opportunity; not because he was keen to be a factory manager, but because he wished to witness the workings of the new industrial society at first hand. He had recently come under the influence of a wealthy Berlin publisher named Moses Hess, who had converted him to communism. Hess had also persuaded him that England was to play a leading role in the social upheavals that would inaugurate a new kind of society in which the proletariat – the urban working class – would be the driving force for change.

Engels spent two years in Manchester, during which he worked strenuously at furthering the family's business interests, while simultaneously devoting his leisure hours to researching and writing about industry and politics, and corresponding and meeting with people who shared his radical views. He also formed an attachment to an uneducated Irish factory worker named Mary Burns, with whom he was to live happily for the next twenty years.

In 1844, Engels published the classic *The Condition of the Working Class in England*. In that year, too, he wrote two articles for the Paris-published *German-French Yearbooks*, setting out the principles of what he called scientific socialism, wherein a future revolution would abolish private property and bring about 'a reconciliation of humanity with nature and itself'. On his next visit to the firm's head office in Barmen, in the Rhineland, he stopped off in Paris for a ten-day meeting with the *Yearbooks'* editor, Karl Marx, whom he had already met briefly in Cologne. It was a visit that would determine the course of both their lives, and have a profound influence on millions around the world for the next century and a half.

Marx and Engels discovered that they were soul mates whose talents and experience perfectly complemented one another's. Marx was essentially a scholar: a social philosopher of huge intellectual power, but hopelessly impractical in everyday matters, and unsuited to holding down a job. Engels was a polished, effective man-of-the-world, and a gifted communicator. Together they formed a remarkable team that lasted all their lives. Engels was also able to provide Marx and his wife Jenny with financial support, without which they would have been in abject poverty.

At the time of their meeting in Paris, Engels was twenty-four and Marx twenty-six. Marx, who was born in Trier in the Rhineland, was a graduate in history and philosophy, and had been the editor of a radical newspaper in Cologne. It was the suppression of this that had led to his move to Paris, where he had met, and been influenced by, the leading French socialists of the day. Unfortunately, the *Yearbooks*, which he had gone to Paris to edit, were not a success, and closed down after two issues. As a consequence of what was published in them, the Prussian government issued a warrant for his arrest, which meant that he could not return there.

Marx and Engels were disciples of the German philosopher, G.W.F. Hegel, who argued that human history embodied a process he called the dialectic. This was a process within which one kind of society or set of ideas (the thesis), engaged in a struggle with its opposite (the antithesis), giving rise to a resolution combining features of each (the synthesis). Hegel also insisted that human nature was distorted by the unnatural relationship between worker and machine, and between workers and the owners of machines: a process he called alienation. It was a proposition that Marx and Engels endorsed enthusiastically.

In 1845, Engels escorted Marx on a tour of England, to provide him with firsthand experience of the workings of the world's most advanced industrial society. In 1847, he and Marx persuaded the Second International Communist Congress, meeting in London, to adopt a programme of their devising, and were authorized to prepare a statement of the programme.

In February 1848, Engels published their jointly written *The Communist Manifesto*. This was based in part on previously published work by Engels, but was mainly written by Marx. It drew on the ideas of earlier socialist thinkers, but advocated a more thoroughgoing form of socialism they called communism. It involved the abolition of all private property (including privately owned businesses), and the division of the proceeds of labour by publicly determined rules, not by contracts between private employers and their employees.

The tone of the *Manifesto* was set by its opening sentence: 'The history of all hitherto existing society is the history of class struggles.' Its most thrilling line was the one with which it ended: 'Workers of all lands unite! You have nothing to lose but your chains! You have a world to win!'

The *Manifesto* did not have much impact when it was published. In 1848, the year of uprisings across Europe, people had other things on their minds. The revolutionary spirit that had never been fully quenched after the defeat of the French Revolution broke out once again in country after country, reinforced in many places by a new sense of nationhood among ethnic minorities in regions such as Italy, Austria-Hungary and the Turkish Ottoman empire.

All of these uprisings were defeated, but Marx and Engels, who had been reunited in England, continued to prepare for the further revolutions they were sure would soon occur. Engels returned to Manchester, where he worked in the family firm – never letting his principles interfere with the furthering of his business interests – until he was able to arrange a comfortable retirement in 1869. He continued to support Marx financially, and when his own finances benefited from the sale of his share in the business, he was able to increase that support appreciably.

Marx, with a modest income assured, was able to devote himself to his studies, and to his propagandist activities. In the quiet of the Reading Room at the British Museum, he assembled a massive analysis of the economics of capitalist societies and the process by which he believed they were bound to be superseded. Engels, from his base in Manchester, sent letter

after letter, answering Marx's questions about the actual workings of business and supplying supporting statistics. The first
volume of Marx's masterpiece, *Das Kapital* (Capital), was published in 1867. The initial response was disappointing, but its
influence spread. It was widely read in its Russian and French
translations, though was not translated into English until after
his death in 1883. He never finished preparing the second and
third volumes for the press, a task completed by his faithful
comrade Engels.

The essence of Marx's analysis of capitalist society was that
it carried within itself the seeds of its own destruction. The continual efforts of employers to drive down wages must eventually
reduce their workers to bare subsistence level. Fiercer and
fiercer competition must lead to a falling rate of profit. The capitalist system of production would stumble from crisis to crisis,
until the final crisis that would usher in the golden age of communism. After which, not only would exploitation of man by
man come to an end, but the state itself would 'wither away'.
Precisely how this ideal communist society would work he did
not say. What he did say was that when it came to pass, human
nature would itself change. Greed and competitiveness, being
the product of a sick society, would vanish from the earth.

Given the worldwide success of capitalist institutions, this
analysis now seems utterly barmy, and it might seem strange
that anyone could have been taken in by it. But it should be
borne in mind that for more than sixty years after *Capital* was
published, the industrialized countries were plagued by a succession of economic crises. When the big one came in 1931,
it really did look as though the entire capitalist system might
be about to implode. Lots of intelligent people thought so. It
was only after Keynes showed how to manage the inherent

tendency of modern economies to career out of control that a way was found of keeping the show safely on the road. And Marx wasn't wrong about the inescapable conflict between the interests of capital and labour. If the rich countries no longer have child chimney sweeps and women coal-haulers underground, it is not because the employers of labour are more enlightened and sensitive than their five-times-great-grandfathers. It is because the generations that followed were prevented by law from continuing with such practices, and because changing patterns of income and costs rendered some of them uneconomic. Appalling exploitation still goes on, of course, but it occurs in far-off countries, hidden from the consumers of the products involved.

Marx's promise of a communist Utopia has entranced countless millions since it was first extended 160 years ago. Most of them have been poor – dreadfully poor. When life is grim, and there are no grounds for reasonable hope, unreasonable hope can be very seductive. And if there really is no possibility of a significant improvement in one's own life, the belief that present suffering can lead to a better life for later generations may be the answer. It is a belief that religions have exploited throughout the ages, and Marxism is best understood as a religion, albeit one without gods. And religion, as Marx said, without any apparent sense of irony, is the 'opiate of the people'.

But whether Marxism, as a guide to living, makes sense or not, is not really what concerns us here. What matters in the context of this book is that it has been one of the greatest influences on the course of human history for the past hundred years. It has left its mark on the life of two great nations – Russia and China – and has spread its influence far beyond their borders. There is no possibility of understanding world history since 1900 without understanding what communism appeared to offer, and what it actually delivered.

3 3

THE PURSUIT OF EMPIRE

As the population of Europe increased, and demand for the products of its industries continued to grow, its nations sought new sources of raw materials. Their gaze fell on Africa, and especially on that part of the continent south of the Sahara. This was a land more extensive than Europe, with 100 million people, and, quite possibly, enormous untapped sources of wealth. Little was known about the interior of the continent before 1850, but during the following thirty years missionaries and explorers penetrated further inland. The information they brought back encouraged both commercial and state interest, and around 1870 there began a feverish race for the annexation of 'unclaimed' territory: the notorious 'scramble for Africa'. As more areas were claimed by European powers, the risk of war over competing claims grew.

In 1884 a conference was therefore convened in Berlin to resolve a number of outstanding disputes, including African colonization. Like guests at a particularly inviting dinner, Europe's statesmen tucked in their napkins, and proceeded to carve up the African continent. The idea that it might already 'belong' to the people who lived there would not have occurred to them; they concentrated on the question of to whom it *should* belong. The fact that it already contained a number of established states, and many ancient nations, did not register, and they drew their straight lines without regard to language, culture or any criterion other than the need to ensure that each European nation received a fair slice. Needless to say, neither the peoples of Africa nor their rulers were asked for their opinion. The arbitrary boundaries that resulted became the source of many conflicts when these artificially created territories later gained independence.

While the Great Powers were parcelling out the land and peoples of Africa, a trial of strength was under way to decide who should control the future of East Asia. The first test of the progress of Japan's modernization came in 1884, only sixteen years after the Meiji restoration. It took the form of a confrontation with China, and the issue in dispute was the government of Korea.

Korea had been a client state of China's for some time, but its location opposite the Japanese mainland, and its resources of coal and iron, made it a natural target for a now outward-looking Japan. As early as 1875, Japan had followed the example of the other industrial nations, and forced Korea to open its borders to Japanese trade. When a division opened up between modernizers and traditionalists in Korea itself, the Japanese sided with the modernizers, and the Chinese with the traditionalists. In 1884, a group of pro-Japanese reformers attempted to overthrow the Korean government, but were frustrated by Chinese intervention. On this occasion the dispute was patched up, but in 1894 the leader of the 1884 coup was assassinated in China, and the Chinese intervened in a renewed uprising against the Korean government. The Japanese saw this as a violation of the agreement and when they declared war in August 1894, most of the world's great powers assumed that Japan would be given a bloody nose. But in the fire of battle, the strength of the newly industrialized Japan and the weakness of its bigger, but more backward neighbour were demonstrated for all to see.

In the treaty that ended the war, China was forced to recognize the independence of Korea and to cede the island of Taiwan to Japan, as well as granting that country trading rights on Chinese territory. This demonstration of Chinese weakness had both external and internal consequences. Externally, it encouraged the European powers to demand further concessions in their turn. Internally, the perceived humiliation sowed the seeds of revolutionary activity that would eventually bring the Manchu dynasty to an end. But it was not only China that suffered humiliation as a consequence of the war. Japan, too, had to face up to the realities of its position in the world. Under pressure from European powers, especially from a Russia concerned at Japanese ambitions, it was forced to give up some of the territory it had won. It was a loss of face that would not be forgiven, and it reinforced the country's determination to achieve the status of a truly great power.

While Japan was flexing its muscles in Asia, another recently reborn power was asserting itself in Europe. In 1897, Germany began construction of a battle fleet, serving notice on Britain that it was not prepared indefinitely to accept a situation in which British naval supremacy could dictate the course of international affairs. Britain took note, and began to look around for ways of counteracting the threat this powerful new state represented to its position in the world. The essence of Britain's attitude, and the way it was viewed by other countries, was later nicely summarized by Winston Churchill, when he said in 1914:

We have got all we want in territory, and our claim to be left
in unmolested enjoyment of vast and splendid possessions,
mainly acquired by violence, largely maintained by force,
often seems less reasonable to others than to us.

In 1899, it was clear that the British had not yet got all that
they wanted in territory. In that year Britain went to war
against the Boers, a people of Dutch ancestry who lived in the
southernmost region of Africa, in the republics of Natal, the
Orange Free State and the Transvaal. The Boers had already
fought one war against the British in 1880–1, but the discovery of gold in the Boer territory of the Witwatersrand in 1886
virtually guaranteed that they would have to fight another. The
war, when it came, was a severe shock to the British, whose
forces outnumbered those of the Boers by nearly ten to one.
What should have been a short campaign turned into two and
a half years of bitter guerrilla fighting. The outcome ensured
British control of what would become the Union of South
Africa, but it cost Britain dearly in both lives and money. The
deaths of 20,000 Boer women and children in British prison
camps cost Britain even more dearly in the damage to its international reputation.

One power not involved in the parcelling-out of Africa
was Russia, which had no need of African colonies: it had all
the opportunities it needed in Asia. But the rise of Japan as a
major player in East Asian affairs underlined the need for
speedy action. The tsar, Alexander III, had conceived a plan for
a trans-Siberian railway, and work had started in 1891. Work
proceeded simultaneously on sections right across Asia, and by
1901 the line extended for 5800 miles, from Moscow to
Vladivostok on the Sea of Japan. At the same time the Russians

obtained a lease of Port Arthur (modern Lü-Shun) on the Liaotung peninsula, giving them a formidable base from which to further their influence in Korea.

This growing Russian threat to Japan's influence in East Asia was something that Japan's rulers were not prepared to countenance. By 1904 they were ready to strike. The Russians, badly led by an ineffective government, and with half their naval forces in European waters, were in no shape to withstand the assault. In a succession of battles on land and sea, the Japanese inflicted defeat after defeat on the Russian forces. This series of disasters culminated in the destruction of the pride of the Russian fleet – which had finally made it all the way from Europe – in a battle in the Strait of Tsushima, off the coast of Korea, in May 1905. It was one of the most decisive naval battles in history, and it signalled a change in the worldwide balance of power.

If Japan's victory over China in 1889 had come as a surprise to military planners elsewhere, it was nothing to the shock they registered at the defeat of this much more formidable adversary. They were forced to recognize the existence of a new member of the Great Powers club, and to reorder their strategies accordingly. The Japanese for their part could walk the world with their heads held high. In a mere forty-two years they had wiped out the shame of having to submit to Commodore Perry and his four gunboats. They had compelled the European powers to relinquish the trading concessions obtained at the time of Japan's weakness. They had asserted their military superiority over their giant Chinese neighbour. And now, sweetest of all, they had decisively defeated a major European power in a fair fight. They could have been forgiven for thinking that if they had achieved so much in a single generation, there really was nothing they couldn't do. In addition, subject peoples everywhere had been given food for thought. If an Asian nation could take on one of the 'master races' and beat them at their own game, could not others do the same?

For educated Chinese, there were no such consolations. Looking back over the experiences of the previous fifteen years – or for that matter, the previous fifty – the vista was one of almost unrelieved depression. Their country, which they had been taught to call, and to think of as, the centre of the world, had suffered humiliation after humiliation. Their nation, which little more than a century earlier had been beyond question the most prosperous, and in many ways the most cultured, in the world, was now assailed with constant reminders of its weakness and backwardness. Its rulers, weary and corrupt, had for years seemed mired in indecision, not knowing whether to modernize as the Japanese had done, or whether such an attempt would bring down even more humiliation on their heads. Beginning in 1901, the government had at last embarked upon a belated programme of reform. It had abolished the 2000-year-old civil service examination system; reorganized the army; introduced a new system of education; and convened regional and national assemblies. But as so often when a fossilized regime embarks upon modernization without a change of leadership, the changes merely intensified the widespread feeling that only root-and-branch reform would do. It was clear to many that the country was no longer being governed with the Mandate of Heaven. According to past precedent, it was time for someone with a new mandate to step on to the stage.

The Manchu (or Qu'ing) dynasty that had ruled China since 1644 was finally overthrown in 1911. It was replaced by a Kuomintang (nationalist) government led by Sun Yat-sen. Sun, a 45-year-old British-educated Christian convert, has been called 'the father of modern China', and is still honoured in China as 'the father of the revolution'. His 'three principles of the people' – nationalism, democracy and the people's livelihood – were adopted not only by the Kuomintang, but by the communist revolutionaries who succeeded them. He had spent many years in exile, organizing Chinese revolutionary cells in Europe and Japan, and he had been involved in several failed rebellions. In 1911, while he was still in exile, a further series of uprisings occurred around the country, and this time they were successful. Sun was invited by the leaders of the rebellion to return to China and assume the presidency. He did not occupy it for long, but he continued to serve the Kuomintang government in other capacities, and would remain its driving force until he died in 1925. In 1911, it seemed possible that China might at last be about to shake off the years of humiliation and weakness, and resume its accustomed place among the great nations of the world. Possible, that is, if one forgot the lesson of 3000 years of history, that the ending of one dynasty was always followed by an interval of civil war and dislocation before the Mandate of Heaven descended upon another.

As the nineteenth century drew to a close, a collection of new technologies came to maturity that would transform human society in both peace and war. The most important of these involved the generation and distribution of electricity, at the heart of which were two early nineteenth-century inventions: the electric generator and the electric motor.

The basic discoveries that led to the development of both these devices were made by the Danish physicist Hans Christian Oersted in 1821, and the British physicist Michael Faraday in 1831. Faraday, following up Oersted's discoveries, demonstrated that the rotation of a wire coil in a magnetic field produced an electric current. He also demonstrated that an electric current passed through a coil could cause a magnet to rotate. These two processes, which are the mirror image of each other, contain the essence of electricity generation – the use of mechanical energy to produce electricity and the use of electricity to produce mechanical energy. The electric power that underpins modern society is the product of a three-step sequence:

1 a machine (steam turbine, water turbine, etc.) generates current

2 a transmission cable carries the current to where it is to be used

3 an electric motor, a lamp, or some other device, uses the current to produce mechanical energy, light, heat, etc., at the point of use.

These three steps, which are so simple to summarize, required half a century of ingenious inventions before the basic principles could be effectively applied. It was not until 1873 that the first commercially practicable electric motor was produced. But in the last quarter of the nineteenth century and the first quarter of the twentieth, these inventions created a second Industrial Revolution every bit as significant as that created a century earlier by the development of the steam engine.

Electricity did not replace the steam engine. On the contrary, it gave the steam engine a new *raison d'être*. Electricity has to be generated, and most of the world's electricity is still generated by steam-driven machinery. This is the case whether the fuel used is coal, gas, oil or nuclear energy. Only where water power is available to drive turbines directly can steam power be dispensed with. The foreign exchange dealer at her computer is as dependent on steam power for her livelihood as was her four-times-great-grandmother working down a mine.

We live in the world that electricity made. Electric light has enormously increased the hours during which work can be performed, and leisure pursued. Electric power has removed the constraints that required industry to be located near coalfields. Electricity has made cinema, radio and television possible. Without it, the computer and the internet would be inconceivable. Electricity *is* the modern world. It is a stunning reflection that, for all practical purposes, it did not exist 150 years ago.

At the same time that electricity generation and transmission were being perfected, another hugely important technology – the internal combustion engine – was reaching maturity. This device, which depends upon the rapidly repeated ignition of a vaporized fuel such as gasoline, had a long history. A key stage in its development was reached in 1861, when the German engineer Nikolaus August Otto made the first engine working on a four-stroke cycle. This opened up the possibility of using the internal combustion principle as an alternative to steam power. But Otto's engine, like all other internal combustion engines at the time, ran on coal gas, which of its nature required supply lines, and could not therefore be used to power vehicles. It was not until petroleum spirit became available in significant quantities, as a by-product of the lighting oil industry, and people started looking for a use for it, that the mobile engine we know today became a practicable possibility.

By 1900, all the important problems involved in the construction of internal combustion engines had been solved, and a number of manufacturers in the United States had begun to produce automobiles on a small scale. The novelty of the product, and the small scale of operation, made these early cars very expensive, and the manufacturers endeavoured to maintain the image of the automobile as a high-priced, luxury object accessible only to the rich. But in 1903, this cosy arrangement was shattered by the formation in Detroit, Michigan, of the Ford Motor Company, the creation of an engineer of Irish immigrant stock named Henry Ford.

Ford had a vision of the future role of the automobile in American life, and his approach to marketing and manufacturing was inspired by it. Unlike his competitors, who fought in the courts to try to prevent him from achieving his vision, he went for the lowest price and the biggest market, based on extreme standardization and streamlined production. In October 1908, he introduced his Model T, the most famous vehicle in automobile history. In 1913, inspired by the example of the Sears, Roebuck assembly lines that employed conveyor belts to fulfil mail orders, he created the world's first assembly line for the mass production of an engineered product. At a stroke, it cut average assembly times from 12.5 to 1.5 hours per vehicle, dramatically reducing the cost of the finished product. With its aid, Ford was able to turn his dream into a reality. During its nineteen-year life, the Model T would achieve sales of 16 million vehicles, half the total sales of the automobile industry worldwide. In the USA 15 million were sold, transforming American life and providing a model of mass production applicable to a vast range of industries.

It was also in 1903 that the first full-size aeroplane with an internal combustion engine took off from a field near Kitty Hawk, in North Carolina. The pilot was a 32-year-old mechanic named Orville Wright, the son of a bishop of the United Brethren of Christ. He and his brother Wilbur designed and built the engine that powered it in their bicycle shop, because no one could make them an engine light enough for the purpose. On its first flight, the plane flew just 40 yards, and was airborne for only 12 seconds. But by the end of the day, they had achieved a sustained flight of 58 seconds. It was all that was needed to prove the practicability of heavier-than-air flying machines.

For the next three years, the brothers refused to fly, partly because of their fear of industrial espionage, but also in exasperation at the refusal of the American army to take their invention seriously. But they continued to build and refine their machines, and their breakthrough came on 8 August 1908, when Wilbur Wright gave a spectacular demonstration of aerobatics in front of an astonished crowd at Le Mans in France. From then on, Europeans, who had been slow off the mark, embarked upon the development of heavier-than-air machines with enthusiasm. Within a year, a 37-year-old French factory-owner named Louis Bleriot had won the £1000 prize offered by the British *Daily Mail* to the first person to fly across the English Channel. By 1911, France had 350 certified pilots, twice as many as the rest of the world, and more than ten times as many as the USA. There followed three years of daredevil adventure, as aviators travelled everywhere, competing in races and flying circuses. But in 1914, something happened to turn aviation into one of the deadliest businesses in the world.

When Henry Ford started up his first assembly line in 1913 the world was a busy place. One of the most striking facts about it was just how many people there were, compared with any time in the past. In the 150 years since 1763, the world's population had more than doubled, from 800 million to more than 1600 million. This was partly due to advances in medicine. Thanks to a better understanding of infection and the importance of hygiene, improvements in sanitation, the introduction of vaccination and the provision of clean water, life expectancies in many countries had increased. This was particularly true of cities in industrialized countries. Before the nineteenth century, cities had been population sinks, where people met an early death. Only constant replenishment from the countryside had enabled numbers to be maintained. Now their populations were advancing rapidly, and in many countries there had been a marked increase in the proportion of the total population living in an urban environment.

In these countries, the fall in death-rates had occurred against a background of maintained birth-rates, with the result that population growth had been particularly rapid. One of the most striking examples of this trend was Britain, where a population of around 7 million in 1763 had by 1913 grown to 40 million, in spite of the emigration of around 20 million people.

Improved hygiene and medical advances would not have

led to increases in population had there not been a corresponding increase in the amount of food available. Between 1763 and 1913, the acreage of cultivated land in the world had increased something like threefold, and in many countries improved techniques had resulted in higher yields per acre of both crops and livestock. As a result, standards of living had improved appreciably, in spite of the worldwide doubling of population.

Not every country benefited from the increase in the amount of food available. Britain's downtrodden colony of Ireland had had a population of 6.5 million as recently as 1840, but thanks to famines and grinding poverty, had lost 5 million to emigration, and now had less than 4 million. Such areas of deprivation against a background of comparative plenty show that there had been a great increase in the inequality of living standards between the better-off nations and those less fortunate.

The increase in global population during the previous century or so had been accompanied by a huge amount of movement between countries. By 1890, these migrations had been going on for seventy years, but they reached a peak in the quarter century between 1890 and 1913. The reasons for this included:

1 the removal of legal obstacles to migration in a number of countries

2 a sharp fall in the cost of ocean travel

3 an agricultural depression caused by imports of cheap grain from countries such as Argentina and America, which created destitution among European farm workers.

The most important factor in these migrations was the fall in transport costs associated with the coming of the steamship, which acted as both a 'push' and a 'pull'. By making it easy to transport foodstuffs over long distances, it rendered much traditional farming uneconomic in the face of competition from countries such as the USA and Australia, throwing workers in older countries out of a job. This was the 'push'. At the same time, it cheapened travel, making it possible for poor people to leave their homes for the chance of a better life elsewhere. This was the 'pull'.

Some of these migrations reached phenomenal proportions. Between 1840 and 1913, something like 60 million Europeans left their homelands to try their luck elsewhere. Around three-quarters of them finished up in North America, where the railroads had opened up the country and land was cheap. Another 10 million or so, mostly Spaniards, Portuguese and Italians, found their way to Latin America. Substantial numbers from Britain and Ireland found new homes in Canada, Australia, New Zealand and South Africa. This was the time when European empires reached their maximum extent, and it was in many ways a golden age of opportunity for European emigrants looking for a new home in countries where they could still feel 'at home'.

It was not only from western and southern Europe that people moved to seek their fortunes in strange lands. In the second half of the nineteenth century, four or five million Russian pioneers made new homes in Siberia. And in South and East Asia, people were similarly on the move in search of a better life, or simply a way of earning a living. Between 1830 and 1913, tens of millions of Indian workers on short-term contracts supplied the labour needed in mines and on plantations in British colonies such as Trinidad, South Africa, Ceylon and Burma. During the same period, perhaps as many as

15 million Chinese peasants, desperate to escape debt, took advantage of the 'coolie' trade, which supplied them as labourers to employers around the world, but especially to the rubber plantations and tin mines of Malaya.

Thanks to increased food supplies, and these great migrations, some areas of the world had registered huge increases in numbers since 1763. The population of Europe, excluding Russia, in spite of its losses to migration, had exploded from around 110 million to something like 350 million. Russia itself, including Siberia, now had a population of 150 million. The population of the USA, on the receiving end of the tide of European migration, had passed 100 million.

Among the nations of Asia, Japan was home to 60 million people: prosperous, well educated and brimming with national self-confidence. China, with over 500 million people, and an illustrious past, should have been one of the world's great powers. But years of war and famine, complacent and ineffective government, and abuse by its foreign tormentors, had reduced it to a shadow of its former self, and left a large part of its population mired in debt and ignorance.

India's population of 350 million – equal to that of Europe – was still subject to the whims of the government of one of Europe's offshore islands. For the time being, India's educated classes had no choice but to allow themselves to be patronized by people whose illiterate ancestors had been running around in skins when their own forebears were creating supreme masterpieces of art and literature. But they would not put up with it for much longer.

Two other vast territories, Australia and Canada, were still nominally part of the British empire, but their inhabitants could not be patronized as the people of India were. British

India had been created by a commercial enterprise, which had obtained control of a densely populated subcontinent by means of superior armaments and diplomatic chicanery. Canada and Australia, by contrast, had been effectively emptied of their native peoples by a combination of European diseases and racial cleansing. They had then been resettled, as the United States had been, by independent-minded European immigrants, who would quickly have asserted their independence if Britain had attempted to treat them as it did those colonies whose peoples had a different skin colour. Canada had been effectively self-governing since the passing of the Government of Canada Act in 1867. A third of its people were culturally and linguistically French, and many of those would have preferred to form a separate nation. But in 1913 separatist sentiments were not so strong as to threaten the survival of the state.

Australia had been a self-governing commonwealth since 1901, with a constitution that gave its individual states, like Canada's provinces, a large measure of control over their own affairs. Like Canada, it was blessed with extensive wheat-growing lands, and was rich in mineral resources. The citizens of both countries enjoyed a standard of living that was the envy of people elsewhere.

The former British colony of New Zealand, too, was for all practical purposes now an independent country. It had been administered separately from New South Wales since 1841, and in 1907 had been designated a 'dominion', and taken its place alongside Australia and Canada as a self-governing territory united to Britain only by ties of friendship and the sharing of a king.

As 1913 drew to a close, the bronzed young sportsmen of Australia and New Zealand, like the sportsmen of all the well-fed nations, were already looking forward to the next Olympic

Games. No women were doing so. Unlike the Greeks, the modern world was not ready for the spectacle of women athletes displaying their physical skills in public. The ancient Greek festival had been revived in 1896 as a result of the enthusiasm of a French aristocrat, Baron Pierre de Coubertin, who had visited the little English town of Much Wenlock at the time of its annual Olympian Games, a mixture of 'manly sports and outdoor recreations' that drew athletes from all over the region. What he had seen there had persuaded him that a similar festival on an international scale might be a means of fostering peace and goodwill. The 1896 games had been such a success that it had been resolved to repeat them at four-yearly intervals. In 1916 they were due to be held in Berlin. But in 1914 an event occurred that committed the nations of the world to a contest of an altogether more desperate kind.

3 6
GLOBAL WAR: ACT ONE

Prince Otto von Bismarck, the founder and creator of modern Germany, suggested in the 1880s that the next major European war would be started by 'some damn fool thing in the Balkans'. It was an uncannily sound prediction.

In June 1914, the heir to the Austrian throne, the Archduke Franz Ferdinand, was in Bosnia, then part of the Austrian empire, to review the imperial troops there. On 28 June, on a sunny Sunday afternoon, he and his wife Sophie paid a visit to the city of Sarajevo. Also in Sarajevo on that day was a party of students and apprentices – members of a revolutionary group called Young Bosnia – with the express aim of assassinating the archduke. One of them threw a bomb at the royal car, but it fell off, injuring a number of bystanders.

A few hours later, the royal couple decided to visit the injured in hospital, and by chance their route took them past one of the would-be murderers – nineteen-year-old Gavrilo Princip – who was hanging around after the apparent failure of the assassination attempt. He fired two shots, killing the archduke and his wife.

After a four-week lull, things suddenly careered out of control. By a tragic irony, the archduke's assassination had removed the one person most likely to act as a restraining influence on those elements in Austrian society that pressed for a showdown with Serbia. The Austrian government sought, and received, an assurance of German support in the event of Russia coming to Serbia's aid. The German government had no interest in Austria's quarrel with Serbia, but had no intention of allowing Russia a free hand.

On 23 July the Austrians accused the Serbian government of involvement in the assassination, and issued a 48-hour ultimatum. This included demands for the elimination of terrorist organizations on Serbian soil, an end to anti-Austrian propaganda and the inclusion of Austrian representatives on the commission of enquiry into the assassination. The Serbian government considered this last demand an infringement of its national sovereignty, and rejected it. The Russian government, still smarting from its humiliation at the hands of the Japanese, felt it could not be seen to desert fellow Slavs in Serbia, and announced a general mobilization. This did not necessarily indicate an intention of going to war, but events were now moving with such speed that statesmen were having great difficulty in distinguishing between sabre-rattling and immediate threats. It was not clear to any of them that a dispute between Austria and Serbia necessarily implied a Europe-wide war. Even as late as 31 July, the British prime minister, Asquith, was expressing to the Archbishop of Canterbury his opinion that 'Serbia deserves a good thrashing'.

Bismarck had always designed his alliances as a way of avoiding war, and his ultimate horror was Germany being drawn into a war on two fronts – east and west – simultaneously. But after his death, his successors had lost sight of this strategy, and had begun to construct detailed plans in the event of such a war, based on the perceived need for swift victory over France before the Russian juggernaut could be mobilized. When the Russian mobilization was announced, the German generals, not wishing to see their Austrian ally destroyed and fearing the growing strength of Russian industry and armaments, saw this as a last chance of dealing with the Russian threat. On 1 August, Germany declared war on Russia, and on 3 August, on France.

To ensure that victory over France would be swift, German plans had always assumed that any attack would be through Belgium. But the neutrality of Belgium was guaranteed by an international treaty to which Britain was a party. When German troops crossed the Belgian frontier on 4 August, it provided the British government with justification to go to war at France's side. So within six weeks of those two shots in Sarajevo, all the Great Powers of Europe were committed to war. The echo of those shots would not completely fade away until the summer of 1945, thirty-one years later, by which time they would have led to two world wars, and the deaths of 60 million people.

At first everything went according to the plans the German High Command had prepared. Within three days, 40,000 French soldiers were dead. Within a month, German guns were within range of Paris. But then, the French armies, under the inspired leadership of their commander, General Joffre, not only held, but began to repel the invaders. At this stage, soldiers on both sides and civilians at home believed that the war would be over within months. But as first the Germans, and then the French and British dug themselves into defensive trenches, the war degenerated into a gruesome struggle in which thousands could die in the attempt to capture a small hill, or a few hundred yards of almost impassable mud. It was a horror that would persist for another three years.

Britain and France did not fight alone. The investment that Britain had made in its overseas empire now produced a human dividend. Troops from Australia, Canada, Ireland, New Zealand and South Africa volunteered in thousands to fight at Britain's side. Soldiers from the overseas colonies – from India above all – fought and died to save the 'mother country' that had ruled over them with less than undiluted kindness for a century and more. France's overseas colonies, too, provided substantial numbers of soldiers who gave their lives so that France could go on exploiting the families they left behind. But in spite of all this help, there were times when it seemed likely that Germany would emerge the victor.

Once the trenches had been dug, the war in the West remained for most of the time confined to a narrow strip of land stretching from the English Channel to the Swiss border. It was a very different picture in the East. There, the armies of Germany and Austria on the one hand and Russia on the other swept backwards and forwards, as first one side, then the other launched major offensives that drove everything before them, and then petered out, as supply lines became over-extended and bad weather intervened. In the West, an assault that had taken months to prepare, and cost scores of thousands of lives, might advance a front line by 5 miles. In the East, a similar offensive might advance it by 200. Between 1914 and 1917, four such great swings of advance and retreat carried the opposing forces deep into one another's territories. For the peoples living in the lands that were captured and recaptured the consequences were often as dreadful as for the combatants themselves.

As the years passed, and the problems of maintaining supplies of food and war materials mounted, it began to appear that the outcome would be decided by whichever side succeeded in starving the other into submission. By 1917, Britain had established a naval blockade that threatened Germany's ability to continue. The Germans, in response, turned to a weapon they had developed years before, but had not yet seriously employed: the submarine. It proved massively effective, but the manner in which it was deployed brought about the intervention that ensured Germany's defeat.

When the war had started in 1914, the United States had held aloof. Europe's family squabbles were no concern of America's. If anything, American opinion had been sympathetic to the Central Powers (Germany and Austria-Hungary) rather than the Allies (Britain, France and Russia). However, the propaganda efforts of the Allies, especially the British, who had the enormous advantage of a shared language, proved effective, and by 1917 there had been a marked swing of opinion in their favour. But this was still a long way from implying any intention of becoming actively engaged.

In January 1917, the German emperor, Wilhelm II, held an audience at which the chiefs of the army and the navy, in the absence of the German chancellor, insisted that unrestricted submarine warfare was essential if the war was to be won. The emperor assented, and the chancellor, when informed, offered no opposition. 'Unrestricted' meant that the decision to attack merchant ships would be determined by their perceived destination, not by reference to the flag under which they were sailing, or the nationality of the passengers they were carrying. The implementation of this decision by itself would have been sufficient to bring America into the war. But the decoding of telegrams in which the German government extended a promise of support to Mexico, in the event of that country becoming involved in a war with the United States, put the matter beyond doubt. On 6 April 1917, the United States declared war on Germany. From that moment, it was no longer a question of which side would lose the war, but merely how long it would take.

Paradoxically, this dawn was followed, for the Allies, by the darkest hour of the entire conflict. In the West, a series of battles around the town of Ypres, involving appalling loss of life, struck a severe blow at British morale and fighting capacity. At the same time the overstretched French army was struck by a series of mutinies. While the shock of these events was being absorbed, the Allies had to come to terms with the disintegration of the Russian war effort in the East.

Compared with Russia, Britain and France were mature democracies. When the war brought a need to impose a degree of authoritarian control, their political systems were able to handle the strain. Russia, however, was barely a fledgling democracy. Following defeat by Japan, the country had experienced a decade of rapid growth, accompanied by a raising of political consciousness. In this atmosphere, the attempt to return to a more autocratic form of government aroused tremendous resentment. The problem was made worse by the character of the country's ruler, Nicholas II, who possessed real power, but lived in a fantasy world, equally distanced from his people and his ministers.

Nowhere did these simmering resentments bubble more ominously than in the capital city of Petrograd (St Petersburg). Between 1914 and 1917, the industrial expansion generated by the war had caused the city's population to increase by a third. Disruptions to the harvest and to the railway system, and hoarding by peasants, had led to severe food shortages. Near-starving citizens staged demonstrations, and the garrison supposedly installed to control them expressed open sympathy. On 11 March 1917, soldiers from the Pavlovskiy barracks mutinied. The next day, 20,000 people took to the streets. The tsar, on the advice of his ministers, abdicated, and a provisional government appointed by the Duma (the Russian parliament) took control of the whole country.

Encouraged by socialist agitators, factory workers and servicemen began forming councils called soviets, based on the model established during the failed uprising of 1905. The most important faction in the Petrograd soviet was a group called the Bolsheviks. Their leader was Vladimir Ilich Lenin, a 47-year-old law graduate and magnificent orator, living in exile in Switzerland. Lenin, who had already served prison sentences for his part in unsuccessful uprisings, was a follower of Karl Marx, but advocated his own version of Marxism, which questioned the ability of the proletariat to bring about revolution, and insisted on the necessity of leadership of the workers by an elite group – the communists – who would enforce discipline and provide direction to the forces of revolution.

The German government, although opposed to the Bolsheviks, smuggled Lenin out of exile in Switzerland, in the hope that his presence in Russia might lead to the withdrawal of Russia from the war. They were right. Lenin's arrival in a 'sealed' train at the Finland station in Petrograd on 3 April 1917 – one of the most momentous episodes in Russian history – initiated a series of events that culminated in the setting up of a Revolutionary Government and the signing of an armistice between Russia and Germany. Lenin was quite clear that he had enough to do in Russia. He had no desire to fight a war as well.

Germany was now in a position to concentrate all its efforts on the war in the West. But its situation was desperate.

Its fighting forces, like those of its enemies, were war-weary, and morale was low. Its ally, Austria, was visibly cracking. The British blockade was causing the civilian population severe privation. America was gathering its strength to deliver a knock-out blow. Either one final offensive could destroy the weakened British and French armies, and deny the Americans entry to the continent, or the war was lost. It was time for the gambler's last throw.

Beginning in March 1918, a series of assaults drove the allied forces back, and by 23 March, German guns were once more shelling the outskirts of Paris. But then the tide turned once more. The industrial resources of Britain and France, and the deployment of American troops, who were arriving in considerable numbers, now began to tell. Guns and shells were reaching the allied side at a rate the Germans could not match. During the next three months, they lost 800,000 men, and their fighting strength was further undermined by an epidemic of influenza that swept through their ranks.

In the end, victory came more quickly than the Allied Command had dared to hope. On 1 October, British forces crowned a series of victories over Germany's Turkish ally with a triumphant entry into Damascus, and on 30 October, Turkey surrendered. At 11 a.m. on 11 November, the guns at last fell silent on the Western Front, and Germany and its allies waited to see what terms their enemies would enforce in the peace that followed.

While victors and vanquished alike were giving thanks for the ending of the agony of war, they suffered a final vicious blow. The influenza epidemic that had wrought such devastation among the demoralized German armies in France raced like a forest fire around the world. Nowhere did it linger for more than a few weeks. By the time it had finished its journey, more than 20 million lay dead in its wake – nearly twice as many as had died in four terrible years of war.

37

AN UNQUIET INTERLUDE

Germany's enemies did not go out of their way to be magnanimous. The terms of the treaty that officially ended the war were thrashed out at a peace conference held in the palace of Versailles, outside Paris, in the spring of 1919. Thrashed out, that is, between the representatives of the victorious nations, not between the victors and the vanquished. The only role allocated to the representatives of Germany was to speak when spoken to, and to sign on the dotted line. This they did in the splendid setting of the palace's Hall of Mirrors on 28 June 1919, when they signified their acceptance of the peace settlement set out in the Treaty of Versailles.

The terms of the treaty came as a shock. When Germany had sought an armistice – that is, an end to hostilities – it was on the basis of the 'fourteen points', a list of objectives drawn up by the American president, Woodrow Wilson. But subsequently, another nine had been added. One of these was an admission of war guilt. Further conditions involved substantial losses of territory for Germany and its allies. Germany was required to relinquish its colonies, including Tanganyika (Tanzania), South-west Africa (Namibia) and a collection of islands in the Pacific. In addition, the population and territory of Germany itself were reduced by about 20 per cent, including the return to France of Alsace and Lorraine. The Turkish Ottoman empire, whose soldiers had fought with courage and skill, was savagely reduced in extent, creating the totally new countries of Syria, Palestine, Lebanon and Iraq.

One of the creations of the Treaty of Versailles was an entity called the League of Nations, with headquarters in Geneva. This was a forerunner of – and partial model for – today's United Nations. A number of territories – Syria, Palestine and Iraq (former Turkish territories), and Tanganyika (a German colony) – were designated 'Mandated Territories'. These were in theory administered by France (Syria) and Britain (Palestine, Iraq, Tanganyika) under the supervision of the League. But this gently seductive label was really just a perfume, to give their annexation by the victors a sweeter smell.

For Britain, Palestine would later turn out to be a poisoned chalice. The country had for years been the scene of unofficial immigration by Zionist settlers: Jewish immigrants who aspired to see the ancestral home of the world's scattered Jews once more a specifically Jewish state. In November 1917, the British foreign secretary, Arthur Balfour, wishing to increase American support for Britain's war effort, and conscious of the political clout possessed by American Jewry, had written to the banker L.W. Rothschild expressing his support for 'a national home in Palestine for the Jewish people'. This became known as the Balfour Declaration. When Britain assumed responsibility for Palestine under the mandate – which it did in order to obtain control over the approaches to the Suez Canal – this became a lever for the supporters of Zionism to exert pressure on Britain.

As part of the post-war settlement, one of the Central Powers – the Austro-Hungarian empire – was totally dismembered. Out of its body, three new countries were carved. Two of these – Austria and Hungary – are still with us. The third – Czechoslovakia – embraced the territories we now know as the

Czech Republic and Slovakia. Poland reappeared as an independent country; restored to its people after years of division between Germany, Austria and Russia. A fourth country, with a name the world had not heard before – Yugoslavia – was created by adding together Serbia and Montenegro, the Austrian territories of Slovenia and Croatia, and the Turkish territories of Bosnia and Macedonia.

Absent from these discussions and suffering from rather than participating in the share-out of the spoils, was a country that would have been on the winning side, had it not withdrawn from the fray: Russia. It had no say in the reshaping of the map of Europe. As a socialist republic, with the stated objective of bringing about revolution in capitalist countries everywhere, it was seen as a threat by the other Great Powers of Europe. In their eyes it was now the enemy.

In addition to the loss of territory, the Versailles settlement contained other provisions that would later play an important part in persuading the German people that they had been the victims of an unjust settlement. Chief among these was an obligation to make financial reparation to the victors.

The idea of reparation now seems inappropriate to that particular conflict. It implies that there was a guilty party, and that there were innocent parties. If one takes the view, as many historians do, that the war was an accident waiting to happen, then the question of war guilt hardly arises. But in the immediate aftermath, with the pain and loss fresh in people's minds, the call for the payment of compensation is understandable. The instincts of the American president, Woodrow Wilson, and the British prime minister, David Lloyd George, were against punitive compensation, but both changed their public positions when they realized they were risking electoral defeat.

The compensation decided upon was set at levels that some commentators insisted could only be met by subjecting the German people to extreme hardship, with dangerous consequences. The most powerful statement of this argument was published six months after the conference, in a book entitled *The Economic Consequences of the Peace* by the British economist John Maynard Keynes. Keynes was proved right. The attempt to meet the targets set by the treaty did cause hardship in Germany. And the resentment engendered left the German people prey to politicians who later exploited their sense of having been the victims of a great wrong.

One consequence of the demand for reparations was a nightmare bout of price inflation that afflicted Germany between 1921 and 1923. Reparations were payable in German marks. But Germany, previously the continent's economic powerhouse, had been impoverished by the war, and by the post-war occupation. The payment of reparations was only possible if the German people were prepared to accept a level of taxation that would have reduced them to near-penury. This they were not prepared to do, and a democratically elected government could not force them. It therefore took the only option open to it, which was to print the money and leave taxation at a tolerable level. But as the German people and the countries receiving reparations tried to spend their marks on the limited amount of German goods available, prices naturally rose. As they rose, people became more and more reluctant to hold money. So they spent it as fast as they could, pushing prices higher, which pushed wages higher, which required more money to be printed . . . And so it went on, in a never-ending spiral. As more money was printed, and the purchasing power of that money shrank, the value of the German mark on the foreign exchanges dropped. In January 1923, France and Belgium, exasperated at the falling value of their reparations receipts, which they believed were being deliberately manipulated by the German government, sent troops into the coalfields of the Ruhr, with the intention of taking their entitlement in kind. This created a deeper economic crisis.

By the end of October 1923 the mark, measured against the American dollar, was worth only one four-hundredth of what it had been worth at the beginning of the month, and a large section of German society, including most businesses, had abandoned money altogether and reverted to primitive barter. The situation was dealt with in the end, thanks to a gifted Central Bank president and a reversion to sense by the country's former enemies. But by then, iron had entered the soul of the German middle classes. They were in a condition that made them vulnerable to any politician who offered a restoration of national pride.

Apart from Germany, most of the industrialized countries of the world experienced increasing prosperity during the 1920s. This was particularly true of the United States, and much of the improvement elsewhere could be traced back to the United States, whose economy, enlarged by the demands of wartime production, but undamaged by fighting, was now the most important influence in international trade and finance. The improvement in industrial efficiency achieved during the war, and the increased capacity created by it, were now harnessed to the production of new products based on inventions made during the previous half century. Some of these had existed before the war, but they had been costly to make, and available only to the rich. Now they were within the reach of more people.

These new products were evidence of a society that had begun to escape from a preoccupation with mere subsistence. The rich had always been above such concerns. What was new was that, for the first time in history, large numbers of ordinary people were able to rise above them. The new products were purchased for comfort and pleasure, rather than out of necessity, and they had a life measured in years, rather than days or hours. These goods were different, so different that a new name was invented for them – consumer durables.

What differentiated consumer durables from more traditional products was that they were based on technologies that had not existed a century earlier. The most important of these were electric power and the internal combustion engine, and it was on these two now mature technologies that the great surge of economic growth in 1920s America was based.

Electricity was the basis of three of the most important contributors to the comfort and pleasure of Americans in the 1920s: telephones, radio and cinema. All three of them created great industries. Cinema, which did not require the customer to buy a durable product, possessed two unique qualities. It created a sense of shared nationhood, counteracting the sense of separateness produced by the great distances characteristic of America. It also created an export industry that spread an image of America around the world, an image that sold both American goods and the American way of life.

But the most important of these new products was the one based on the internal combustion engine: the automobile. It not only transformed people's everyday lives; it also created a new approach to manufacturing that combined assembly line production with extreme standardization. Together, these two novel concepts dramatically lowered the costs of car manufacture, and, moreover, were transferable to a whole range of other industries.

As the 1920s progressed, and these new industries got into their stride, the USA experienced a remarkable boom. This generated a stock market bubble of extraordinary proportions, inflated by irresponsible bank lending. And this in turn created a state of euphoria that infected, not just the woman in the street, but people who should have known better. It was tulip time all over again.

But a new element had now entered the economic equation. Hitherto, financial manias, and the crashes that followed them, had principally affected those involved in speculation, with only secondary effects on the economy at large. But the invention of consumer durables introduced a new source of instability: postponable expenditure. Cars weren't like food: no one had to buy them. Or at least, no one had to replace them at a particular time. If people lost confidence in their financial future, they could always delay replacing their cars and their radios. In this case, the thousands employed in making them would be thrown out of work, with dire consequences for the economy at large.

In June 1929, the legendary financier Bernard Baruch told the *American Magazine* that 'The economic condition of the world seems on the verge of a great leap forward.' Later that year, the country's most eminent economist, Professor Irving Fisher of Yale University, entered the history books with his observation that 'stock prices have reached what looks like a permanently high plateau'. A few days later, share prices on the New York Stock Exchange began to fall. And they fell, and they fell, and they fell – for three years. By the end of 1932, they had fallen by 70 per cent.

This collapse of share prices is still referred to as the Great Crash, and will be until we have another like it, after which we will call it the Crash of 29. It was the trigger for the Great Depression that followed it. Between 1929 and 1933, America's Gross Domestic Product (GDP) – roughly speaking, the national income – fell by 30 per cent. Industrial production fell by almost 50 per cent. By the end of 1933, a quarter of the country's workforce was unemployed. This was no short-term affliction. It permanently scarred a whole generation. As late as 1938, the proportion out of a job was still 20 per cent. Had it not been for the war that came soon after, there is no knowing how long the American economy might have continued to run with a large part of its capacity unemployed.

America suffered badly, but it did not suffer alone. The international economy in the 1930s, apart from the economic isolation ward of the Soviet Union, was a highly integrated one. The countries of the world did not just take in one another's exports, they took in one another's booms and slumps. Moreover, the American economy in the 1920s was the source of 40 per cent of the world's manufactured goods. As the dole queues lengthened in America, they lengthened in every other non-socialist country. At the low point of the depression, in the industrial countries as a whole, 40 million people were out of work. And the precipitous fall in the prices of industrial raw materials ensured that the countries that provided them shared in the pain.

The suffering caused by this commercial debacle was the result of ignorance. In the 1920s, the science of economics was still in a primitive state, and decision makers everywhere were guided by a mixture of prejudice and homely common sense that left them helpless in the face of the powerful tides sweeping through the international economy. This limitation is illustrated by the buzz word that was on everyone's lips at the time: over-production. The idea was that industry had become so good at producing things that markets were no longer able to absorb them. For some reason, no one ever got around to coining the word underdemand.

It was not until 1935 that the way to avoid, and escape from, such problems was explained by John Maynard Keynes – the same person who had warned of the likely consequences of the Versailles settlement. His analysis was set out in his book *The General Theory of Employment, Interest and Profit*. Unfortunately, it was a book that required its readers to forget 'common sense', and to do some hard thinking instead. It did for economics what Copernicus's *On the Revolutions of the Heavenly Globes* did for cosmology. It had been common sense that the sun went round the earth. It was also garbage. It was equally common sense that governments ought to cut back on their spending during recessions. Thanks to Keynes, we know now that that, too, is garbage.

The book's argument received a cool reception, not helped by the fact that many of the best minds of Keynes's generation were in the throes of a love affair with Karl Marx's *Das Kapital*. That work of 1867 provided an armour-plated defence against ideas based on real-life business experience, even when those ideas were transmitted by one of the finest intellects of the age.

To be acquainted with Keynes's thought processes is one of the greatest delights a business education has to offer. It is like the delight a mathematician gets from the work of Newton, or a physicist from the work of Faraday. The pleasure is intensified by the quality of Keynes's writing. Here he is in

The Economic Consequences of the Peace, on the state of mind of the participants in the conference:

> The future life of Europe was not their concern; its means of livelihood was not their anxiety. Their preoccupations, good and bad alike, related to frontiers and nationalities, to the balance of power, to imperial aggrandizements, to the future enfeeblement of a strong and dangerous enemy, to revenge, and to the shifting by the victors of their unbearable financial burdens onto the shoulders of the defeated.

It is easy now to see that Keynes was one of humanity's great benefactors. The techniques of economic management he promoted now form part of the toolkit of every central banker and every minister of finance. And if we feel confident that we know how to prevent short-term recessions from developing into long-term depressions, it is to a large extent due to him. But the world would have to go through the fire of another war before his ideas would be accepted by those most in need of them.

One of Keynes's great achievements was to persuade people of the importance of confidence: confidence of investors, confidence of builders, confidence of shoppers, and so on – what he called 'animal spirits'. The most important piece of advice contained in the *General Theory* can be summed up in the saying 'When you're in a hole, stop digging.' Conventional thinkers in the 1920s could not see that by reducing spending at such times, governments were reducing the level of business activity still further, putting more people out of work, and further undermining confidence.

One country was protected from the waves of financial panic, business depression and bank failures that swept the globe between 1929 and 1933: Soviet Russia. Lenin's 'dictatorship of the proletariat' – the temporary state of affairs that was to precede the coming of the socialist millennium – had never come to pass. Lenin himself had suffered a stroke in 1922, and had died in 1924. His place had been taken by Josef Stalin, a hero of the 1917 civil war, who from his key position as general secretary of the Communist Party organized the elimination of his rivals for power, and thereafter ruled as undisputed master of Russia until his death in 1953. He became ever more tyrannical and paranoid. Though he transformed Russia's industrial base, creating the infrastructure that would make possible the Russian army's victories in the next world war, it was at a very high price.

In Stalin's Russia, where stock markets did not exist, where the pursuit of private profit was outlawed and where factory building, farm management, output targets and shop prices were all subject to the supervision of an all-seeing, all-controlling state, the problems that afflicted the capitalist world could not arise. No privately owned bank collapsed, because no privately owned bank existed. No shareholders saw their life savings wiped out in speculative investments, because there were no opportunities for speculative investment.

As highbrow intellectuals in capitalist countries, and their unemployed, lower-brow fellow citizens, contemplated the devastation in their own countries, this model of a supposedly socially oriented, greed-free, goal-focused society – 'the Socialist Sixth of the World', as one best-selling book called it – began to appear very attractive. Communist parties experienced a boom in membership. Had they known the truth, they would have been less enthusiastic. The central planning that made booms and slumps impossible created stupendous follies of ill-advised capital expenditure. The forced collectivization of agriculture destroyed individual initiative and incentives to work, leading to famines in which millions died. The activities of the secret police, and their informers, led to the deaths of millions more. The fear of being accused of harbouring officially disapproved theories paralysed scientific research and speculation. Those who did voice opposition disappeared, either murdered or despatched to Siberian prison camps.

One starry-eyed visitor who came home in 1919 from a carefully arranged Russian tour, the American journalist Lincoln Steffens, is still remembered for the deathless phrase 'I have seen the future, and it works.' It would not be until the Twentieth Party Congress in 1953, when the lid was safely closed on Stalin's coffin, that the gruesome truth would be revealed to the people of Russia, and to the world. Looking back now, a more appropriate reaction might be 'We have seen the past, and it was a nightmare.'

3 8

GLOBAL WAR: ACT TWO

In Germany, the despair generated by unemployment and business failure, in a country still wounded by the previous decade's inflationary nightmare, opened the door to dramatic political change. In an election in 1930, the Nazi (National Socialist German Workers') Party, led by a hypnotic 41-year-old public speaker named Adolf Hitler, campaigned on a platform of national regeneration, and won 102 seats, a fifth of the total, in the German parliament. Austrian by birth, Hitler had started out as a lonely, failed artist. Originally rejected as unfit for military service, he had served in the war as a corporal, and been wounded, gassed and decorated for outstanding bravery. He was obsessed with ideas of racial purity, which were developed in *Mein Kampf* (My Struggle), written while he was serving a prison sentence.

In the next election, in July 1932, against a background of 8 million unemployed – 40 per cent of the workforce – the Nazis won enough seats to make them the largest group in parliament. President Field Marshal Paul von Hindenburg offered Hitler the post of chancellor (first minister). On assuming office, Hitler exercised his right to hold another election. The Nazis campaigned vigorously, underlining their message with terror tactics, while sympathetic police looked the other way. Forty-four per cent of the electorate voted for them, but they secured under half of the votes cast, and under half of the seats in contention. However, with the help of alliances with other parliamentary groups, Hitler lobbied for extraordinary powers, which were granted in March 1933. He saw to it that there were no more elections. He assumed the title of *Führer* (leader), and became the undisputed ruler of Germany; a position he would occupy, at the head of an increasingly authoritarian regime, for the next twelve years.

Hitler had based his election campaigns on three propositions: that Germany was being denied its rightful place in the world; that it would have to fight for that place; and that, in order to do so, the country must be made strong. He added spice to his argument by telling his listeners that their country was the victim of an international conspiracy, in which the most active and influential force was what he called 'International Jewry', a worldwide alliance of Jews, of which there were many millions in Germany and neighbouring countries.

On achieving power, Hitler succeeded in making some impression on Germany's unemployment problem with public works such as motorway construction. He also embarked upon a programme of rearmament. At first, this was much more modest than he pretended it was, since he had no desire to undermine his position by diverting production from current consumption. The weapon he developed most assiduously was propaganda. A particular effort was put into the staging of the Olympic Games in Berlin in 1936, with the intention of demonstrating the power of a reinvigorated Germany, and the superiority of the 'master race'. Everything went brilliantly until the closing stages of the competition, when a 22-year-old black American athlete named Jesse Owens left the cream of European youth trailing in his wake, as he swept to gold medal victories in the 100 metres, 200 metres, long jump and relay. It was not quite the climax to the festival that the *Führer* had planned.

In military terms at least, things continued to go well. In March 1938 Hitler annexed Austria. Early in 1939, while his armed forces were still not fully ready for war, he manage to bluff the British into acquiescing in his occupation of what is now the Czech Republic, while Slovakia took the opportunity of declaring its independence. The British government at last woke up to the fact that here was someone seriously intent on military adventure. Seeing Poland as Hitler's likely next victim, Britain and France issued a public guarantee that they would come to its aid in the event of German aggression. They could not actually have done so, given Poland's location, but they entertained the not very confident hope that the threat of war with Britain and France might deter Hitler from launching an attack.

On 1 September 1939, German forces invaded Poland, and on 3 September Britain and France declared war on Germany. The Germans quickly overran the western half of Poland, while Stalin, who had signed a non-aggression pact with Hitler, took the opportunity to annex the eastern half, as a protective cordon against a possible future attack on Russia itself.

With his armed forces now equal to his ambitions, Hitler next turned his attention westwards, and in quick succession his armies overran Belgium, Holland, France, Denmark and Norway. But he did not succeed in obtaining mastery of the air over the English Channel, and he was forced to abandon plans for an invasion of Britain. Had he rested content with his conquests thus far, he could have created a European empire that might have lasted a long time. But in June 1941, in a move eerily reminiscent of Napoleon's similar adventure 120 years earlier, he turned on Russia. This decision was undoubtedly rooted in his racial obsessions. He regarded all Slavs, Russians included, as an inferior race. He saw them as potential slave labour, and their rich lands as a source of the agricultural and industrial materials his empire needed. The timing of the assault took Stalin completely by surprise. He had no illusions about Hitler's true attitude to Russia, but he believed – he had to believe – that he would have time to build up his country's strength.

For the attack to succeed, Russia had to be defeated within a matter of months. All Hitler's victories had been achieved by *Blitzkreig* (lightning war) – the overwhelming of an enemy by massive air and ground offensives. His strategy did not allow for victory after prolonged fighting, for the simple reason that Germany's industrial resources could not have delivered it. But he had allowed himself to become involved in the military misfortunes of his Italian ally, Mussolini, in the Balkans and in the Mediterranean, an involvement that lost him a vital six weeks, and seriously depleted his air power. At first, like Napoleon's, his forces swept all before them, and very soon they, too, were besieging Leningrad, and at the gates of Moscow. But once again, Russia's winter and its capacity for enduring suffering proved the undoing of a foreign invader. The Russians suffered eight months of appalling losses and incessant defeats, but at Stalingrad in 1942 they achieved a stupendous victory that marked the turning of the tide.

On 11 December 1941, Hitler had perpetrated a second blunder. President Franklin Roosevelt of the US had been rendering assistance to the British cause that went beyond a strict interpretation of existing legislation. Hitler, irritated at such involvement by a neutral power, and fired by a Japanese attack on British and American territories in the Pacific a few days earlier, formally declared war on the United States. In doing so, he wrote a suicide note, not only for himself, but on behalf of the short-lived empire he had created.

Relations between America and Japan had been deteriorating for years, as a consequence of a Japanese invasion of China in 1937 and the entry of Japan in 1940 into an alliance – known as the Axis – with Germany and Italy. In July 1941, encouraged by Russia's involvement elsewhere, Japan began a campaign of imperial expansion by invading the French colony of Indo-China. The US replied by placing an embargo on the supply to Japan of aviation fuel and all materials of war. This gave encouragement to the militaristic element who believed that a war with America was inevitable, if Japan was ever to assume its 'rightful' place as the leading power in Asia. But opinion in government circles was finely balanced, right up to the moment when the war actually began.

The Japanese assault on America in 1941 began at 7.55 a.m. on 7 December – a quiet Sunday morning – with a surprise attack on the United States Pacific fleet, which was lying at anchor in Pearl Harbor, in Hawaii. The devastation was almost total, most of it occurring in the first thirty minutes. By the end of the day, five battleships had been either sunk or destroyed, and a number of other battleships and cruisers seriously damaged. Japanese losses amounted to about 50 planes, 100 men and a few submarines.

The success of the attack on Pearl Harbor gave Japanese forces a free hand in the Pacific, which they exploited to mount invasions of European colonies in Burma, Malaysia and Indonesia, as well as virtually every island in the western Pacific. A hugely significant event occurred in February 1942 just two months after the engagement at Pearl Harbor, when Japanese forces captured the supposedly impregnable British naval base of Singapore, with the surrender of 70,000 British, Indian and Australian troops. For most Japanese, it was a source of intense pride that their forces had triumphed over the powers that had lorded it for so long over so much of Asia. But those in government circles who had advised against the attack on Pearl Harbor remained convinced that Japan, too, had written a suicide note.

Like the German attack on Russia, Japan's offensive swept all before it for six months or so. The turning point – the Pacific equivalent of Stalingrad – came at the Battle of Midway, a titanic battle between opposing airborne armadas that was fought 1300 miles to the north-west of Hawaii from 3 to 6 June 1942.

The mobilization of the American economy and the organization of an invasion of Europe took some time, during which the Russian people continued to bear the main burden of the war on land. But on 6 June 1944, Allied troops landed on the beaches of northern France, and began the rolling back of the German forces in Western Europe. In January 1945, Hitler committed suicide in his bunker in Berlin. Four months later, on 8 May, the formal surrender of the German commanders on both eastern and western fronts brought the European war to a close.

As the victorious armies had approached, and crossed, the frontiers of Germany, a new horror had been brought to light. Allied governments had long been aware of the large numbers of Jews incarcerated in concentration camps, and of the dreadful crimes committed against them. Little detail had emerged, however, and the world at large remained ignorant. But as camps such as Auschwitz, Belsen and Buchenwald were overrun, it became clear that a programme of extermination had been carried out on an industrial scale, and with macabre efficiency: against Jews in particular, but also against Romanies. The total can never be known with any precision. But whether the number of Jews who met their death in these gas chamber death factories was 4 million or 5 million (6 million, the figure often quoted, may be an exaggeration) is really beside the point. In its combination of sheer scale and systematic, insane racism, it remains an obscenity with few parallels in the history of the world.

With the end of the war in Europe, America's leaders addressed the question of how, and at what cost, the war in the Pacific might be concluded. They knew that they faced an inch by inch conquest of a series of Pacific islands, followed by a sea-borne invasion of the Japanese mainland, which was defended by forces for whom death in defence of the imperial homeland was the ultimate honour. But the Americans also knew that they had an alternative.

In October 1939, the physicist Albert Einstein had written to President Roosevelt, to convey his belief that it might prove possible to harness the energy within the atomic nucleus to produce a bomb of extraordinary power, and his fear that the Germans might succeed in doing so. Roosevelt's reaction had been to authorize a programme – which became the biggest industrial project the world had ever seen – to find out whether it was possible to produce such a weapon, and if so, to make one. At the time of the German surrender, the bomb was almost ready, but no one could be sure that it would work, or what the consequences might be if it did. At 5.30 a.m. on 16 July 1945, a test bomb containing 19.84 pounds of uranium and plutonium was detonated at Alamogordo Air Base in New

Mexico. It worked, with a force equivalent to 20,000 tons of TNT, leaving a crater half a mile wide.

A question now arose: was it permissible to employ a weapon of such indiscriminate and overwhelming destructiveness? Those advisers who longed to find out what the new weapon could do supported those who genuinely believed that it was the preferable alternative, and the decision was taken to use it. What the Americans did not know was that at that very moment, even more agonized discussions were taking place in Tokyo, as to whether the war should be continued. These discussions always came back to the same point: without a guarantee of a continuation of the emperor's rule, surrender was inconceivable. And the Americans had made it clear that this was a condition they would not accept.

Like a Greek tragedy, the war moved swiftly to its conclusion. At 8.15 a.m. on 6 August, a bomb identical to the one tested in New Mexico was detonated above the city of Hiroshima, creating a firestorm that incinerated more than 80,000 people, and leaving a wasteland where a proud city had once stood. To make sure the message had been fully taken on board, another, somewhat different bomb was detonated on 9 August over Nagasaki, with similarly devastating effect.

The inconceivable now became the unavoidable. On 15 August, the emperor himself used the radio to tell a nation that had never heard his voice that the war was at an end. On 2 September, his representatives attended upon General Douglas MacArthur of the United States Army on board the battleship *Missouri*. Under Commodore Matthew Perry's 100-year-old flag – specially flown over for the occasion – they signed articles of unconditional surrender.

The end of the war in 1945 brought a rearrangement of the international political system even more dramatic than that brought about by the ending of the First World War in 1918. There was no peace conference this time. Germany and Japan had been utterly defeated, and their task was merely to wait to be told what was going to happen to them. Britain's contribution to the achievement of victory was politely recognized by the inclusion of its wartime prime minister, Winston Churchill, and his successor, Clement Attlee, in the discussions between the Americans and the Russians. But compared to Russia and America, Britain was a spent force. A huge proportion of its accumulated wealth had been expended in the six-year struggle. Its armed forces were dwarfed by those of its allies. And its empire was clearly on the verge of disintegration. Britain's 200-year reign as cock-of-the-walk that had been the reward of its flying start in the Industrial Revolution was finally at an end.

The most dramatic immediate change was the loss of Britain's Indian empire. The campaign for Indian independence had been gathering strength since the end of the nineteenth century. Under the charismatic leadership of Mohandas Gandhi, a Hindu lawyer who had lived for twenty years in South Africa, it had maintained steady pressure on successive governments, forcing the pace of the movement to self-rule in the face of Britain's reluctance to relinquish control of its most splendid possession. Japan's conquests of the British colonies in South-east Asia had undermined British prestige in India, and greatly encouraged those who were agitating for independence.

The end of British rule, when it did come, came quickly. Britain's newly elected Labour government announced its intention of ending colonial rule by 1947. It was perhaps an unrealistically short time-scale for such an enormous change, but it was deliberately chosen in an attempt to force India's political leaders to face up to the implications of independence, and in the hope that it would instil a spirit of compromise.

Unfortunately, the principal cause of dispute did not lend itself to a compromise solution. The problem was that India was the home of two major religions: Hinduism and Islam. Hinduism had the greater number of adherents, but the followers of Islam were a substantial majority in some areas, and each had large numbers of followers in regions where the other was in a majority. The Congress Party, led by Jawaharlal Nehru, supported a 'one-country' solution. The Muslim League, under its leader, Mohammad Ali Jinnah, believed that this would merely ensure that the interests of the Hindu majority would dominate the country's future. To prevent this, Jinnah pressed for a 'two-country' solution: the creation of an Indian state, comprising those areas with a Hindu majority, and a separate state – 'Pakistan' – embracing those with a Muslim majority. Convinced that no compromise was achievable, and determined to adhere to its timetable, the British government announced that a two-country solution would be enforced, and that the hand-over of power would take place as announced. Despite Ghandi's warning of the likely consequences, the Muslim areas in the north-west were joined to the

Muslim territory of East Bengal, more than a thousand miles away to the east, to form the new Pakistan. In 1947, in an atmosphere of general goodwill between the former colonies and their departing former rulers, the two new countries duly came into existence.

The consequence that Ghandi had feared now came to pass. In a massive exchange of populations, 15 million people were uprooted from their homes, and in the associated riots, more than 200,000 died. It was a sad accompaniment to what was otherwise a memorable event in Indian history, and its echoes would haunt India–Pakistan relations for years. The Pakistan that was created in 1947 did not retain its unity for long, since its two constituent parts had very different linguistic and cultural traditions. In 1971, mounting dissension between East and West Pakistan would lead to war, and with help from India, the eastern portion would break away to form the independent republic of Bangladesh.

1948, the year after India and Pakistan achieved their independence, saw the creation of the state of Israel, which was formed out of part of the British mandated territory of Palestine. Although Britain was still in a sense bound by the Balfour Declaration of 1917, the commitment to the creation of a 'Jewish National Home' did not necessarily imply a Jewish state with a substantial amount of territory. Even in the 1940s, after fifty years of legal and illegal immigration, Arabs still made up two-thirds of the population of Palestine. Britain, left to its own devices, would never have contemplated the displacement of the Arab population on the scale that subsequently ensued. But there was no question of Britain being left to its own devices. Pressure from Jews around the world, pressure from an American government responding to the influential Jewish element in its own electorate, and the emotions aroused world-wide by the revelations of genocide in the Nazi concentration camps, eventually made the British position untenable. Any temptation to procrastinate was discouraged by a systematic campaign of terrorism waged by the extreme Zionist group Irgun Zwai Leumi (the Hebrew National Military Organization).

The creation of the state of Israel was the fulfilment of a dream: the dream of millions of Jews for generations past. But it contained the seeds of a nightmare for Jews and non-Jews alike in years to come, as the resentment of Israel's Arab neighbours at this cuckoo in the Arab nest continued to fester.

While India and Pakistan were taking their first steps as independent nations, the future of China was being determined in civil war. After the Japanese surrender in 1945, communist forces under the leadership of Mao Zedong had gained control of northern China and much of Manchuria. In January 1949 they captured Beijing. By April they had taken control of Chiang Kai-shek's Nationalist capital, Nanking. Two million refugees were evacuated by the United States seventh fleet to the island of Taiwan, where a Nationalist government was installed. On 1 October 1949, the communist People's Republic of China, headed by Mao and Zhou Enlai, was formally proclaimed.

In November of the same year, Chinese forces intervened in a war between communist North Korea and the American-backed Republic of South Korea. The lines across which Chinese- and American-backed forces faced one another were part of a division that by now extended all the way around the world: a division between the so-called 'communist bloc' on the one hand, and countries friendly to, and supported by, America on the other. This division had originated very soon after the war, with the drawing down of what the British statesman Winston Churchill called an 'Iron Curtain' across the middle of Europe, between the countries that had been liberated by Russian forces, and those liberated by the Western allies. East of this 'curtain' were Russian-occupied countries, including Poland and Hungary, and the East German Republic (the former Russian Zone of occupied Germany). These, together with Russia and China, made up the communist bloc. Elsewhere in the world there were other countries sympathetic towards, and supported by, Russia. Ranged against them were the countries sympathetic towards, and financed by, the United States. In American terminology, these made up the 'free world', a somewhat elastic concept, as the only criterion for inclusion was lack of sympathy for Russia and its friends. Provided that this was satisfied, any country, no matter how tyrannical or corrupt its government, was, in American eyes, entitled to the label 'free'.

This polarization into 'us' and 'them', 'democracy versus tyranny', lasted for the next thirty years. By and large, the countries of the free world were more liberal and democratic than the countries of the communist bloc, but this was coincidental. What mattered was maintaining the power and freedom of action of America and its friends. That didn't necessarily make it bad, but it does no harm to call things by their proper names. The 'free world' is a weasel phrase that was, and is, used to cover up much that is not very free at all.

This division hardened into what became known as the Cold War. It was a situation in which 'hot' wars were fought out between smaller nations acting as proxies for Russia and America, but no wars were fought between these powers themselves. After the dropping of those atomic bombs on Hiroshima and Nagasaki, war between superpowers had become a much more intimidating prospect. The idea of a single bomb with the explosive force of 20,000 tons of TNT would have been difficult to grasp before one fell on Hiroshima. But within ten years of Hiroshima's destruction, some strategists were already referring to bombs of that size as 'tactical' atomic weapons. Such is the mind-numbing power of modern science when applied to purposes of war.

When the Americans revealed that they had atomic weapons, and subsequently cast the Russians in the role of enemies of freedom, the Russians felt compelled to develop atomic weapons of their own, in simple self-defence. But when Russia got its bomb, the perceived threat to American (and British and French) interests, and the appetites of American (and British and French) military contractors, ensured that America (and Britain and France) would acquire bigger bombs. The Russians exploded their first bomb in 1949. In the 1950s America, Russia (and Britain and France) demonstrated their cleverness by building hydrogen bombs, which use Hiroshima-type bombs as triggers. Very soon, China had joined this big boys' club. Then it was the turn of India and Pakistan, both of which, of course, needed atomic weapons to defend themselves against their evil adversaries. The Israelis, surrounded by nations that longed for their destruction, had to have them, too – but in their case, everyone is supposed to pretend that their nuclear arsenal does not exist. One day, Israel's enemies will not have nuclear weapons, in the same way that Israel doesn't have them. What will happen then is anyone's guess.

The military strategists, who play games to work out the limits of sanity – and the consequences of insanity – in the conduct of modern war, have a name for this amassing of monstrously effective weapons. They call it mutually assured destruction, known by its acronym MAD. They aren't joking. Somehow, in the half century since the number of nuclear powers first rose above one, we have managed to avoid setting one off, either in anger, or by mistake. We can only hope our luck continues to hold.

One country that was not involved in the nuclear arms race was Japan. The new constitution drawn up by the country's American occupiers, and enacted in 1951, explicitly prohibited Japan from making preparations for war, or entering into military alliances. Instead, the nation's security from foreign attack was guaranteed by America. This enforced freedom from military commitments saved Japan from the burden of military spending, and the diversion of scientific manpower into military applications, that was to be such a source of weakness for many countries, Britain in particular, during the 1960s and 70s. Free to concentrate on civilian applications, Japanese industry, with its highly educated and disciplined workforce, and nourished by an unlimited supply of labour made available by improved productivity in its agricultural sector, now delivered an 'economic miracle'. This was kick-started by the demands of America's war in Korea, which soaked up huge quantities of Japanese-made equipment and supplies at gratifyingly high prices.

The Korean War ended in July 1953, with an armistice that recognized the right to existence of the American-backed Republic of South Korea, and effectively accepted that America had won this not-so-cold round of the Cold War. Thanks to the war, Japanese industry was now ready to take on the world. It was a world hungry for the consumer durables that had hitherto been the preserve of well-heeled Americans. And thanks to reductions in the costs of sea transport, it was a world that was wide open to exports of Japanese products. As well as the familiar products of the 1930s – automobiles, radios, refrigerators and washing machines – these now included a whole range of devices – calculators, televisions, and so on – based on the new science of electronics that had been born during the war. During the late 1950s, and right through the 1960s, Japan's GDP grew at a rate above 10 per cent a year. It was a sustained effusion of economic growth of a kind that had never before been seen. And while the nation's workers strained every muscle to meet this insatiable demand, the whole country became one great building site, as wartime rubble gave way to sleek modern offices, factories and warehouses.

In 1964, Japan celebrated its emergence from the shadow of war and international disgrace with a triumphant staging of the Olympic Games, the first time they had been held in Asia. Tokyo had been chosen as the venue for 1940, but war had intervened. Now one of the defeated nations set itself the challenge of providing the facilities required to host 5000 international athletes and hundreds of thousands of visitors. When 8000 white doves were released into the sky at the opening ceremony on 10 October, a whole nation rediscovered its pride. In a moment of great poignancy, the Olympic flame was lit by a nineteen-year-old youth born in Hiroshima on the very day that it was obliterated. When the home team went on to win sixteen gold medals – a total bettered by only the USA and the Soviet Union – the whole world took notice.

Japan's economic miracle was unique in the pace of its progress, but something very similar was happening at the same time in central Europe, where its wartime ally Germany was performing its own breathtaking transformation act. Strictly speaking this was happening in *West* Germany, since the pre-war state was now divided between the two new republics that lay on either side of the Iron Curtain. At the end of the war they had both been places of devastation, where people grubbed around for sustenance, and lived where, and by whatever means, they could. But by the mid-1950s, a gap had opened up between the standards of living of the peoples of the two republics that would grow wider and wider as the years went by.

The key to West Germany's phoenix-like rebirth out of the ashes of defeat lies in the behaviour of the country's American conquerors. Seldom in history has a nation paid such close attention to the lessons that history has to teach, and it is difficult to think of another occasion when the study of history has paid such a handsome dividend.

In 1919, America had made two mistakes. It had turned its back on a devastated Europe, and it had acquiesced in the punishment of its defeated enemies. In the late 1940s, it avoided both mistakes. Admittedly, its actions were not wholly altruistic. It was clear that if American turned its back on Europe, the consequence would be if not a Russian invasion then at least a creeping subversion of many of the continent's non-communist states. The Americans therefore decided upon two courses of action that guaranteed that this post-war Europe would have a very different history from the Europe of the 1920s and 30s. It continued to maintain a sizeable military presence on the continent, contrary to previous American policy; and it made money and supplies available for the regeneration not just of its war-weary allies, Britain and France, but, even more so, of its defeated enemies, Italy and Germany. The consequence was a remarkable economic recovery in all these countries, and in Germany in particular.

Britain, still not fully free of its imperial delusions, made the mistake of trying to play the part of a Great Power, and committed itself to levels of military expenditure that limited its industrial renewal. But even so, the country could not fail to share in the increased prosperity experienced by its trading partners.

In the 1950s, West Germany, protected, like Japan, from the temptations of military expenditure, and supported by substantial American subsidies, embarked upon the most spectacular economic expansion in its history. To some extent, this recovery, was, like Japan's based on the export of consumer goods, but it also exploited the country's established expertise in the manufacture of industrial plant and machinery, for which, in a world recovering from war, there was a similarly insatiable demand.

German industry did not have Japan's advantage of a Korean war on its doorstep, but it found a substitute that was able to deliver as great an advantage, one that, unlike a war, would continue to deliver its benefits indefinitely. The project of Western European economic union was conceived, and driven forward, by two of France's leading politicians, Robert Schuman and Jean Monnet. There was an idealistic element in their programme, but even more important was the desire, understandable in any Frenchman, to ensure that Germany would never again threaten Europe's peace. Their hopes had been encouraged in 1948, when the Benelux group of countries – Belgium, The Netherlands and Luxemburg – formed a Customs Union. But the breakthrough came in 1952, when the Benelux countries, France, Germany and Italy handed control of their coal and steel industries to an international body, the European Coal and Steel Community. With the confidence gained from this, economic unification moved forward at a remarkable rate. In 1957 representatives of the six countries signed one of the most momentous treaties in European history – the Treaty of Rome – and on 1 January 1958, the European Economic Community, or Common Market, formally came into existence.

40
PEACE AND PROSPERITY – FOR SOME

The experience of the developed world in the decades following the Second World War was utterly different from that in the comparable period after the First. There was no runaway boom, no worldwide stock market crash and no long-drawn-out depression. The mistakes made earlier were plain to see. The principles of economic management identified by Keynes were understood, and, in some countries, consistently applied. Thanks to intelligent policies, and the availability of new technologies, most industrialized countries experienced something never before known: a long period of rapid economic growth without major setbacks. A particular feature of the world economy in the post-war period was the increase in international trade. In the twenty years between 1950 and 1970, the volume of trade between countries increased at an average rate of 7 per cent a year. By the end of those twenty years, the level of world trade was four times what it had been at the beginning.

The annual rate of increase in international trade was double the rate of increase in world output, because a steadily increasing proportion of output was being imported and exported. The makeup of this trade was also markedly different. Fifty years earlier, agricultural products had accounted for most of the traffic. Now it was manufactured goods, exchanged between the specialized industries of Japan, Europe and North

America using the newly developed technique of container shipping that reduced handling costs to a fraction of what they had been.

A consequence of this rapid economic growth was a widening of the gap between rich and poor nations. Although the industrialized countries imported increased quantities of food and raw materials from what became known as the 'undeveloped' countries, those imports became a smaller and smaller proportion of total world trade, and trade between the 'developed' countries became a larger and larger proportion. As a result, the bargaining position of the poorer countries became progressively weaker. As the prices of their food and raw materials fell relative to the prices of industrial goods, they were less able to pay their way in the world, and they got caught up in a vicious circle of mounting debt and growing deficits.

These less developed countries were not only disadvantaged by their inability to exploit modern industrial technology, they were also unable to afford modern medicine, either in drugs or in equipment. This created another gap between them and the more fortunate nations: a gap in health care. Since a healthy workforce meant an effective one, this deficiency further lessened these countries' ability to compete in a demanding global market-place.

It didn't help that many of these countries were struggling to adjust to life as newly independent nations. In Africa and South-east Asia in particular, former European colonies were having to cope with life in a highly competitive world with inadequate government machinery, and without local business talent or locally-based business corporations. It left them sitting ducks for powerful and rapacious corporations based in the rich countries.

As if this was not enough, many of these countries were made still poorer by the ravages of post-colonial wars. Artificial boundaries drawn in the eighteenth and nineteenth centuries, when the European powers carved the world up between them, had created 'invented' countries that contained peoples of widely differing cultures and language groups. When the colonial powers withdrew, these disparate groups naturally contended for influence, or for their own separate nationhood, and a number of these disputes degenerated into civil wars. Some brought further misfortunes in the shape of foreign intervention. Among the most gruesome such entanglements were the conflicts that followed the withdrawal of the French from their colonies in South-east Asia.

Japanese victories in the region, especially the eviction of the British from Singapore, had greatly damaged European prestige, and given a boost to national independence movements. After the Japanese defeat, the British – in Burma, Malaya and Singapore – the Dutch – in Indonesia – and the French – in Indo-China (Vietnam, Laos and Cambodia) – reoccupied their former colonies. But by 1957, they had been driven out. The French fought with particular tenacity to hold on to their colonial possessions, but their spirit was broken in 1954, when, despite American support, they were defeated in a six-month-long battle near the Vietnamese city of Dien Bien Phu.

For the people of Vietnam, and of other poor countries caught up in the manoeuvrings of the Great Powers, the Cold War had appalling consequences. But for the inhabitants of the industrialized countries it was really just a sideshow. The fear of another world war was real, and in a world bristling with nuclear weapons the implications were horrific. The Cold War itself, however, presented no threat to the comfort of most of the industrialized countries, and no obstacle to a continued improvement in their standard of living.

A particular feature of this age of prosperity was a massive investment in scientific research, and the development of new products, by both governments and private corporations. A third Industrial Revolution had been inaugurated in the 1940s by the development of the new science of electronics, in particular the invention of the electronic computer. Computers were developed to meet the wartime need for code-breaking, but rapidly found new applications in the post-war period. The computer brought about a transformation of two activities that were fundamental to both business and war: computation and information processing. With the aid of computers, tasks that had hitherto required armies of office workers could now be performed by machines supervised by a handful of operatives, and the cost of performing such tasks was massively reduced. In addition, the highly educated people who would otherwise have spent their lives as clerks or number-crunchers were freed to do work that machines could not do. The result was a huge improvement in the quality of life in any country that was already rich and organized enough to be able to employ the new technology. The computer also made possible a totally new approach to the control of industrial processes. Manufacturing operations could now be performed at high speed, and with extraordinary precision, by machines that required no human operators. The employment of robots, the stuff of science fiction as recently as the 1930s, became an industrial commonplace.

Computers also transformed scientific research. Calculations that might have taken teams of mathematicians hundreds of hours to carry out could now be performed by a single machine in minutes. But the scientific applications of electronic processing went far beyond mere number-crunching. Scientists were now able to construct models of natural processes, such as epidemics or earthquakes, and to study their workings in speeded-up experiments.

Advanced computers, combined with developments in control mechanisms, also made new kinds of weapons possible. Within a quarter of a century of the destruction of Hiroshima, the idea of dropping an atomic bomb from an aeroplane would seem as quaint and old-fashioned as riding to war on a horse. Once Russia and America had their stocks of hydrogen bombs, the arms race between them turned into a contest to develop the most effective delivery systems. At the end of the war, Germany had had by far the most advanced rocket propulsion industry in the world, and both Russia and America kick-started their weapons delivery programmes by exploiting the expertise of German engineers. Both countries soon had inter-continental ballistic missiles (ICBMs) targeted on one another's cities, and maintained in a state of constant readiness. This really *was* MAD (mutual assured destruction).

America was so rich that it could support the enormous cost of such programmes and still provide a high standard of living for most of its citizens. But Russia was a poorer country, one that had suffered huge devastation during the war. The level of military expenditure involved in this arms race was a luxury it could not really afford. The diversion of so much expertise, and such large resources, into devising high-quality killing machines deprived civilian industry of the resources it needed. The situation was made much worse by the way in which Russia's economy operated. Subjected to initiative-stifling central planning and lacking the incentive to improve performance that competition provided in capitalist economies, this 'socialist paradise' was in fact a nightmare of waste and inefficiency. It was a system that had been capable of winning a war – just. But it was grotesquely ill equipped to prosper in times of peace.

One of the most pernicious effects of the tyranny that ruled Russian lives was the damage it did to the spirit of enquiry. Scientific theories that did not follow the party line were not only resisted; they resulted in punishment for those propounding them. The damage that this did to Soviet science is illustrated by the case of Trofim Lysenko, one of Russia's most influential scientists and director of the country's Institute of Genetics from 1940 to 1965. Lysenko insisted that the genetic character, and therefore the yields, of food plants such as wheat and rye could be transformed within two or three generations, by subjecting them to an appropriate environment. This was music to Stalin's ears at a time when grain yields were a matter of desperate importance to the economy. Anyone who questioned this ridiculous proposition or showed sympathy for Mendelian theories of inheritance risked being exiled to Siberia, and many such ended their lives in prison camps. Even Stalin's death in 1956 did not end Lysenko's ruinous influence. It was not until 1965 that Stalin's successors felt strong enough to remove him from office.

Stalin was not so stupid when it came to military science. In this area it was failure, not unorthodoxy, that risked exile, or worse. So it was in military applications that Soviet science scored its greatest triumphs. The effort put into the development of weapons delivery systems was so fruitful that for a time Russia was able to pull ahead of America in space research. In 1957, Americans suffered a stunning psychological blow when

Russia successfully launched *Sputnik*, the world's first artificial satellite. This was followed by a further triumph on 12 April 1961, when the Russian cosmonaut Yuri Alexeevich Gagarin made the world's first manned space flight. These shocks forced the American president, John F. Kennedy, to announce his intention of achieving an American landing on the moon by 1970. It was an extraordinarily daring, not to say rash, commitment, but once it was made, there could be no going back on it. In the event, the promise was fulfilled with several months to spare, when Neil A. Armstrong, commander of the *Apollo 11* mission, stepped out on to the lunar surface on 20 July 1969.

The huge effort necessary to achieve this had required no sacrifice of the high living standards of the majority of Americans. Throughout the 1960s, the American economy continued to race ahead. The success of the lunar mission gave a phenomenal boost to morale, and this sense of national self-worth was reinforced by the equally obvious triumph of the 'American way of life', as proved by the country's prosperity. But hardly had these feelings had time to register, when the country was reduced to turmoil by a development that raised troubling new questions about America's role in world affairs.

When the French had withdrawn from Vietnam, that country had become part of the front line in the Cold War. For the people of Vietnam, the war was anything but cold, as the forces of the communist North and the anti-communist South fought across their lands and through their villages. America, in particular, found itself more and more deeply mired in an anti-guerrilla war it seemed unable to win, and that opened up a desperate divide within its own people. On one side were those opposed to what they considered to be a brutal, essentially colonial war against a poor but courageous adversary. On the other were those who saw the war as part of a worldwide communist conspiracy, and who subscribed to a 'domino' theory: if South Vietnam were abandoned to communist rule, the other states of South-east Asia, and perhaps many countries further afield, would go the same way. The consequences for the people of Vietnam were horrific. By the end of 1968, a greater tonnage of bombs had been dropped on North Vietnam than fell on Germany and Japan combined in the Second World War.

In the end, the burden of this war, coming on top of the enormous effort involved in the space programme, proved too great, even for the world's greatest military power. The damage to the American economy, and the rifts opened up in the country's social fabric, could not be sustained. In January 1973, a ceasefire was agreed in Paris, and in 1975 the American government withdrew all aid to South Vietnam, and left the country to its fate.

4 1
MIRACLES AND MAGIC WANDS

A striking feature of the industrialization process is the increasing speed at which it has occurred over time. After Britain achieved 'take-off' around 1780, the country took sixty years to double its output per head of population (its per capita output). America, half a century later, was able to do so in under fifty. When Japan's turn came, later in the nineteenth century, the corresponding time-scale was only thirty years. And when South Korea embarked upon its industrial revolution in the 1960s, it was able to perform the trick in little more than a decade. In the twenty-five years between 1970 and 1995, South Korea increased its per capita output tenfold, implying an average annual growth rate of 10 per cent for a quarter of a century.

Statistics like this can have an unsettling effect on those who do not really understand them. Commentators who should have known better, hypnotized by the performance of South Korea, and of other East Asian economies that managed similar transformations, invented something called 'Asian values' and suggested that if Britain, for example, did not adopt them it would descend into irreversible decline. It would be difficult to think of a more grotesque misinterpretation of economic phenomena. It wasn't a matter of 'values' at all. It was about possessing a well-educated workforce. It was also about improving agricultural productivity, so that people who would otherwise have been working on the land were available to work in offices and factories. Most of all, it was about the advantages of the latecomer: being able to invest in the latest technology, rather than being stuck with old-fashioned plant and production methods.

Unfortunately for Marxists, and their dreams of a communist millennium, it was also about harnessing people's natural acquisitiveness, by giving one's own nationals, and foreigners, the chance to make money, and to hang on to most of what they made. It took most of the second half of the twentieth century for the message to get through to the disciples of Karl Marx that the desire to make money was not only natural, but was the essential driving force of a thriving economy in any age. It was not until the Chinese government recognized this in the 1980s that China was able to embark upon its own economic miracle, and begin the remarkable expansion that is now in full swing.

South Korea's 'take-off' was to an important extent powered by the expansion of heavy industries such as shipbuilding. But there are other ways of performing an economic miracle. A different kind of example was provided by Ireland, just a few years later.

In the 1950s, Ireland (that is, the Republic of Ireland, not the part of the island that remained British) was neither a rich country nor a very poor one. It had been self-governing for a generation, following its escape from British colonial rule in the 1920s. But although it was formally free to make its own way in the world, it was not going anywhere very fast.

Ireland at this time was to a large extent still a peasant society. It lacked natural resources, such as coal and iron, and it was nursing some terrible scars. The defining event in the country's modern history had been the potato famine of the 1840s. Ireland, perhaps more than any other country, had benefited from the importation of the potato into Europe around 1600, in the wake of Pizzaro's conquest of Peru. In a cool, damp climate, and on the poor soils to which their English conquerors had banished them, the rural Irish had found in the potato an easily cultivated and highly nutritious staple. Thus nourished, the country's population had exploded. Starting from perhaps 500,000 in 1600, it had trebled by 1760 to reach 1.5 million. Then in a mere eighty years, between 1760 and 1840, it increased sixfold to 9 million. But this was not the expansion of a prosperous economy. Ireland was a virtually cashless society, whose people had no means of buying alternative foods if their potato crop failed. Crushed by some of the most iniquitous laws ever enacted by a powerful state against a subject people, and prevented by those laws from having any say in the running of their own country or pursuing any kind of commercial enterprise, they clung to their poverty-stricken existence. Their condition was summed up in 1839 by the French geologist Élie de Beaumont, when he observed that

> Irish misery forms a type by itself, of which neither the model nor the imitation can be found anywhere else. In all countries, more or less paupers can be discovered; but an entire nation of paupers is what was never seen until it was shown in Ireland.

The potato, supplemented with occasional cabbage and fish, provided a more nutritious diet than the bread that was the staple of most of Europe's poor. While the potato thrived, this miserable existence could be maintained but in 1846, the potato died – and nineteenth-century Ireland died with it. In June 1845, during a run of cold wet summers, a blight, *Phytophthora infestans*, probably of South American origin, and possibly introduced by peelings dropped overboard from an American ship, appeared on potatoes on the Isle of Wight, off the coast of southern England. It caused devastation throughout Europe, but in Ireland the devastation was total. The Inca had had hundreds of different varieties of potato, making them much less vulnerable to plant diseases. But the Irish had only one. When the blight struck, the country's potatoes rotted in the ground, and its starving people rotted alongside them. Perhaps a million people died from starvation and the famine-related diseases that followed. Another million and a half emigrated in the years immediately after. By the outbreak of the First World War, at least 5.5 million people had left Ireland, to seek a better life elsewhere. And by definition, these were the young, the fit and the adventurous: the people the country could least afford to lose.

It was a country still suffering the after-effects of three centuries of oppression and misfortune that set about the task of transforming its future in the 1960s. The result was a triumph, a true 'economic miracle', one that serves as an object lesson in what can be achieved when a country gets lucky, and its people are given the chance to exploit their luck to the full.

Ireland in the 1960s had four things going for it: a well-educated population; the English language; privileged access to the British market; and close ties with America after a century of emigration. In a brilliant stroke of policy, the government introduced a generous system of industrial subsidies and total tax exemption for ten years for foreign firms setting up in the country. This kick-started an industrial revival, but the country's economy really took off after it joined the European Common Market in 1973.

Common Market entry transformed Ireland's existing advantages into an unbeatable package. It could now offer not only privileged access to the British market, but to the European market as well. The icing on the cake – a very thick layer of icing – was the subsidies available under the Common Agricultural Policy. These had been designed to bribe French farmers into accepting the Common Market, but were now available to fill Irish farmers' pockets, and to ease the transformation of an agrarian economy into an industrial one. For good measure, the country's fairy godmother, in an effort to make up for all the bad times, tapped her wand on Ireland's seas and up came natural gas. As the country prospered, the tide of emigration turned. Ireland's young people no longer had to leave, and other countries' young people began to arrive. Cinderella had gone to the ball after all – and what a ball it turned out to be!

Although it would be stretching the concept somewhat to describe Ireland in the 1950s as an 'underdeveloped' country, its 'economic miracle' is an instructive illustration of what it takes to make a quick transformation from underperformance to outperformance. If one considers the advantages that Ireland was starting with – a highly educated workforce, a sound political infrastructure and privileged access to lucrative markets – and if one factors in huge capital inflows from public and private sources overseas, it is easy to see where the miracle came from. It is also easy to see why many countries in Africa and Latin America might find it a little more difficult to pull the trick off.

4 2

AN EMPIRE OVERTURNED

By the early 1970s, the division of the world between two rival power blocs – America and its allies on the one hand, and America's perceived enemies, led by Soviet Russia, on the other – had been in existence for so long that it had come to seem almost a law of nature. Stalin had died in 1953, but his successors, afraid of what might happen if they were to let go of the rigid controls that held the Russian empire together, had continued both his external strategies and his internal systems. And disastrously, from the point of view of the Russian people, they had embarked upon a massively increased arms programme that would continue for twenty years, eventually bringing the country's economy crashing about their ears.

This increase in arms spending, which the country could not afford, was a response to the perceived threat of America's own hugely increased arms programme. This, in turn, was the product of a hysteria that saw Russia as a dangerous force, intent on world domination. Nothing could have been further from the truth. What the Russians wanted, more than anything else, was to be left alone to get on with solving their own desperate problems and modernizing their outdated and impoverished economy. But the sabre-rattling and war-games-playing of their ideological adversaries created an atmosphere in which arms spending seemed unavoidable. Their sense of isolation and encirclement was increased by the change that took place in relations with China. In 1968 and 1969 Russian and Chinese troops were involved in a number of clashes along their lengthy shared frontier. Then in 1970, the Chinese demonstrated their wish to distance themselves further from their former ally by initiating diplomatic exchanges with America itself. Yet while the Russians were busy convincing themselves that they were the victims of encirclement, the Americans, still smarting from their defeat in Vietnam, continued to subscribe to the notion that they were the nation at bay. This was not a notion that the manufacturers of America's guns, ships, planes and rockets were likely to discourage. There were enormous sums to be made out of ministering to this fear of external attack.

The result was the inauguration of what some have called the second Cold War. There seemed little reason to think that the existing alignment of nations might come to an end in the near future, and few informed observers expected that it would. But like the pressures that build up between the earth's tectonic plates in advance of an earthquake, forces were at work, in Russia and elsewhere, that were to transform the international balance of power.

The first shift that signalled the emergence of a new age occurred in 1973, when a war – the Yom Kippur War – broke out between America's close ally, Israel, and the Russian-supplied forces of Egypt and Syria. Several oil-producing states of the region were members of a consortium known as OPEC (the Organization of Petroleum Exporting Countries), and in order to exert pressure on Israel, they cut oil supplies and threatened an embargo on any country supporting Israel. The consequences of their action astounded them as much as it did the rest of the world. Up to that moment, oil had remained in plentiful supply, and its cheapness was a factor contributing to the economic boom that the industrial countries were enjoying. But the enforced reduction in supplies at a time of record demand (the Vietnam War was in full swing) led to an immediate, sharp jump in the price of oil. This revealed to the OPEC countries, and to the rest of the world, the hitherto unsuspected strength of their bargaining position. As a result, they were able to enforce a new pricing structure, which transformed them overnight from poor countries at the mercy of international oil companies to rich ones, with the huge international influence they have possessed ever since.

Another beneficiary of increased prices was the Soviet Union, which had huge oil reserves of its own. Although few outsiders were aware of it, this piece of good fortune came at a desperately important time. The Russian economy was still very inefficient, and this inefficiency, together with the costs of the Cold War, was not only depressing the standard of living of the Russians themselves, but undermining Russia's ability to control its subject peoples, both in Eastern Europe and within its far-flung empire. Radio and television meant Russians and the citizens of satellite countries knew about the prosperity enjoyed elsewhere, and the resulting dissatisfaction posed a real threat to the authorities. The foreign currency that Russia could now earn from exports of its own newly discovered reserves of oil and gas at inflated prices made it possible to import food and other goods that relieved what could otherwise have been a very dangerous situation.

For the OPEC countries, the transformation in their international status was breathtaking. Most importantly, it was not dependent upon the continuation of high prices. They had small populations, and enormous revenues. When prices fell a few years later, as new sources of oil came on-stream at a time of recession in the industrial countries, they were able to live off their now massive foreign exchange reserves – which brought them enormous influence overseas – until the next boom, which came along in 1979. When the massive price rises that this boom caused created yet another international recession, they were once again able to sit out a period of depressed prices. But Russia was not in this fortunate position. Every rouble of oil revenue was needed, and each price collapse intensified the pressures within a still impoverished empire. These pressures reached crisis levels when oil prices suffered an extended depression between 1984 and 1986.

The confrontation between Russia and America, which placed such heavy costs on Russia in particular and carried such risks for world peace, was finally brought under control by the ability of two men to believe in one another's good faith. In two meetings – in Reykjavik in 1986 and in Washington in 1987 – President Mikhail Gorbachev of Russia and President Ronald Reagan of America were able to shut out the voices of their more excitable advisers for long enough to arrive at an accord that effectively brought the Cold War to an end.

The idea that the Cold War might really be over took a while to sink in. There was no sudden reduction in the output of weapons. And there was no reduction at all in the amount of spying on both sides. But much of the heat had gone out of the situation, and the chances of a nuclear incident had been reduced. Whether, and when, the accord would have been followed by an actual reduction in armaments, we will never know, because events now took a dramatic course.

In 1987, Gorbachev published a book in which he advocated a programme based on the principles of *glasnost* (openness) and *perestroika* (restructuring), and proceeded to introduce elements of democracy and economic liberalization. Almost inevitably, after seventy years of frost, when the ice began to break, it broke too slowly for some, and too quickly for others, and Gorbachev found himself under attack from both sides.

It was a situation that was beyond the ability of anyone to control, and the Russian empire proceeded to unravel at a speed that left even the most starry-eyed optimists breathless in disbelief. In 1989, amid great rejoicing, the wall separating West Berlin from communist East Berlin was torn down by demonstrators. Within months, all the satellite states of Eastern Europe had broken away from Russia. Gorbachev, with great coolness and courage, had refused to take military action to prevent them. In October 1990, East and West Germany were reunited, and Germany could look forward to resuming its natural place as the leading European power west of Russia.

Meanwhile, dramatic changes were under way in Russia itself. In 1990, religious freedom was enshrined in law, and the constituent republics of the Union were given a greater degree of independence. In November 1991, the Soviet Communist Party, which had guided the nation's affairs for more than seventy years, was banned. Just one month later, the Soviet Union broke up into fifteen independent states.

It had been one of the greatest political upheavals in the history of the world. And it had happened with scarcely a shot being fired.

43

A NEW CHINA

The wave of prosperity that washed around the industrialized world in the quarter century following the Second World War passed one great nation by.

In 1949, when the communist People's Republic was founded, China had a population of nearly 600 million. Most were peasants, with a standard of living no better than their grandparents had known. The country had a strong government again, but this alone was no guarantee of prosperity. The task confronting the Chinese government was a daunting one. The war with Japan had been long, and the sufferings of the Chinese people immense. In all, the war had cost China somewhere between 15 and 20 million dead, and left much of the country's infrastructure in ruins. And there was none of the massive American aid available to help with reconstruction that enabled Germany and Japan to lay the foundations of their 'economic miracles'. It did not help that for thirty years after the war the economic policy of this dictatorship was guided more by ideology than by any rational analysis of how recovery might be engineered. The country's leader, Mao Zedong, had come to power with his own vision of how the Marxist millennium might be brought about. Unlike Marx, Mao believed that the best hope of the revolution lay in the peasants, not the urban proletariat, and he focused his attention on the disciplining and organization of these peasants, who made up most of the nation's workforce.

Agriculture was the lifeblood of China's economy. In the years immediately after 1949, it performed with gratifying efficiency, as land reforms encouraged farmers to take an interest in improving output. But in 1955, Mao introduced a programme that began to have the opposite effect. This was the forced collectivization of agriculture. A policy with disastrous consequences in Russia in the 1930s, it produced no better results in 1950s China.

In 1956, Mao made a speech encouraging people to come forward with criticisms of the way the country was being run. Within twelve months, half a million critics who had been naïve enough to take him at his word were languishing in prison. In 1958, he aroused great enthusiasm with his announcement that China was embarking on a programme to be known as the 'Great Leap Forward'. This involved the reorganization of collective farms into still larger units called 'communes', in which new kinds of social relationships, at odds with Chinese tradition, were enforced. It also encouraged the creation of large numbers of inefficient backyard industries and unrealistic output targets, which gave priority to quantity of output, rather than quality, providing a powerful incentive to lie about the actual levels of production achieved.

It was an absolute disaster: 'Great Leap Backward' would have been more accurate. It failed because China's ideology and isolation from the rest of the world meant it had no access to the resources that could have helped it modernize its infrastructure. International borrowing, export earnings or links with foreign companies who would put up the capital were not possible in Mao's China, no more than they had been in Stalin's Russia. The contrast with the country's successes in the 1980s and 90s is an object lesson in how to, and how not to, make industrialization work. For Mao, as for Stalin, the end justified the means. What neither of them understood was that their professed ends were unattainable by their favoured means.

One of the consequences of the national self-deception involved in the Great Leap Forward was a degree of wishful thinking that led to massive exports of grain; grain that China could not in fact spare. The result was a series of appalling famines between 1958 and 1961, in which at least 20 million, and possibly nearer 40 million, people died.

Mao's next assault on the country's economic and social fabric came in 1966, when he initiated a programme of social reconstruction and re-education known as the 'Cultural Revolution'. This was designed to destroy institutions or attitudes inherited from the past that were considered obstacles to the creation of the new China on which the leader's eyes were set. People were encouraged to inform on their neighbours, with the result that very soon the country echoed to the sound of hysterical public denunciations, and forced confessions, reminiscent of medieval witch trials. These reached their climax in 1968 and 1969, in a frenzy of denunciation and public humiliation, organized by out-of-control vigilantes known as 'Red Guards': baby-boomers who had known nothing but communist rule. During this explosion of insanity, hundreds of thousands of skilled professionals were removed from their posts, and forced to undergo 'political re-education' while performing manual labour in the fields. This created such devastation that in 1970 the army stepped in, in defiance of Mao, pulling the country back from the very brink of national dissolution.

Mao was progressively sidelined, but the nightmare did not end until his death in 1976, by which time he had established a reasonable claim to have killed more of his own people than any ruler in history. After his death, a rational appraisal of the country's needs once more became possible, and a programme of national regeneration was embarked upon. Under a new leader, Deng Xiaoping, who had twice been purged by Mao for his liberal views on the economy, a degree of economic freedom was introduced. This made it possible for farmers once again to profit from their labour, and for businesses to operate on a commercial basis. At the same time, state-owned industries were reorganized on lines that emphasized quality of output as much as quantity, and made possible the sort of modern management systems taken for granted in other industrial countries. For the first time in the nation's history, it was acknowledged that there was a world outside with much to teach, and that China had much to learn. And as the door swung open, foreign companies swarmed in, attracted by the mouth-watering opportunities offered by this huge, undeveloped country, and encouraged by the sort of generous tax breaks that were working such magic in Ireland.

There was no equivalent political liberation. The Party was determined that the lid would remain tightly clamped on any criticism of the regime. But as one would expect, in a country with more than 2000 years of mercantile activity behind it, the economy now began to motor. As farming productivity improved, the threat of famine receded, and millions of farm workers, surplus to requirements, flooded into the towns, swelling their populations and providing an unlimited supply of cheap labour to staff the newly built factories. As with South Korea, there was no need to retrace the path of earlier Industrial Revolutions. Factories and offices could employ the latest technology, stealing a march on older industrial countries that were locked into less efficient machinery and systems that they could not profitably replace. Within a few years, this combination of low wage costs and advanced technology was making China a power to be reckoned with in international trade, earning it large amounts of foreign currency. It also brought overseas corporations to the country's door, offering expertise and money in return for a chance to be involved in what promised, in the not far distant future, to be the biggest market in the world. Between 1978 and 1998, the Chinese economy expanded at an average rate of 8 per cent a year; a twenty-year burst of growth, at the end of which its annual output was nearly five times what it had been at the beginning.

For most of this period, the army and the Party succeeded in releasing the commercial energy needed to keep the pot of enterprise boiling, while withholding the political freedom that might cause it to boil over. Just once, a little over half-way through those twenty years, something happened that stopped the nation's breath, and raised the possibility that the whole experiment might be about to fall apart.

In May 1989, the Great Square of Tiananmen, in the heart of Beijing, was the scene of an amazing series of mostly peaceable demonstrations by farmers, workers and students, involving up to a million people. They were the culmination of an outburst of dissatisfaction at rising prices, lack of democracy and a whole complex of crises that seemed to be beyond the power of the government to solve. The atmosphere was heady with political discussion, made free by the belief that sheer numbers made it impossible for the authorities to intervene. On the evening of 2 June, things turned rough, as unresisting soldiers were manhandled by some of the more excitable characters in the crowd. The following night tanks entered the square and nearby Chang'an Avenue. By morning the square was clear.

Even today, it is still not known how many people were killed or seriously injured on that never to be forgotten night. Nothing like it has happened since; but the Chinese authorities have never since been confronted with such a problem. It was like the clubbing of a disobedient child: an act so violent that the rest of the family are frozen into submission.

The shadow of 1989 still hangs over this otherwise bubbling society. At the time of writing, the combination of commercial opportunity and political control still seems to be working. The government of this last of the world's great territorial empires have the example of what happened to the Russian empire in the 1990s to remind them of the risks they run. And they have the advantage of working within the framework of a society that has been cultivating the public virtues of discipline and respect for authority for 2000 years. The success achieved by this unique experiment during the past thirty years has been astounding. Whether this combination of economic advance and political repression can be maintained for much longer is a difficult question to answer.

The return to prosperity of Germany and Japan after the Second World War was hastened by the intelligent reaction of America's rulers, who had learned the lesson of the Versailles Treaty, and were determined not to sow the seeds of a future war, as that settlement had done. It was a magnanimous response that fully deserves all the praise that has been lavished upon it. But it was also an act of enlightened self-interest. America had nothing to gain from a repeat of the 1920s and 30s, and a great deal to lose.

Unfortunately, a comparable magnanimity was not displayed at the moment of American victory in the Cold War. The reaction of many influential people to the breakup of the Russian empire was characterized by triumphalism. The 'free world', they seemed to believe, had 'won', and it was the Russians' duty to accept the consequences with a good grace, and get on with reorganizing their society in accordance with a more acceptable model. That this was a proud nation with a long history, and an illustrious record of achievement, that merited sympathy and respect in its hour of need, seems not to have entered some people's minds. Instead it was treated like a latter-day Klondike, teeming with natural resources, just begging for a gold rush. Not all Russians were disadvantaged by their experiences in these chaotic years, of course. Fortunes were made and power bases built up which will probably dominate Russian life for many years. But for ordinary Russians, it was a time of suffering and national humiliation.

The reaction of some Americans went further than mere celebration of the victory of the 'American way of life' over the practitioners of a rival philosophy. For some – among them people of undoubted intelligence – it was a triumph of 'American values' and American ways of organizing society over all alternative versions, past and present. In 1992, a former State Department official, Francis Fukuyama, coined a phrase to describe what had happened: 'the end of history'. Many were encouraged by this seductive concept to believe that the combination of capitalist organization and representative institutions that had arisen in America in the 200 years since the Declaration of Independence was the natural end of human society, and all that now remained to do was to arrange its installation in those parts of the world that had not yet seen the light. Within the American government a group of gung-ho dreamers set to work to plan for the coming of this new millennium. They called their enterprise the 'Project for the New American Century'. It was a label so bizarre as to be beyond the reach of irony.

This certainty that America was the torchbearer for an advance by a grateful world into a glorious future did not allow much margin for disappointment. It was therefore inevitable that when America's own vulnerability was demonstrated in 2001 the nation was rocked back on its heels.

On 11 September of that year, television viewers in America, and across the world, had their programmes interrupted with news flashes from New York, where a plane had crashed into one of the Twin Towers of the World Trade Center in Lower Manhattan. As they watched, a plane appeared from out of the picture, and crashed into the other tower. Minutes later, both towers slid to the ground. It was one of the most horrific illustrations imaginable of what has been christened the 'global village': the new world that technology has created, in which everyone is a neighbour, and faraway disasters are real-time, fireside viewing. No one watching needed to be told that there had been substantial loss of life. Nor did they need to be told that something more significant than the collapse of two large buildings had just been enacted before them.

News quickly followed that a third plane had crashed into the Pentagon in Washington, the nerve centre of America's military command, and that a fourth had crashed in open country in circumstances that suggested it might have been bound for the White House.

It transpired that the planes had been hijacked by terrorists belonging to an organization known as al-Qaida. The leader of al-Qaida was a well-born Saudi named Osama bin Laden, whose motivation appeared to be a hatred of what he considered the pernicious influence of American culture on the life of Islamic countries, intensified by resentment at America's unswerving support for the state of Israel.

The shock-effect of this event was enormous. There was a nation-wide wave of grief at the murder of some 3000 people, the majority of them American citizens, who had been guilty of nothing more blameworthy than going about their daily business. But there was something else: a horrified realization that America, which had been fighting wars around the globe for more than a century, but had itself remained inviolate, was vulnerable in ways that could not have been imagined. America discovered that it was exposed to attacks from overseas enemies of a kind that its defence arrangements were not

designed to meet. The most powerful nation on earth, possessed of a nuclear armoury of stupendous proportions, could
be dealt a massive blow by a small group of highly committed
operatives armed with nothing more technologically advanced
than Stanley knives.

In 2002, American forces launched an airborne invasion of
Afghanistan, where bin Laden was believed to be hiding. The
damage and dislocation caused, and the number of Afghan
civilians killed, were considerable, but the American authorities were satisfied that the disturbance caused to the terrorists'
organization and the toppling of the Taliban regime that ruled
the country made the operation worthwhile.

An influential element in American government circles had
for some time harboured an ambition to 'take out' the brutal
ruler of Iraq, Saddam Hussein. There were, of course, equally
murderous dictators elsewhere in the world, but Saddam was
conspicuously unfriendly to both America and its ally Israel, and
was the ruler of a country that possessed enormous reserves of
oil. In the heightened and confused atmosphere following the
attack on the Twin Towers, the American government was able
to establish a connection in the public mind between Saddam's
regime and something called 'international terrorism'. There was
no evidence of any connection between bin Laden and Saddam
– if anything, rather the reverse – but the case was sufficiently
murky to enable the White House to win over enough of the
electorate to mount the invasion it had been planning. The passing of ambiguous United Nations resolutions and the commitment of a sizeable British force in support gave the assault the
appearance of an international operation in defence of world
peace. The issue was further clouded by claims that Saddam
was harbouring 'weapons of mass destruction' that posed an

imminent threat to countries hundreds, if not thousands, of miles away. It was later established that no such weapons had ever existed, but by then the allegation had served its purpose.

The attack – code-named 'Iraqi Freedom' – was launched on 20 March 2003. Iraqi resistance was quickly overcome, but by the time the Anglo-American army of occupation was fully installed, enormous damage had been done to the country's infrastructure, and huge numbers of Iraqi civilians had met their deaths. The invading powers understandably declined to attempt to estimate the total numbers killed and injured. There can be no doubt, however, that by 2007, the war itself, and the occupation that followed, had been the direct cause of thousands of civilian deaths. To these could be added, according to taste, some or all of several hundred thousand more caused by the combined effect of fighting between various Iraqi factions in the chaotic years that followed, by the direct actions of the occupying forces and by sickness and disease that would not have occurred had the country's infrastructure not been so seriously undermined.

The fact that the attack on the Twin Towers had been launched by Islamist fundamentalists had particularly unfortunate consequences. It was bad enough that it enabled the American government to manufacture the label 'the war against terror', which it was then able to use for any military action against an Islamic country. What was worse was that it gave encouragement to wilder elements in the American body politic eager to push the idea that the world was the scene of a 'clash of civilizations'. As a substitute for thought, it was a winner. As a contribution to the understanding of the dangerous age we now find ourselves in, it was, shall we say, rather less than helpful.

Judged by sheer numbers, the history of the human race during the past few centuries is a story of stunning success. The population of the world in 1913 was 1600 million, having doubled in the previous 150 years. It is now approaching 7000 million, having quadrupled in less than a century. China alone now has 1300 million people, almost as many as the entire world a century ago. India, where the fertility rate per woman is nearly twice China's, is home to over 1000 million, and is forecast to overtake China by 2050. The Indian subcontinent as a whole is already more populous than China.

The growth rate of world population peaked around 1970. Since then, it has slowed down. Current forecasts suggest that world population will level out at about 10,000 million around the year 2050. If it does so, it would then be a million times what it was when our story began some 100,000 years ago.

The massive increase in world population since 1913 is not the result of runaway birth rates. Fully half of it is the result of people living longer. This in turn is the result of effective public health. In 1913, very few countries had public health systems worthy of the name. But as the twentieth century progressed, the knowledge acquired after more than a century of scientific research began to be applied widely. From the beginning of the 1950s, in particular, antibiotics, vaccination and improved sanitation brought about a dramatic improvement in survival rates. Average life expectancy worldwide in 1913 was about thirty-six years. By 1950 it had crept up to forty-five. Between 1950 and 1970, it increased very sharply in country after country. It has continued to increase since then, albeit at a rather more sedate pace, with the result that the average life expectancy for children born today is close to seventy. And this is a worldwide average. In some healthy, rich countries – for example Japan – the average life expectancy is now over eighty.

In some developing countries, such as Taiwan and South Korea, the fall in death-rates was followed quite quickly by a fall in birth-rates. This led to an increase in the ratio of working population to total population that played an important part in the 'economic miracles' these countries experienced in the 1970s and 80s. Women who were not occupied with babies were available to work outside the home.

An important factor in the reduction in birth-rates in many developed, and developing, countries has been the introduction of the contraceptive pill, which first made its appearance in the 1960s, and has since transformed the lives of hundreds of millions of women worldwide. In China, following the death of Mao Zedong in 1976, the government introduced a policy of one child per family, with penalties and incentives powerful enough to change behaviour profoundly. In the quarter-century since this policy was introduced, China's birth-rate has fallen by two-thirds.

In many poor countries, however, most notably in Africa and Latin America, birth-rates have remained high, leading to increases in the numbers of dependent children, and limiting the ability of women of childbearing age to participate in the workforce. This is one more factor operating in these countries to reduce the potential for economic growth.

The combined effect of improved public health and maintained birth-rates has been to dramatically increase the population of parts of the world. Sub-Saharan Africa, with a population of barely 100 million in 1913, is now home to 700 million, while Central and South America, which had a combined total of some 80 million, now come in at over 500 million.

Every so often during the past two centuries, the increase in global population has caused anxieties about our ability to continue to feed ourselves. Thanks to scientific advances during the past fifty years – the 'Green Revolution' in agriculture – this is one cause of concern that has largely been put to rest. We can say with confidence that, in theory at least, there is no reason why we should not be able to feed a population of 10,000 million forty years from now. A particularly striking illustration of the ability of modern farming methods – including the generous application of nitrogenous fertilizers – to deliver increased food supplies is provided by the experience of China, where average food production per head of population is now about twice what it was forty years ago.

Our ability to meet future demand for food will depend on the nature of the diet that is demanded. Most industrialized nations have celebrated their increased prosperity by indulging in the sort of meat-rich diet that poor people cannot afford. Eating meat is an appallingly inefficient way of using cultivable land. It requires a much greater acreage to grow crops to feed animals that are eaten by humans than it does to grow cereals, fruit and vegetables to feed human beings direct. If we are to provide 10,000 million people with a decent standard of living, we will find it much easier to do so if they can be convinced of the benefits of a vegetarian diet. If they cannot, then the price of meat (and fish) will long before 2050 have to rise to levels that a sizeable proportion of the world's population cannot afford, and they will have to make do with a vegetarian diet, whether they like it or not.

The world is a much more unequal place today than it was in 1913. The past century has witnessed a dramatic improvement in living standards in the richer countries. In many poor countries, by contrast, living standards for the mass of the population are little better than they were then. There are still at least a billion people living in countries that have so far been unable to get a foot on even the lowest rung of the ladder of economic development. And while famine and malnutrition are proportionately less common than they were in 1913, the absolute number of people suffering from malnutrition is greater now. The people of Africa are still at the bottom of the heap. Having drawn the short straw so often in the past thousand years, they look like doing so for a long time yet.

At the same time that world population has been exploding, there has been a significant change in the proportion living in towns. Industrialization and agricultural improvement are two sides of the same coin. Modern manufacturing, and the service industries that support it, require large workforces that have to be located in towns. Improvements in agricultural technology reduce the number of workers needed on farms. So, as a country industrializes, the percentage of its population engaged in agriculture must fall, and the percentage of its population living in towns must increase. As the proportion living in towns increases, the size of those towns also grows.

In the middle of the eighteenth century, as the first Industrial Revolution got under way in Western Europe, the population of its two greatest cities, London and Paris, reached the then amazing figure of 700,000 each. The figure would have been larger still, had death-rates not been so appalling. As various countries embarked upon their respective Industrial Revolutions, their rural populations, too, flooded into the cities. As improvements in public health took hold, and poor city dwellers lived longer, city populations exploded, and their numbers began to be measured in millions. Tokyo, Mumbai, Shanghai, Beijing, London, New York and Mexico City are just some of today's cities with more than 10 million people apiece. And some of them are still growing fast, as people flood in from the countryside in search of work. According to United Nations estimates, as recently as 1950 only 29 per cent of the world's population was living in an urban environment; the figure is now more than 50 per cent. In other words, in the world as a whole, there are now more people living in towns than outside them. Nor is there any reason to expect this process to slow down in the near future.

It is not just the number of human beings in the world that has been increasing at a rapid rate; so has the volume of inter-action between them. This is true in two quite different senses: in the frequency and speed of information exchange, and in the amount of simultaneously shared experience (such as television news, films and propaganda).

An important factor in this has been the spread of the world's leading languages. The number of languages in the world has been falling for the best part of 3000 years, and the rate of language death is faster now than it has ever been. There are still about 5000 different languages worldwide: Australia is home to around 200, Papua New Guinea boasts over 800. But many are spoken only by a small number of people – and old people at that. On average, a language is lost, somewhere in the world, every other week.

Of the world's nearly 7000 million people, more than half share just ten languages. One, Mandarin Chinese, is the first or only language of more than a billion people, and three other fast-growing languages – English, Spanish and Hindi – are each spoken by more than half a billion. The expansion of the internet and the influence of television and film seem likely to accelerate further the spread of these four, both as first languages and as second languages in business and scientific exchange.

The introduction of the personal computer in the 1980s and the development of the world wide web in the 1990s have so transformed the process of information exchange that we

45.1 Top Ten Spoken Languages

Year		Number of Speakers (millions)
1	Chinese (Mandarin)	1050
2	English	510
3	Hindi	490
4	Spanish	420
5	Russian	280
6	Bengali	210
7	Portuguese	190
8	German (Standard)	130
9	French	130
10	Japanese	130
	TOTAL	3540

The numbers shown are those speaking each language as their first, or active second language. Arabic does not figure in this list because of the mutually unintelligibility of many of its dialects.

Source: N. Ostler, *Empires of the Word*, (HarperCollins, 2005) p.526

can truly say that we live in a different world from that of only a quarter of a century ago. It is now possible to communicate instantly, at negligible cost, with people on the other side of the world. One can explore the contents of the world's media, and the world's libraries, without getting out of one's pyjamas. It is possible to publicize one's opinions and one's needs for literally all the world to see. These things are miraculous by the standards of any past age. If we choose to do so, and have the means, we really can live in a global village.

As this interaction increases, so does the number of discoveries and inventions, and the speed at which new technologies spread around the world. This in turn brings about further acceleration of the rate of change in the workings of society. In every generation in industrial countries for at least the last 200 years, older people have said, 'Things can't go on changing at this rate.' They were right – things didn't go on changing at that rate. In the industrialized world things change, and will almost certainly continue to change, at an ever-increasing rate.

There is a new technological revolution under way at the moment, based on the discoveries made in biology and biochemistry during the past fifty years. It is usual for there to be a lapse of half a century or so between the fundamental discoveries that create a new technology and the beginning of their commercial exploitation. The discovery in 1953 of the structure of the DNA molecule by Francis Crick and James Watson of the University of Cambridge was one such discovery, and we are now just at the beginning of what could be a century of innovation in the field of genetic engineering. This will not only revolutionize the diagnosis and treatment of human diseases; it will make possible massive increases in food production, by creating new, high-yielding varieties of plants and animals, and preventing plant and animal diseases.

Just over the horizon, there is yet another industrial revolution, based on nanotechnology: the technology of the extremely small. It is impossible to say what the ramifications of this will be, but they will be huge. And after that? We don't know. But it would be ridiculous to suggest that we just happen to have reached a stage where there are no new discoveries to make and exploit. We have to assume that for a long time to come, human beings will acquire ever more knowledge of the way the world works, and increasing control over both our physical environment and our bodily processes. As we do so, we will have to get used to a faster and faster rate of change in both technology and social relationships. That first Industrial Revolution in the eighteenth century came up with the process of continuous invention, and there is no reason to suppose that it will come to an end for a very long time. Unless, of course, something unpleasant should intervene to bring the entire process to a halt. What that might be, we consider in the next chapter.

This transformation of the technology of everyday life has been matched by a similar transformation of the technology of war. Thanks to its industrialization, war, too, has become more unequal. The rich countries of the world now possess weapons of such sophistication and power that they can visit death and destruction on poor countries on an industrial scale, while suffering negligible casualties and damage themselves. The citizens of these rich countries can sit, TV dinners on their laps, watching it happen, while their human sympathies are shrivelled by a medium that serves up real-life tragedy and soap opera in almost identical format.

For the moment, such countries are free of the threat of wars in which they themselves might suffer extreme damage. As far as they are concerned, war is for export only. And in spite of the huge arsenals of weapons of mass destruction these countries keep in readiness, their peoples sleep peacefully, knowing that incineration and dismemberment are, for the time being, fates reserved for the inhabitants of countries that have committed the sins of being poor and being weak.

One has to suspect that this is a temporary state of affairs. The smugness of America's more imperially minded politicians and intellectuals is reminiscent of their British equivalents 150 years ago, before the realities of a changing balance of power broke in on *their* self-serving delusions. It would come as no surprise to students of nineteenth-century history if the growing strength and self-confidence of China, India and Russia were to bring this so-called 'new American century' to an end in much less than 100 years. If that should happen, the world would be back to the competing power blocs of the late nineteenth century. And we have seen what that led to.

The particular political systems these great nations finish up with will not be the determining factor in world affairs during the coming years. The coming power struggles will not be about political principles. They will be driven by the same forces that have always governed such contests: competition for natural resources; competition for trading influence; and, above all, pure fear – that same primitive fear of the 'other' that has governed human relations since our ancestors first stood up and looked across the wide savannah.

4 6

A BACKWARD LOOK

In 1922, the British writer H.G. Wells published his best-selling *A Short History of the World*. It ended with the following:

> As yet we are hardly in the dawn of human greatness. . . .
> Can we doubt that presently our race will more than realize
> our boldest imaginations, that it will achieve unity and peace,
> that it will live . . . in a world made more splendid and lovely
> than any palace or garden that we know, going on from
> strength to strength in an ever widening circle of adventure
> and achievement?

Wells penned those words just four years after the conclusion of a terrible war. The memory of the obscene carnage on the world's battlefields was still fresh in his readers' minds. How could he have been so blithely optimistic? He was a highly intelligent and sensitive man, with exceptional powers of imagination. He understood what terrible things human beings were capable of in desperate situations. The trouble was, he was a comfortably-off citizen of one of the richest countries on earth; a country whose ruling classes had experienced an uninterrupted improvement in their personal comfort and prosperity for more than two centuries.

Fine writer and visionary though he was, Wells was a product of his time. It was only within the previous hundred years or so that scientists had begun to piece together the history of the earth, and the origins of the human race. It was only sixty years since Darwin had published his *Origin of Species*, and barely thirty since his *Descent of Man*, the first coherent study of human origins. Darwin had chosen the title with care, so that people might understand that he was concerned only with elucidating the structure of humanity's family tree, and not promoting any idea of 'progress'. In the last edition of the *Origin of Species* that he personally supervised, he had used the word *evolution* for the first time. But what he meant by evolution was continuous change, not continuous improvement.

Unfortunately, with Darwin out of the way, it was open house for everyone who had misunderstood him, or who wanted to invoke his name to support their own crackpot theories. In no time at all, the industrial countries were awash with theories of 'social evolution', a historical process by which human society supposedly advances towards higher and higher forms of organization. Unsurprisingly, the highest form to date turned out to be the kind of organization displayed by the society in which social evolutionists occupied such comfortable and prestigious positions.

Wells was not a Christian, but he was born into a society deeply imbued with Christian philosophy. When he wrote his *Short History*, his world-view, like that of most of the people around him, was still shaped by Christian habits of thought. Christianity is a millenarian religion that has been teaching for nearly 2000 years that history has meaning: it is a linear process with a preordained end. This feeling was intensified in the more prosperous Christian countries by the scientific and industrial revolutions. These developments encouraged the leaders of intellectual fashion – by definition drawn from the class that had most benefited from these revolutions – to believe in a golden future.

Belief in the 'march of civilization' ought to have been killed off by the horrors of the First World War, but for many people, the effect was quite the opposite. The shock was so great that the patient went into denial. The war was seen instead as a tragic interlude, a wakeup call for a world that had grown complacent. Now was the time, it was thought, for men and women of goodwill to create new kinds of international institutions, to ensure that nothing like it could ever happen again. To console the grieving for the losses they had suffered, a rationalization was invented: 1914–18 had been 'the war to end war'. We know better now. Whether we are any wiser is a matter of opinion.

In the face of the evidence of the past hundred years, we should have abandoned fantasies about the onward march of civilization. But this kind of thinking still lingers – only the language changes. Some put their faith in something called the 'enlightenment project', a collection of loosely connected notions and historical experiences to which intellectuals in some rich countries ascribe great significance. In this variation on the 'march of civilization' view of history, the ways of organizing society developed in Western Europe and North America since the seventeenth century are seen as inherently superior to any other, and therefore must prevail, provided only that their practitioners keep their nerve.

This linear view of history as a progression towards a golden future is shared by both Christianity and Marxism, and also by 'enlightenment liberals', some of whom are neither Christians nor Marxists. But there are other ways of interpreting human experience. Other cultures, for example the Maya and pre-communist China, have seen history as a 'cyclical' process, in which similar sequences of events recur over long periods, and in which there is no ultimate destination.

Some have even suggested that the way in which a society views history can itself affect the way its story unfolds. A society that sees history as a linear process, particularly if it also embodies a belief in 'progress', is perhaps more likely to look for ways of making discoveries and improvements. Unfortunately, such societies are also in danger of believing that 'history is on our side'. And it is a short step from this to the belief that 'the end justifies the means', an attitude that has led to many of the atrocities that have disfigured human history.

But the cyclical view of history has its own dangers. It may avoid the kind of horrors that are perpetrated by people who carry with them the certainty that History, or God, is on their side. But it is a belief that easily slips into fatalism: an acceptance that suffering (especially other people's) is an inescapable fact of life, and that attempts to influence the course of history are doomed to fail.

Looking back over the story told in these pages, one has to question whether history has any pattern at all, linear, cyclical or any other. Perhaps the story of the human race is best understood as a journey through particularly hazardous terrain, in the dark, in a not very well-serviced vehicle, with a succession of drivers of varying competence, in assorted states of inebriation. Some of the passengers have a clear idea of the destination they are aiming for, but not all of them have a realistic view of their chances of reaching it by the route they have chosen.

Any student of history cannot help but be struck by the number of setbacks the human race has suffered during the past 150,000 years, and just what fragile creatures we are, both individually and as a species. In the face of the stupendous forces that nature has at its command, a little humility is called for when speculating about the future. To take just one example, there is an immense plume of molten rock and gas bubbling away beneath North America. Two million years ago, it was under Idaho. Now it is under Yellowstone National Park, in north-west Wyoming. The plume hasn't moved. It is the continent that has moved, as it is carried along on one of the earth's tectonic plates. This unexploded bomb may not go off for a long time. It tends to do so, on average, once every 600,000 years. On the other hand, it could blow within the next few years. If it should, the human race would almost certainly suffer a calamity such as it has not experienced since the eruption of Mount Toba, in Sumatra, 74,000 years ago. That one created a six-year 'nuclear winter' that had a dramatic effect on the distribution of plants and animals around the world, and brought the human race close to extinction. A similar eruption in Yellowstone would probably dispose of most of North America's human population, and the resulting climate pollution would make any form of civilized existence over most of the rest of the world difficult.

That is an example of the kind of threat we can do nothing about. But there are others that are still within our power to counteract. One is the threat of a major pandemic, like the Black Death of the fourteenth century, or, slightly less frightening, the influenza that raced around the world in 1919. In a world where we are disturbing every corner of our natural environment, where people are travelling and mixing on a scale never before known, and where we are embarking on experiments in genetic manipulation not only of animals and plants, but of viruses and bacteria, the possibility of something new and horrible emerging to devastate populations worldwide is very strong.

We were provided with a dramatic illustration of the power of new diseases to wreak havoc among human populations by the appearance of the AIDs/HIV virus in the mid-twentieth century. It has already caused one of the most deadly pandemics in human history, and its career is still far from over. This is an experience that carries a number of messages. The first of these is that evolution is still going strong. The virus, and the human disease it causes, were unknown thirty years ago. It had been working away in the bodies of our primate cousins in Africa for a long time before it made the adaptations that enabled it to home in on us. And it is still evolving, as it battles with the drugs with which we are attempting to treat it.

Another message this disease underlines is the huge part that good and bad luck play in the history of nations. It is the people of poor countries, especially poor countries in Africa, who have suffered, and continue to suffer, the biggest share of this terrible affliction. Lack of education, inability to afford protection, and the prohibitive cost of medicines and medical care, all conspire to ensure that the countries that are already mired in poverty are the ones made still poorer by this terrible, yet largely preventable, disease.

Although some of the rich countries of the world have suffered significant numbers of AIDs-related deaths, these have not been high as a proportion of the population. And the disease remains a manageable element in the lives of such countries. But we may be sure that it is only a matter of time before something even more damaging emerges from who knows where. So long as the human species exists, it will suffer pandemics, and every so often we may expect to be visited by a Big One.

Another threat that hangs over us is human-induced climate change. Even a generation ago, the evidence was still so tentative that it was perfectly respectable, even sensible, to question its significance, and to oppose proposals for large-scale changes in the patterns of production and consumption in the industrialized world. It may still be respectable, but it is no longer sensible. If there had not been so much corporate money riding on the outcome of the argument, it would have been treated as an open and shut case years ago.

We have learned two things in recent years that make any continued foot-dragging in this matter extraordinarily unwise. First, we now know that some past climate swings have occurred very quickly. Ice Ages have sometimes been replaced by interglacials – and vice versa – in a matter of years, rather than centuries. And that was without any push from large-scale human activity. Second, climate change models suggest that the present margin of safety between a gently changing climate and a rapid tip-over into something more frightening is quite small. It really does look as though it would need only a modest reduction in the snow cover in northern latitudes (reducing the proportion of the sun's heat reflected back into space) and a modest increase in the carbon dioxide in the earth's atmosphere (preventing that heat from escaping into space) to start a runaway rise in global temperatures. The science does not offer 100 per cent certainty, but the risks are so great that we should surely try to ensure that our margin of safety is a generous one.

Unfortunately, we face two problems when we try to tackle major issues such as global warming, pollution or arms control. One of these is as old as the human race. The other has been around for some time, but has only become serious during the last two centuries.

The age-old problem is the balancing of immediate personal freedom against long-term communal good. Most of us are prepared to accept some restrictions on our freedom of action, recognizing that we gain from the simultaneous restriction of other people's freedom. Few people burst a blood vessel if they are prevented from taking a gun on board a plane, or are searched to make sure they are not trying to do so. They are happy to have their own freedom to carry guns restricted, in return for the safety they enjoy as a result of other people's freedom being similarly restricted. Unfortunately, whatever opinion polls may say, it is doubtful whether they are equally ready to have their motoring, their foreign travel or their access to central heating restricted, or made significantly more expensive. We can only hope that the change of heart comes before it really is too late.

But challenges such as climate change are complicated by another problem, one that we have hardly begun to tackle: that of corporate power and motivation. Tobacco companies spent years, and millions of dollars, rubbishing medical research that suggested a link between smoking and lung cancer. Energy companies in particular, but others as well, have a similar vested interest in denying the reality of human-induced climate change and will fight to prevent the action necessary to contain it. In much the same way, arms companies, and their friends in high places, have a vested interest in nourishing fear, and in manufacturing enemies. In a world without fear, weapons would be very difficult to sell, and arms companies would be in danger of going broke.

These malign influences do not arise because company directors as a class are more venal, or personally less honest than other people. It is because a socially responsible business – like a flying pig – is a contradiction in terms. Pigs are not designed to fly, and privately owned business corporations are not designed to serve the public good. This is not to characterize them as public enemies, merely to recognize them for what they are: devices to enable their shareholders to maximize their earnings, and their senior executives to maximize their power *and* their earnings. Even if a particular board of directors, bizarrely, wished to abandon the maximization of profit and place equal emphasis on increasing public welfare, they could not do so, because the resulting deterioration in short-term profits would lead to a collapse of the company's share price, and the arrival of other managers with more stock market-friendly attitudes.

Having devoted so many words in this book to the benefits that humanity has derived from giving capitalist enterprise its head, and the damage that has been done by ideologies that denied those benefits, it is only fair to point out the huge potential for harm that uncontrolled profit-seeking carries with it.

Adam Smith, that wise philosopher and father-figure of the science of economics, is revered by economists and businessmen for his explanation of the benefits that accrue to the community – as a by-product, not by intention – from genuine competition between firms operating in the same market. But what Smith emphasized with equal force was the damage to the public good that must result if businesses are allowed to operate without regard for the wider consequences of their pursuit of profit maximization. Appropriate legislation and public bodies with adequate powers are needed to keep this pursuit within reasonable bounds. It isn't rocket science. Laws like those that punish the adulteration of food do not interfere with business efficiency. They prohibit abuse, while preserving the level playing field that competition requires. Legislation that forced businesses to take drastic measures to reduce their emissions of greenhouse gases, and other forms of pollution, would not offend against the principles of free competition. And it might possibly give the human race a chance of making it to the year 2050 in reasonable shape and with not too seriously reduced numbers.

Controlling the abuse of the power of national monopolies is a bit more difficult, but the obstacle is usually lack of will on the part of governments, rather than any technical difficulty. It is when we have to deal with powerful businesses whose operations spread across continents that the problem becomes really challenging. But even there, the key to success is to nail the lie that unfettered business is essential to the public welfare. In a global economy, unfettered businesses, and businesses whose operations are concealed from public scrutiny, are monsters that can only do more harm than good. Any argument that seeks to defend them by appeal to principles of free competition originating in the study of small markets is pure humbug.

But that's enough for one small book. Let's end with a look on the bright side. Human history has delivered any number of triumphs, and – for the lucky ones – huge advances in wealth, in welfare and in control over the environment. And barring the most terrible accident, there must be wonderful surprises still to come. Less than 100,000 years ago, the human race numbered only around 10,000 people, wandering around in small bands on the African savannah. Now there are over 6000 million of us, in just about every corner of the world. In spite of this huge number, the luckier ones – and that's quite a lot – are decently fed, and enjoy luxuries of housing, health care, food and drink, travel and entertainment that our great-great-grandparents could barely have dreamt of.

As these words are being penned, athletes around the globe

are training for the 2008 renewal of the Olympic Games. What was a one-day festival in a field in southern Greece will be an international celebration involving 10,000 competitors, played out before 1000 million spectators. The fact that the Games are taking place in the Chinese capital, Beijing, is symbolic of that great nation's rapid emergence from more than two centuries of comparative decline.

Provided that no disaster occurs to prevent the Games being held, we may be sure that they will be a triumph of organization, and that Chinese athletes will take many of the medals on offer. Africans, and men and women with recent African ancestry, will also make frequent appearances on the winners' podium. There will almost certainly not be as many 'white' medal winners as there have been in the past. The domination of games and sports by the nations that invented them has gone for ever. Other nations can now afford the food and the time needed to become good at them. But no matter what our ancestry, and whatever our colour, we will all be able to take pleasure in the winners' achievements. We are all Africans, after all, even if some of us *are* paler than others.

Most dates BC are approximations only – the earlier the date, the cruder the approximation.

BC

6 million   Split between hominid and chimpanzee lines

4 million   *Australopithecus Afarensis* living in East Africa

2.5 million *Homo habilis* living in South-east Africa

1.6 million Earliest known *Homo erectus* (in Africa)

500,000   Split between *Homo sapiens* and Neanderthal lines

250,000   Earliest Neanderthals (not in Africa)

200,000   *Homo erectus* still living in China, Java and the Caucasus

150,000   First modern humans in Africa
                 (or later, depending on definition of 'modern')

100,000   Total human population *c.* 10,000 (all in Africa)

60,000   Migration of small founding population out of Africa
                 (ancestral population of all modern humans outside Africa)

50,000   First modern humans in Australia

30,000   First modern humans in Western Europe
                 Total human population *c.* 500,000
                 (none in the Americas)

18,000   First modern humans in Central Asia

13,000   First modern humans in the Americas

9000–8000   Domestication of food plants in Fertile Crescent

7000   Domestication of food plants in China

6000   World population around 10 million

5000   Sahara begins to dry out

4000   Eridu in Mesopotamia has 5000 inhabitants
World population around 30 million

3500   Earliest known image of a wheel
First city-states in Mesopotamia

3000   Beginnings of agriculture in Central America
Cuneiform writing in use in Mesopotamia
Bronze first made

2700   Uruk (Mesopotamia) has 50,000 inhabitants

2500   Uruk has 200,000 inhabitants
Indus Valley civilization thriving
Great Pyramid of Giza, in Egypt

2000   Horses first ridden (Central Asia)
Agriculture established in the Central Andes

2000–1500   Greek speakers invade Greece from the North

2000–1000   Polynesians colonize Western Pacific

1800   Iron first made (in Anatolia, Turkey)

1500   Earliest Chinese writing
Nomad cavalry in Central Asia
Aryans invade India from the north-west

1100   Phoenicians using alphabetic script

1000   World population around 120 million
Olmec culture flourishing on Gulf of Mexico
Aryans in India adopt settled agriculture

800   Homeric epics written down

776   Traditional date of first Olympics

551	Birth of Confucius
Between 550 and 420	Birth of Gautama (the Buddha)
507	Cleisthenes lays foundations of Athenian democracy
500	Iron in widespread use in India Deep water rice paddies in the Yangtze Valley Rome is a city-state with 50,000 inhabitants
401	Athens is a city-state with 60,000 voting citizens and a population of 500,000
326	Alexander the Great embarks on his conquests
321	Maurya dynasty established in India
300	Rome has a population of 100,000; Carthage has 250,000
268–233	Reign of Asoka
221	China united at end of warring states period
214	Completion of China's Long Wall (precursor of the Great Wall)
200	Trace harness in use in China
146	Destruction of Carthage
100	Silk Road in use Chinese deep-drilling for brine and natural gas
85	Chinese sowing seed with multi-row seed ploughs
6–4	Birth of Jesus
AD	
30	Death of Jesus
100	Chinese using paper and porcelain
150	Roman empire extends from Scotland to the Persian Gulf – population of 50 million and a regular army of 300,000

313	Edict of Milan establishes toleration of Christianity throughout Roman empire
320	India reunited under the Gupta dynasty
324	Constantinople made capital of Eastern Roman empire
380	Christianity official religion of the entire Roman empire
391	Japanese conquer three Korean kingdoms
410/415/ 476	Rome sacked by Visigoths/Vandals/Goths
500	Golden age of Tiahuanaco (population 50,000) Golden age of Teotihuacán (population 150,000) Mayan civilization in full flower Japan's population reaches 5 million
570	Birth of Muhammad
611	Completion of China's Grand Canal
622	Muhammad's flight to Medina (the hegira)
632	Death of Muhammad
638	Muslim forces capture Jerusalem
664	Muslim forces capture Kabul
711	Muslim forces enter Spain
768	Charlemagne crowned king of the Franks
800	Charlemagne crowned Holy Roman Emperor Maoris reach New Zealand
800–900	Introduction of heavy plough and collar harness to northern Europe
900	Chinese using gunpowder and the magnetic compass
1000	Chinese using paper money
1050	Split between Western and Eastern Christianity

1066	Norman French invasion of England
1071	Seljuk Turks defeat Byzantine army at Battle of Manzikert
1095	Pope Urban II launches First Crusade World population around 300 million China's population at least 80 million
1099	Crusaders take Jerusalem and massacre population
1100	Cahokia (Mississippi) has 20,000 people
1177 and 1229	The Milanese construct the Naviglio Grande and Muzza canals
1214	Genghis Khan takes Peking
1240	Mongols destroy Kiev and make Russia their tributary
1260	Kublai becomes Great Khan
1300	Venice has a population of 200,000
1348–50	The Black Death in Europe
1368	China's Ming dynasty founded
1405-33	Zheng He's voyages
1434	Van Eyck's *Arnolfini Marriage*
1453	Copernicus's *Revolutions of the Heavenly Spheres* Ottoman Turks capture Constantinople
1455	Gutenberg's Great Bible
1492	Columbus reaches the West Indies
1497	Vasco da Gama sails round the Cape to India
1498	Switzerland becomes a republic
1504	Michelangelo's *David*
1517	Martin Luther challenges the Church
1519–22	Magellan's ships sail round the world

1521   Cortés completes the conquest of the Aztec empire

1525   Mughal dynasty founded in India

1533   Pizarro captures the Inca capital of Cuzco

1545   The Spanish discover the silver deposits of Potosí

1547   Ivan IV crowned tsar of Russia

1599   Shakespeare's *Twelfth Night*

1620   *Mayflower* expedition founds New Plymouth
First Negro slaves landed at Jamestown, Virginia

1638   Russian fur traders reach the Pacific

1644   Manchus end the Ming dynasty

1652   Dutch settlers arrive in South Africa

1674   Dutch colony of New Amsterdam becomes British colony of New York

1687   Newton's *Principia* publicizes his theory of universal gravitation

1707   The Act of Union unites England and Scotland

1709   Abraham Darby introduces coke-fired smelting of iron

1750–70   England's Industrial Revolution achieves 'take-off'

1763   End of Seven Years War between Britain and France
World population nearly 800 million, of which half lives in India and China; Paris and London each have 700,000 people

1766   James Watt patents his steam condenser

1769   Cook discovers New Zealand and the east coast of Australia

1776   Adam Smith's *Wealth of Nations*
America's Declaration of Independence

1787   End of the American War of Independence
Constitutional Convention, Philadelphia creates the USA

1788	The First Fleet transports convicts to Australia
1789	The French Revolution
1807	Abolition of the slave trade in the British empire
1808	Argentina achieves independence from Spain
1812	Napoleon's retreat from Moscow
1819	The American steamship *Savannah* crosses the Atlantic
1821	Bolívar's victory at Boyacá prepares the way for the independence of Colombia, Ecuador and Venezuela
1822	Brazil achieves independence from Portugal
1825	Liverpool and Manchester Railway
1835	First use of the word 'socialism'
1839–42	First Opium War
1844	Morse demonstrates the electric telegraph
1848	Publication of *Communist Manifesto*
1853	American naval squadron under Commodore Perry compels Japan to admit foreign traders
1858	Government of India Act abolishes the East India Company
1859	Charles Darwin's *Origin of Species*
1861–5	American Civil War
1863	Slavery abolished in the USA Completion of the unification of Italy
1870–1	The Franco-Prussian War
1871	Germany united under Prussian king
1873	First commercial electric motor
1882	New York's Pearl Street power station brings electric lighting to the USA

1896	First modern Olympic Games (in Athens)
1901	Unification of Australia Marconi sends a radio message across the Atlantic
1903	Wright Brothers' first flight at Kitty Hawk
1904–5	Russo-Japanese War
1910	Britain's self-governing colonies in Southern Africa form the Union of South Africa
1912	China becomes a republic
1913	Henry Ford's first assembly line
1914–18	First World War
1917	Russia's October Revolution
1924	Death of Lenin; Stalin succeeds him
1929	The Wall Street Crash
1933	Hitler comes to power
1934	Chinese communists complete their Long March
1935	Keynes's *General Theory*
1939–45	Second World War
1944	Famine in Bengal kills 3 million people
1945	Atomic bombs destroy Hiroshima and Nagasaki
1946	The University of Pennsylvania's ENIAC computer Civil war breaks out in China between nationalists and communists
1947	India and Pakistan achieve independence
1948	Founding of the Chinese People's Republic
1949	Inauguration of the state of Israel
1953	Crick and Watson establish the structure of DNA End of Korean War

♦ TIMELINE ♦

1958	Inauguration of the European Economic Community
1966	Mao Zedong launches the Cultural Revolution
1969	First Moon landing (*Apollo 11*)
1973	Yom Kippur War between Israel and Egypt Vietnam War ends
1980–8	Iran-Iraq War
1982	The Canada Act establishes Canada as an independent state free of legal ties with Britain
1989	Demolition of the Berlin Wall
1990	Tim Berners-Lee invents the world wide web
1991	End of communism in Russia
2001	Completion of the Human Genome Project Destruction of New York's Twin Towers
2003	Anglo-American invasion of Iraq

FURTHER READING

The publication dates shown are not necessarily those of first publication. Later editions have been cited where these contain new material, or are likely to be more readily obtainable.

ATLASES

These three atlases are strongly recommended, both for their splendid maps and for the superb quality of the accompanying commentary:

Haywood, **John**, *The Penguin Historical Atlas of Ancient Civilizations*, Penguin Books, 2005
Ancient cultures worldwide, from the Agricultural Revolution in the Fertile Crescent to the Maori settlement of New Zealand.

Ruthven, **Malise**, with **Nanji**, **Azim**, *Historical Atlas of the Islamic World*, Oxford University Press, 2004
The spread of Islam and the development of Islamic culture, from Muhammad's first missions to the present.

Smith, **Dan**, with **Bræin**, **Ane**, *The State of the World Atlas*, Earthscan, 2003
A picture of the world at the beginning of the twenty-first century, covering such topics as water supply, climate change, human rights, tourism and military spending. Packed with statistics.

OVERVIEWS

Blanning, **T.C.W**. **(ed.)**, *The Oxford Illustrated History of Modern Europe*, Oxford University Press, 1996
A profusely-illustrated collection of essays by eminent historians covering the period from the French Revolution to the fall of the Berlin Wall.

Miles, **Rosalind**, *The Women's History of the World*, Harper Collins, 1990
A look below the surface of traditional history writing, to uncover the day-to-day reality of women's lives, and the often overlooked contribution of some notable women to the course of human history.

Overy, **Richard (ed.)**, *The Times Complete History of the World*, sixth edition, Times Books, 2004
This magnificent work is a combination of atlas and historical encyclopaedia. Purchased new, it is expensive, but good value. Bought second-hand, it is a bargain to treasure.

Roberts, **J.M**., *The New Penguin History of the World*, Penguin Books, 2004
Arguably the best outline of world history currently available.

Woodruff, **William**, *A Concise History of the Modern World*, Abacus, 2005
A survey of world history since 1500, with particular emphasis on the twentieth century.

IN-DEPTH TREATMENTS

The following, listed in the order in which the topics appear in this book, are recommended for further study:

Diamond, **Jared**, *The Rise and Fall of the Third Chimpanzee*, Vintage, 1992
Prize-winning examination of the relationship between humans and other primates, with reflections on the possible future consequences of our primate instincts.

Dunbar, **Robin**, *The Human Story: A New History of Mankind's Evolution*, Faber, 2004
Fascinating speculations on the origins of consciousness, language, religion, etc., by a leading evolutionary psychologist.

Pinker, **Steven**, *The Language Instinct*, Penguin Books, 1994
An enthralling study of the way that children and adults acquire language, and an exploration of the argument that language is instinctive, rather than invented.

Oppenheimer, **Stephen**, *Out of Eden: The Peopling of the World*, Constable & Robinson, 2003
The timing and the pattern of the spread of modern humans out of Africa, as revealed by genetic analysis.

Smith, **Bruce D**., *The Emergence of Agriculture*, Scientific American Library, 1995
A detailed history of the domestication of animals and plants worldwide.

Temple, **Robert**, *The Genius of China*, Prion, 1998
The amazing achievements of early Chinese technology, as revealed by the researches of Joseph Needham.

McNeill, **William H**., *Plagues and Peoples*, Blackwell, 1977
The part played by disease in the history of humanity since 500 BC.

Ziegler, **Philip**, *The Black Death*, The Folio Society, 1997
The spread of the Black Death in Europe and its effects on European society.

Oliver, **Roland**, *The African Experience*, Phoenix, 2000
A history of Africa from the appearance of the first hominids to the 1990s.

Fritze, **Ronald H**., *New Worlds*, Sutton Publishing, 2002
An illustrated account of the great voyages of discovery, 1400–1600.

Bernand, **Carmen**, *The Incas: Empire of Blood and Gold*, Thames and Hudson, 1994
A beautiful small book, highly illustrated, containing an account of Inca society and Pizarro's conquest, with extracts from contemporary documents.

Mann, **Charles C**., *1491: The Americas before Columbus*, Granta Publications, 2006
A riveting reappraisal of pre-Columbian North America, challenging the traditional view of the continent as an almost empty land of primitive cultures.

Taylor, **Alan**, *American Colonies: The Settling of North America*, Penguin Books, 2002
A masterly survey of the settlement of North America, from the first crossing of the Bering Strait in 13,000 BC to the end of the eighteenth century.

Hobhouse, **Henry**, *Seeds of Wealth*, Shoemaker and Hoard, 2004
How five agricultural products – timber, wine, rubber, tobacco and coffee – influenced human history. The section on timber has particular relevance to Britain's Industrial Revolution.

Hobhouse, **Henry**, *Seeds of Change*, Shoemaker and Hoard, 2005
A similar treatment of six more plants: quinine, sugar, tea, cotton, potato and coca.

Pope-Hennessy, **James**, *Sins of the Fathers: The Atlantic Slave Traders 1441–1807*, Phoenix Press, 2000
A detailed history, based on contemporary letters and journals.

Williamson, **Edwin**, *The Penguin History of Latin America*, Penguin Books, 1992
This book provides a good introduction to the period of Spanish and Portuguese rule, but its principal virtue lies in its detailed account of the post-independence history of the countries of South and Central America.

Keay, **John**, *India: A History*, HarperCollins, 2000
A good book for anyone wanting a detailed treatment of the whole of Indian history, from the Aryan invasions to the late twentieth century.

Judd, **Denis**, *The Lion and the Tiger: The Rise and Fall of the British Raj*, Oxford University Press, 2004
An excellent short history of the British in India, from 1600 to 1947.

Pomeranz, **Kenneth**, *The Great Divergence: China, Europe and the Making of the Modern World Economy*, Princeton University Press, 2000
A detailed analysis of the various explanations that have been advanced to explain why it was Europe, and not East Asia, that took the lead in the Industrial Revolution.

Longworth, **Philip**, *Russia's Empires*, John Murray, 2005
The ups and downs of Russian history, from prehistory to Putin.

Hughes, **Robert**, *The Fatal Shore*, Vintage, 2003
The classic account of the history of convict transportation to Australia.

Reynolds, **Henry**, *The Other Side of the Frontier*, Penguin Books, 1982
The story of Aboriginal resistance to the European settlement of Australia, from the Aboriginal point of view.

Weightman, **Gavin**, *The Industrial Revolution: The Creation of the Modern World 1776–1914*, Atlantic Books, 2007
A fascinating account of the inter-relationship of the lives of the industrial pioneers of the eighteenth and nineteenth centuries, and the process by which their ideas and inventions were spread around the world.

Crump, **Thomas**, *A Brief History of the Age of Steam*, Constable & Robinson, 2007
A fascinating account of the part played by the steam engine in the Industrial Revolution of the eighteenth and nineteenth centuries.

Chancellor, **Edward**, *Devil Take the Hindmost*, Macmillan, 1999
Quite simply the best book there is on the subject of financial bubbles and crashes, from the tulip mania to the Asian crisis of the late 1990s.

Galbraith, **J.K.**, *The Great Crash 1929*, Penguin Books, 1975
The classic account of the Wall Street Crash, by a great economist who lived through it. Still as fresh and funny as it was when it was written.

Buruma, **Ian**, *Inventing Japan*, Phoenix Press, 2006
A short but compelling account of the course of Japanese history from Commodore Perry's mission in 1853 to the stock market crash of 1997.

Strachan, **Hew**, *The First World War*, Pocket Books, 2006
A brilliant piece of story-telling, describing the course of the war from the assassination of Archduke Ferdinand to the signing of the armistice.

Taylor, **A.J.P.**, *The Origins of the Second World War*, Penguin Books, 1991
Taylor's brilliant and controversial account of Hitler's rise to power and the events that led to the war of 1939–45.

Mitter, **Rana**, *A Bitter Revolution*, Oxford University Press, 2004
A history of China from 1919 to the dawn of the twenty-first century.

Short, **Philip**, *Mao: A Life*, John Murray, 2004
A masterly biography of one of the towering figures of the twentieth century.

Pearce, **Fred**, *The Last Generation*, Eden Project Books, 2007
A lucid explanation of the mechanics of global climate change, and a cool, utterly convincing analysis of the threat that global warming represents to the continuance of civilized life as we know it.

INDEX

Page numbers for tables, diagrams and maps are in *italics*.